Assessing Corporate Political Risk

ASSESSING CORPORATE POLITICAL RISK

A Guide for International Businessmen

David M. Raddock

with contributions by

Henry Albinski, William Coplin and Michael
O'Leary, Gustavo Coronel, Hermann Eilts,
Fariborz Ghadar, Zvi Gitelman, Felton
Johnston, Robert Slater, and Kim Woodard

ROWMAN & LITTLEFIELD
PUBLISHERS

ROWMAN & LITTLEFIELD

Published in the United States of America in 1986
by Rowman & Littlefield, Publishers
(a division of Littlefield, Adams & Company)
81 Adams Drive, Totowa, New Jersey 07512

Library of Congress Cataloging-in-Publication Data
Main entry under title:

Assessing corporate political risk.

    Includes index.
    1. Risk management. 2. Risk management—Case studies.
I. Raddock, David M. II. Albinski, Henry Stephen.
HD61.A87   1986   658   85-19618
ISBN 0-86598-114-0

88 87 86 / 10 9 8 7 6 5 4 3 2 1
Printed in the United States of America

For my father, Jay J. Raddock,
and for all the people in my life
who believe in taking risks.

Contents

Tables and Figures

Acknowledgments

I wish to acknowledge the numerous academicians, foreign service officers, National Security Council staffers from present and past administrations, members of the Department of Treasury and the Department of Commerce's International Trade Administration, and various loan officers and economists at the World Bank—all of whom have helped enrich my work over the last several years. I am particularly grateful to the individuals who contributed to this book.

My expression of gratitude to my wife is more than perfunctory. Annette has endured more agony than ecstasy in connection with the preparation of this volume.

Thanks also to Janet Johnston, my editor, for her stylistic and substantive criticism of the manuscript.

I appreciate the cooperation of Robert E. Ebel of the ENSERCH Corporation, and acknowledge the lessons he taught me about the corporate culture. I benefited from my tenure at ENSERCH, which nevertheless cannot be held accountable for my ideas or for the opinions I have expressed about any given country. Similarly, each contributor bears sole responsibility for his own statements.

Introduction

Venezuela's nationalism and its adherence to Andean Pact regulations that restrict foreigners' shares in joint ventures are well known. But even Venezuela has made exceptions in cases deemed to be of special benefit to the country. A housing construction company negotiated such a deal; it was so proud of itself that it began to turn out press releases back home about how the project bore a U.S. "trademark." Venezuela thereupon aborted the contract.

In 1974, the People's Republic of China was torn between a pragmatic approach to modernization and the xenophobia, or "we can do it all by ourselves" mentality, of the radical faction under Jiang Qing (Mme. Mao). A major Western civil engineering firm at that time undertook to build a project there. When it came time for construction, the company noticed that all the foreign brand names had been sandblasted off imported components. The specifications had been obliterated with them.

These are examples of the problems that can arise from ignorance about a country's political culture or from an encounter with an unfriendly ideology. Political risk analysts are in the business of alerting international corporations to such problems. Indeed, they must not only look at the dangers inherent in political culture, ideology, or the political process itself, but they must be sensitive to the interraction between politics and the commercial and financial environment. Since the Iranian Shah's overthrow, corporations have become much more attentive to host countries' political and social environments. But because true social revolutions are historical rarities, risk analysts and potential analysts of political risk ought not to derive too much capital from the Iranian experience. Instead, as the multilateral lending institutions and the major international banks wrestle with the current debt crisis in Africa and Latin America, we should concern ourselves with concretizing the specific variables that bear watching and be aware of the fact that often an interrelationship exists among the different disciplinary approaches.

In this book I set forth an integrated approach to political risk analysis and risk management. Part I presents not a specific methodology, but rather a collection (with illustrations drawn from more than 20 countries) of the questions I have found to be necessary for the international businessman to use in assessing foreign investment and trade conditions.

Part II's five case studies—the Soviet Union and Eastern Europe, People's Republic of China, Venezuela, Saudi Arabia, and Australia—have been chosen for their geographical representativeness and for their general interest. Each of the country studies can stand on its own, and each also exemplifies the key variables discussed in Part I. Although Part I is replete with case examples that serve to illustrate the variables of risk analysis in a meaningful way, the actual case studies of specific countries in Part II will provide examples of the problems discussed in a fuller context. Some of the chapters place more emphasis on just two or three of the variables discussed in Part I. The fact that *political culture* seems to be a favorite suggests that the contributing authors ascribe special importance to national characteristics and behavioral idiosyncracies of different peoples—a notion that should be borne in mind by those who would elect to reduce the technique of analysis to quantitative models. Other chapters attempt to do full political/economic risk analyses; to the latter category belong the chapters on Saudi Arabia, Venezuela, and Australia.

The most interesting aspect of the five case studies is that all the authors, save one, had never before done work in political risk analysis. All are eminent social scientists, and all are considered experts on the contemporary politics of the countries about which they have written. If the businessperson cannot learn from them as much as the authors themselves learned from viewing the world through a corporate prism, the chapters to follow will have been a misbegotten exercise.

These country studies are representative of a wide range of geographic regions. The Soviet Union/Eastern Europe chapter, on the one hand, and the People's Republic of China, on the other, will demonstrate the structural and ideological diversity among communist systems and the trans-ideological importance of each nation's cultural and social characteristics. It is especially noteworthy that China, which was railing against the West two decades ago, is now more hospitable to Western investment and trade than the presumably more self-assured Soviet Union. Yet it is a moot point which nation is more stable politically than the other. In reading Mr. Gitelman's chapter on the Soviet Union and bloc countries, the businessperson should note that heterogeneity of political cultures and attitudes toward doing business with the West extends beyond the two communist powers to Bulgaria, Romania, Poland, and the other countries which were once lumped together in the communist monolith.

Australia was selected because it is a developed country with a distinct cultural affinity to the West. Mr. Albinski's treatment of the country in terms of the party in power and the party out of power, interest groups and coalitions, and issues of social change demonstrates how political risk analysis should be applied to developed countries with democratic forms of government.

Venezuela and Saudi Arabia are of keen interest to the politically concerned and the intellectually curious. Why has so much oil wealth left the Venezuelan republic, a reasonably long-lasting Latin American democracy, with such doubts about its legitimacy? Saudi Arabia is a fairly equitable society, yet it shares some of the same social problems as prerevolutionary Iran; moreover, it is vulnerable to other sources of violence and instability in the Gulf area. The authors of both country studies end on an optimistic note about their homes away from home.

Part III on methodology and models is intended to illustrate how some of the variables discussed can be organized and codified. The reader is left with two questions: Is modeling practical without incorporating important variances from country to country? Doesn't the use of models or numbers often serve as a bit of trickery to deceive us into thinking that basically subjective judgments are "scientific" evaluations? Finally, Part IV offers some suggestions for risk management in terms of proper financial structuring and in selecting, when necessary, the appropriate type of political or commercial risk insurance cover.

I have drawn little from the fields of political risk analysis and strategic planning because none of the books, collections of short essays, articles, or costly conferences has more than skirted the subject or told part of the story. In this new field, we all still are innovators.

"Aren't you afraid that you'll be giving away trade secrets and doing yourself in?" asked a friend from the Department of State. Of course, I would be delighted if a reading of this book would enable a businessman to become a political risk analyst. Such an outcome is unlikely, however. But I would be truly satisfied if the reader (learner and fellow practitioner alike) gains some new conceptual insights.

I apologize for not discussing to a greater extent the state of the art, the organization of corporate and bank political risk operations and the collection of data. Much of this material already has been covered elsewhere and the rest will make subject matter for future books (not written by me).

Because this work is written primarily for the interested businessperson, I have avoided the use of footnotes and have discouraged the contributors from using citations unnecessarily. The discussion of how to do country risk analysis in Part I is illustrated with specific examples drawn from my own study of the political and economic dynamics of countries throughout the world. I would like to emphasize that while these remarks may seem to be stated as fact, they represent only *my interpretation*. Moreover, I would like the reader to bear in mind that by the time of publication events may have rendered specific statements subject to reinterpretation.

part one

AN INVENTORY FOR POLITICAL RISK ANALYSIS

chapter one
An Overview

Political risk analysis, an important dimension of international planning, defines for a corporation or bank the aspects of a given country's political/ economic environment that might be detrimental to the organization's interests. The political risk analyst arrives at these judgments from a knowledge of the organization's political and economic vulnerabilities and from an understanding of the relevant conditions in a targeted country. A potential investment, sale, or loan might be jeopardized by war, revolution, insurrection, expropriation, civil strife, terrorism, restrictions on repatriation of capital and profits, delays in payment, currency devaluation or (for banks) default or delinquency in repayment of interest and principal. Beyond this general list, a corporation or a commercial bank might identify more specific risks that inhere to a particular project or its timing. This chapter will assist the businessman and banker to understand a broad range of political, economic, and commercial risks that, in their interplay, could be troublesome to the potential foreign investor or creditor. An inventory or checklist is described to serve as an analytical framework for assessing the business environment of an unfamiliar country and for monitoring changes that might have a deleterious effect on business interests.

THE INTERRELATIONSHIPS BETWEEN POLITICS AND ECONOMICS

As the Iranian revolution ran its course during 1978 and 1979, high-level management in international corporations began to realize the importance of keeping abreast of the political situation in countries in which they had exposure. Corporations with long gestation projects in Third World countries, such as oil companies, were particularly affected. Those banks concerned with default on their financing as well as with providing advice to their corporate clients were shocked out of complacency. Whether to examine the implications for foreign business of strike, revolt, regulations, or revolution, political analysis took on a new importance in both strategic planning and protecting existing assets. Many of these business organizations—particularly the international banks—already had economists or entire economics departments studying the business investment climate. As they studied the implications for the growth or degeneration of a business deal in a given country, it became apparent that political or social factors were inseparable from macroeconomic and commercial questions, and they began to recruit political scientists (usually with a background in geographical areas).

A few years later, in a recession that took a particular toll on developing countries in the Third World, the international debt crisis emerged. Maxi-devaluations, currency controls, import restrictions, delays in payment, expropriations of banks and bank-owned companies, and failure to meet repayments on private debt became commonplace from Latin America to Africa. Now, high-level management seemed inclined to swing back in the opposite direction. Some made statements to this effect: "What's needed these days is proper financial planning to alert us to the risks against which a corporation or bank really can protect itself!"

Some corporations actually fired many of their political analysts. The rationale might have been articulated as follows: What good are they any-way? Even if they can identify a political problem, there is little we can do about it. The people in the field say that what we consider political problems are no worse than the ones we face back home in the U.S.A. And, besides, how often do social revolutions like the one in Iran occur?

In actuality, a balance must be struck in international strategic planning and risk management; economics and politics comprise an integrated equation for measuring national environmental risk to foreign direct investment, sales, or outstanding loans. Political/social analysis, a review of business climate or commercial conditions, and financial/economic analysis all have their own sets of variables. *But they are interrelated.* (Some of the ways in which the three categories affect one another will be demonstrated later.) But it is important to remember that each of these categories is inherently relevant. For example, in the political category, not only a revolution or surge of nationalism can lead to an expropriation or regulation of a company's assets. Terrorism, civil disorder, labor agitation, anti-Western foreign policy, popu-list trends, a breach in communication between the local level and the center, conflicts arising from tensions between parochial and modern institutions and attitudes, and other situations can have possible negative consequences for a foreign business deal. Any of these conditions might have a direct impact on the personnel, installations, and operations of an enterprise overseas. Even if a political factor (such as erosion of middle-class support for the government) or an economic variable (such as pervasive subsidies) does not have an immediate or direct impact on doing business in country x, an analysis of all the relevant conditions and a discussion of various ways they might combine to produce a worst-case scenario will educate the operations executive in the field. He will have in hand not just a set of possible "outcomes" for his country of responsibility, but a prism through which to monitor events as they unravel on the spot. Therefore the analysis can serve not merely as a background study replete with projections, but as an analytical tool.

ASSESSING RISK

Many risk analysts state that they prefer a qualitative rather than a quantita-tive approach to examining the political risk for foreign business in a given country, and they may go even further and suggest that they have no explicit formula for the work they perform. Indeed, every country and political culture is unique, and sometimes these unique characteristics have a direct bearing on the business environment. Nevertheless, political risk analysis, as an art or technique, does not preclude an explicit structure. If it is indeed an art, it is not free-form art. General descriptions of how to do it and what questions to ask are indeed possible.

Since most high-risk countries are in the developing world, the variables discussed here have a distinct Third World orientation. For example, while social revolution is discussed at some length, such a political outcome would not be appropriate for the Netherlands or Australia. Nevertheless, if these variables are considered to be a total inventory of possible risks, they can be applied to European countries and even to the United States.

The variables below should be considered from two standpoints. First, what is the probability that the problem will occur, or does it already exist? Second, what would be the impact of such a problem or turn of events on foreign business in general and on a particular project? No matter how serious a problem, if it does not have a markedly negative impact on a particular business deal, the problem is not insurmountable. If the problem is attacked in this structural manner, it is easy to attach numerical (quantitative) ratings to *probability* and *impact* and then to add a further weighting to the *relative importance* of the risk indicator or variable in the country in question. This is not really a quantitative adaptation of the inventory of variables below, but rather a deliberate manipulation of numbers to reflect the analyst's subjective judgment. Our discussion of the salient questions in political risk analysis will become a menu for managing political risk.

chapter two
Assessing Domestic Politics

VARIABLES OF RISK

Leadership Succession

In all countries, particularly those with authoritarian political systems, leadership succession is a very important political problem. It becomes a political risk when procedures for a smooth transition of political leadership have not been constitutionally established or have not gained legitimacy among the elite (particularly in some Third World societies where the masses are politically naîve) or among the people at large. A leadership succession crisis, generated by an uncharted change in leaders, causes uncertainty and turbulence at different levels of society. In countries where military governments have disrupted the civilian political process and rule through coercion, it becomes imperative to rebuild the civilian electoral process. In Pakistan, as the projected elections of February 1985 approached, the question was whether President Zia ul-Haq, who had seized power in a military coup, would be able to manage local and national elections on a non-party basis (the intention being to exclude the PPP, the left-leaning followers of executed former President Zulfikar ali Bhutto) and to integrate military control into grassroots civilian government. If, after seven years, Zia could not successfully bring off the promised election, his own staying power might be jeopardized. More important, although Zia had adroitly managed the political tensions that surround a government lacking legitimacy, what would happen when he left the political scene? A less competent successor might find himself in quicksand.

In cases where the departed leader has established himself on the basis of his own eminence or charisma, a lack of institutionalized procedures for succession assumes an even greater importance. In parts of Africa and Asia, the death of an individual who has guided the country through independence and into modernity might not only cause a leadership vacuum, but might amount to a social identity crisis. The inhabitants may fall back on old tribal or traditional identities or become so psychologically disoriented as to resort to anarchic behavior or emigration. Jomo Kenyatta's successor in Kenya was nearly assassinated in an aborted air force coup; in Ghana civilian rule has been unsuccessful since the death of Nkrumah. In a still more interesting case, when local leaders were discredited during China's Great Proletarian Cultural Revolution, people were thrown into a state of chaos. The apotheosis of Mao Zedong may have been an attempt to steady and unify society. (Some types of radical leadership change do not necessarily represent crises. In many Latin American countries, for example, a *coup d'état,* or *golpe,* against another military leader or against a legitimate civilian government is a normality. In these cases, there is stability in instability.)

A corollary to the question of succession after the death or departure of an important leader (one who has a broad following) is the power vacuum his absence creates. What other leader has the strength to take his place and to cultivate the loyalty of a broad constituency? For example, if Burma's *de facto* political leader Ne Win were to depart from the scene, the president and chairman of the State Council, San Yu, probably would have difficulty governing the country. The man Ne Win had been grooming as his successor was imprisoned for corruption, and it is unclear just what sort of power base San Yu has been able to develop on his own. And looking still further ahead (San Yu himself is over sixty), as the generation of Ne Wins and San Yus that fought in the wartime Burmese Independence Army disappears, a real power vacuum could follow.

To go full circle, a power vacuum created by the absence of strong leadership can also cause a military takeover. If an election is won by a weak compromise candidate who is unable to reverse an economic decline, the military conceivably could intervene.

The international business planner must also focus on *impact*. What effect would a succession crisis have on the type of foreign business in question? Perhaps none, if a project is not closely linked to the person of a departed leader. But consider that major construction projects undertaken in Ghana to enhance Nkrumah's prestige were particularly vulnerable after his ouster. A military coup to fill a power vacuum in Peru in the near future may not seem to have major repercussions for foreign investment (after all, most military coup governments are rather conservative and pro-West); but if the more populist segment of the Peruvian armed forces were to take over, foreign businessmen, banks, and multinationals could be in trouble. In Burma, an inadequate new leadership might be unable to hold together a country that is already fraught with ethnic divisions and liberation struggles. Absent a stable social environment, how can business be carried on as usual?

The political risk analyst must ask, are efforts being made in a potential host country to groom successors? Autocratic rulers may seem to want to cultivate protégés, but they also seem to have singular difficulty in reconciling themselves to political mortality and in delegating power to others. It often happens that if an emerging figure in the political elite becomes too popular or seems to be developing his own constituency, he is relegated to obscurity. For example, when Indonesia's Suharto was reelected to another five-year term in 1984, he demoted his popular Minister of Defense Mohammed Jusuf (the man tipped to be his successor), to Chief of Audit. In another case, President Ahmadou Ahidjo of Cameroon retired formally and passed the mantle to his chosen successor Paul Biya. Ahidjo apparently expected to continue pulling the strings from behind the scenes, but Biya wanted to develop his own power base and establish himself as a leader in his own right.

Three years later, after Ahidjo's surrogates attempted two coups, mentor and protégé have brought the country to the brink of civil war.

Another question to ask: If there is a succession struggle, are some factions better positioned than others? In Indonesia, for example, where interpersonal relations and cross-cutting alliances are so important, it is crucial to tie into the right political group through an informal network of friends and acquaintances. If the Indonesians with whom one works closely are in a high-profile group that is identified with the current leadership hierarchy, such a position can be advantageous in the short term, but might be a liability if an opposing faction took over. On the other hand, an alignment with Indonesians whose political linkages are middle of the road may gain less in dollars and cents in the short term, but will be safer in the event of a succession crisis.

A final problem for the political risk analyst or strategic planner is to examine the evolving attitudes and policies of the key political protagonist(s) as they pertain to foreign investment and trade in his product or service area. He must also gauge the development of a consensus for that particular perspective. In other words, after the faction(s) that are apt to accede to power are identified and their positions with regard to foreign investment in general and the enterprise in question are considered, the support of their power base or constituency must be considered. (What cannot be learned from published materials often can be obtained through personal interviews).

In Turkey the military (which had come to power during the violence of the 1970s) allowed the reconstruction of a constitutional civilian government through the election of November 6, 1983. We anticipated that the opposition Motherland Party's candidate Turgut Ozal would be chosen prime minister. The military junta, or National Security Council, resigned their commissions and remained as a governing advisory council under President (formerly General) Kenan Evren. The potential for a tug-of-war between the two ruling bodies still exists. The military is more bureaucratic and interventionist but has shown no firm commitment to inducing wary foreign businessmen to invest. The paucity of investment to date in large measure reflects the awareness on the part of foreign investors of the hostility of past Turkish governments and bureaucracies toward foreign capital, as well as a recognition of the Turkish people's antagonism toward foreigners. If Turgut Ozal (known for his open-door economic policy and the creation of a Foreign Investment Department in the Prime Minister's office when he was serving as Deputy Prime Minister under the military) maintains his grip and strengthens his power base, the outcome of this still somewhat rocky leadership transition could prove most favorable to Western business. But Ozal must also make a concerted effort to build a consensus among his constituency for his liberal policies toward foreign capital.

Other than undermining an enterprise (which can include nationalization and expropriation of a company or default on a debt), a leadership succession crisis can impede business as usual and jeopardize personnel living in the country. A power vacuum in the absence of proper leadership can cause anomic civil disorder and chaos. Witness the case of mob violence in India—even in Calcutta where the Sikhs are a very small community—after the assassination of Indira Gandhi. The awareness that elite factions are competing for the rule of the country can lead to unreasonable assertiveness on the part of interest groups, including widespread strikes. A foreign company's installations and expatriate employees can be endangered. To further illustrate the interrelationship between political and economic risk, a political leadership crisis can induce a lack of confidence among the people that extends to a mass run on banks and capital flight; concomitant currency controls would paralyze a foreign company's operations.

The question of leadership succession crisis usually applies to Third World countries where real leadership has been embodied in one person with whom the people have come to identify closely, where there are no established procedures for leadership transition, or where such procedures have not obtained sufficient legitimacy to ward off an interloper. In a more general sense, however, "leadership succession" can also apply to the routine process of change in leadership or party administration in a more developed country. Spain is an interesting case study.

Since the death of Franco in November 1975, Spain has developed into a democracy—in form, a constitutional monarchy. Although Spain has since withstood two coup attempts by groups within the military and security forces, the country's democratic institutions are fragile and not yet tested over time. It is still too early to be sure about the steadfastness of democratic institutions in Spain and her people's (particularly the military's) commitment to them. Felipe Gonzalez's socialist (PSOE) government won handily in the October 1982 election and is very popular. All the other leading parties in the *Cortes* (parliament) are fundamentally centrist. The fascists per se have a constituency of only about 1 percent of the voting public; the communists (PCE) have only four seats in the *Cortes*. Therefore the threat from either the far left or the far right is negligible. In the most hypothetical sense, if in an economic crisis the country were to veer to the extreme right, the military might intervene. Or if the very popular Prime Minister Gonzalez were to be assassinated, the military would certainly take over. (Of course, these scenarios are unlikely even in a very young democracy like Spain.) The likely political scenario for the next three years is that the system will renew itself with the reelection of the PSOE and Felipe Gonzalez. The election will take place in 1986 after a referendum is held on Spain's participation in NATO. The possible development of a coalition between the remnants of the old centrist UCD and the right-wing Popular Alliance could be beneficial to the system by giving them just enough more seats to make them feel they are moving forward. The PSOE will consolidate its pragmatic socialist position, remain in NATO by appeasing its left wing through concessions that may damage certain types of foreign investments, but in general continue to remain hospitable to foreign investment. Thus, in Spain the leadership succession process is a matter of transition rather than crisis, but it has implications for business nonetheless.

Crisis of Legitimacy of a Regime

Whereas the previously discussed leadership succession question tends to revolve about the uncertainty of the process of change from one leader to his successor, a legitimacy crisis occurs when the very form, procedures, and institutions of a government fail to establish credibility among the people or lose that trust after a prolonged period of failing to perform their designated functions. The December 1983–January 1984 bread riots in Tunisia raised the question of leadership succession in that country. The aging and ailing President Habib Bourguiba, who had held office since 1957, had had a nearly charismatic hold on his people in his earlier days. Of more fundamental significance than the succession problem was the ongoing erosion of the legitimacy of the Bourguiba government. Bourguiba's senility was increasingly discrediting him before his own people; his wife's involvement in palace politics with the prime minister, other cabinet ministers, and the head of the ruling Destourian Party was shaming the office and the image of the republic; his government's ineptness in economic management and the implementation of equitable, or at least politically clever, austerity measures had triggered riots; the largest trade union was increasingly appearing to be the handmaiden of the Bourguiba regime; and the nation's party system had been undermined by the apparent rigging of the election of 1981. Under all these circumstances, the question of leadership succession was unimportant when the *legitimacy* of the whole apparatus of political power was collapsing. The system ultimately would be able to maintain itself only through coercion. If radical change were to occur, it would take the form of a grassroots social revolution, launched perhaps by some Islamic organization, or of a top-down military coup. The latter development would represent an upheaval: the assumption of a completely different role on the part of the army and an overhauled political system. In either scenario, even if nationalization and expropriation were not in the offing, foreign business operations would experience some degree of turmoil, uncertainty, and stress.

The legitimacy of a regime is so difficult to measure and quantify (in part because cultural limits of tolerance of system failure vary) that it is extremely difficult to convince senior management to limit or withdraw an investment or even to pay attention to what is happening. Regional marketing officers, too, may not see the dangers before them. In Colombia, the real issue is the political system's legitimacy. American businessmen interviewed in summer 1984 were sure they understood the situation because they had been posted in the capital city and could observe daily events. A representative of the American Chamber of Commerce argued that investment conditions in Colombia could not be better because the economy seemed to be on a slight upswing (he had not been charting long-term trends), an anticipated maxi-devaluation had not taken place and did not seem imminent, and the recently elected government seemed to be resolving a long-standing and widespread problem of guerrilla terrorism. Not long afterward it became apparent that guerrilla violence had continued, and the country's president announced that the treasury was on the verge of bankruptcy. Apparently, many in the American business community in Colombia had acquired a distorted perspective because of their proximity to piecemeal events (they saw the parts rather than the whole) and because of a natural, unconscious bias when a vested interest is at stake.

For years, a crisis of legitimacy has been mounting in Colombia, which is ruled by a rather tight oligarchy and where guerrillas and bandits have roamed unsuppressed in spite of the best efforts of the military. Like others earlier, the last presidential election and interim elections indicated voter apathy and disaffection. During the presidential election, the media touted a large voter turnout, but actually only 53 percent of those eligible to vote went to the polls. Indeed, a swing vote perhaps exists which is not necessarily populist but leftist in orientation. A general disgust with the system's incapacity to deal effectively with worsening economic conditions has compounded the ongoing erosion of faith in the legitimacy of political institutions. Even a liberal trend in the opposing party's primaries, which seemed to augur well for a greater participation of the middle class in the country's political process, is apt to be overtaken by economic decline and a rise in social violence. Further, pervasiveness of the phenomenon of corruption from an illegal drug trade has corroded the political parties, the state bureaucracy, legislature, and the judicial branch. When the system loses its legitimacy altogether, it will become extremely vulnerable to guerrilla terrorism and greater political assertiveness by the military. The conceivable outcome after several years—a creeping military, or military-backed, civilian takeover.

Any new political system accumulates legitimacy, or credibility, only gradually over time. Similarly, failures of the system to perform as expected, such as a Watergate scandal or an inability to set right a foundering economy, tend to diminish, or at least call into question, this legitimacy. A cliché of political science likens legitimacy to credit in a bank. Once a regime loses its creditworthiness—and this happens only after many failures to carry out the essential mandate of its constituency (sometimes this group is only an élite and does not include a politically inactive majority of the people)—it may have to "pay its money up front" with force of arms. The more a regime has to resort to force to quell a riot, quash an attempted coup, or suppress guerrilla activity, the more it demonstrates its weakness. And sooner or later it is replaced. It is up to the risk analyst, whether he or she works for a bank or an international corporation, to be aware of a political system's bankruptcy, to identify those groups prepared to mount a challenge to the ruling elite, to gauge their relative strengths, and then to anticipate the timing.

Rising Expectations or Hopes for Social Mobility and the Frustration Thereof

As members of a capitalist society, most of us want and strive to better ourselves. Even members of societies that theoretically are more equitable want to be better than equal. In Third World countries, a peasant's fantasies often embrace visions of the modern sector and the promise it might hold for him. In a world in which a radio or a television can be found in almost every village and in which transportation networks make travel to the city a possibility, peasants do not necessarily stay on the traditional farm and eke out a subsistence living. Instead they move to the cities, often to discover that they are not easily employable. There they endure their crowded neighborhoods of slums and hovels because they hope to become regularly employed workers. In many developing societies, a gainfully employed worker is indeed considered part of the broader middle class. Once an individual has attained middle-class status, he moves to a better neighborhood and continues to look upward.

Frustration can occur at any point in the upward mobility of members of a developing society. It stems from the promise of economic and social rewards, or even the fleeting taste of those rewards, and then their lack of attainment. Never to experience "progress" is less disturbing psychologically than to experience it and then undergo a setback. In the cities of developing countries, frustration of upward mobility is often compounded by such phenomena as psychological uprootedness, poor housing conditions and social services, population density, and growing political awareness in the crowded urban slums and barrios. At bottom, it springs from inflation, lay-offs, and denial of opportunity for advancement. When similar frustrations are shared by many, they can become political. The collective frustrations can be manifested through the legitimate utilization of the electoral process to oust one administration, or they can be expressed more explosively through bread riots, work stoppages, isolated strikes, or general strikes. The more compelling the sense of personal frustration and the less receptive the authorities to consider such grievances, the more likely seems to be the possibility of some sort of civil disorder.

What types of developments in a given country could alert the analyst to possible trouble? First, an example of a political act that *could* have been destablizing. When Betancur ran for the presidency in Colombia, he fired expectations about new housing for the urban poor in Bogota. After his election, the new government received 1.5 million applications for the 50,000 units that were to be built. Conceivably, 1.45 million people in Bogota now might be prime recruits for a social protest movement.

In developing countries, as in the United States and the rest of the developed world, the middle class is particularly vulnerable to inflation and economic recession. Members of the middle class tend to be the most mobile and the most easily frustrated in their attempts to climb the ladder of success. Moreover, in developing countries, "middle class" represents a new-found status for a large proportion of people, and they are afraid of losing it. Colombia, for example, is now experiencing its worst recession in 40 years, and unemployment has reached a level of at least 12 to 14 percent. It has had a particularly troublesome impact on the middle class. Although labor is weak and fragmented in Colombia, the white-collar government workers have been very militant. Indeed, some of the more virulent strikes in developing countries have been among postal and transportation workers and teachers. In Nigeria, the firing of many government workers within months of the Buhari coup in December 1983 seemed only to have contributed to the erosion of middle-class support for the new military government. (In 1976, it clearly had been demonstrated how dependent an earlier military regime in Nigeria had been for its survival on the middle class.)

Rising expectations are particularly acute among the educated in secondary schools and universities. Many of these young people represent the first generation in their families to obtain an education, usually at considerable sacrifice to their parents. Their families share the expectation that they will enter the technocracy. In Cameroon, hundreds of university graduates are looking for appropriate positions, but neither the bureaucracy nor the industrial base can accommodate them. Could they not constitute a source of antisocial or political instability in the system? In Turkey's transition to democracy, its economy is doing relatively well. The irony is that because of its progress and prosperity, Turkey will have to deal with a large pool of educated people who will be seeking an important role for themselves in the adult world. If they are frustrated in their search, and if they should join forces with the many disgruntled professors who were fired after the earlier military takeover in 1980, they could become a source of real political pressure on the system.

Disaffection of Middle Class, Professional Support from the Regime

In developing countries suffering from economic and social deterioration, the middle class can be pivotal. Historically, in any prerevolutionary situation, this class has been comprised of waverers. Let the government overreact to mass violence with inordinate violence of its own, and these equivocal supporters can become radicalized. Any one of our readers who ever has stood on the edge of a political demonstration as a neutral observer probably is aware of the effect of a bullying and billying squad of police appearing on the scene with the explicit mandate to break up the crowd; one can have one's head turned easily with a few swings of a stick.

Moreover, any dissatisfied "counter-elite" is usually drawn from the educated, frustrated, young members of the middle class. As revolutionists in China, Mao Zedong, Zhou Enlai, and Deng Xiaoping, if not strictly middle class in origin, all belonged to the group of newly educated in their country. The M-19 guerrilla organization in Colombia has been comprised of educated, middle-class students who feel excluded by age *and* class from the political process. These people hold great expectations both about advancement in economic status and participation in the political process; in many instances, able to turn over their shoulders and see their own family's poor origins, they want to be part of a process of social change that will ensure a future for themselves and their children.

Just as a middle-class loss of confidence can indicate an erosion of a system's legitimacy, its forbearance can shore up the established order. In some Latin American countries, a conservative, Roman Catholic middle class may put up with infringements of human rights to avoid a period of extreme disorder and chaos. The majority of the Argentine middle class apparently was willing to endure the anti-Peronist police terror of the military junta for quite some time (because the military seemed to be a preferable alternative at first to the tyranny of guerrillas and Peronist terrorists in the streets) before their sympathies significantly turned in the direction of the families that had suffered seemingly unjustifiable "disappearances" of their close relatives. It took the crunch of economic chaos and the humiliation of defeat in a war with the British for the Argentine middle class to abandon the military government.

Because the movements of a Third World country's middle class can be like shifting sands, they should not be overinterpreted. Nevertheless, the appropriate bank officers or operations executives of a corporation should try to gauge their sentiments, particularly at a time of significant social or economic change. This intelligence information can be garnered from newspapers targeted at this class, from informal conversations with shopkeepers and the like, and from knowledgeable sources in the community. Sometimes this shadowy information can suggest positive evolutionary trends within the political-social system. In Turkey, middle-class enthusiasm for the new civilian regime bodes well for its future. Even in Mexico, where middle-class disaffection from the political order (Mexico has been a virtual one-party system under the PRI) has been reflected in the much-increased vote for the opposition party, Partido de Accion National (PAN), the pressure on the PRI government may have a salutary effect. At least, we know that some of the middle-class alienation anticipated as a result of the economic crisis is being channeled through alternative, nonviolent, and nonrevolutionary modes of expression.

Historical Propensity to Default, Nationalize, or Expropriate Gradually through Increased Regulations

Short of robbery, the gravest risk to a bank is default on a loan. The multinational corporation fears the outright expropriation of its equity and assets by a foreign country or the host government's takeover of the local company under the pressure of mounting regulations and restrictions. Such unfavorable outcomes for multinationals can be influenced by a host of variables: the nature of the industry (for example, is it considered strategic?), the ideology of the ruling political elite (for example, has a certain type of social revolution just taken place?), economic conditions and domestic and international political issues (such as, does a company planning an investment in Nigeria have a high profile in South Africa?). But it is also extremely important to look at the host country's history of performance with regard to expropriation and default or, more specifically, the attitudes of the host country's differing political groups concerning these matters.

Countries with a recent history of severe government intervention in foreign business and expropriation in certain areas often are slow to lose their xenophobic attitude toward international investors. Even when a new government seeks to open the economy and encourage foreign investment, it may find itself beset by hostile pressure groups and an unwilling popular constituency. Other countries have so consistently avoided encroaching on the foreign business sector that an awareness of this history should serve as an incentive to do business there. Of course, as Third World countries become more politically conscious and eager to compensate for the depredations wrought by foreigners on their countries in the past, they will national-ize such strategic areas as mining and petroleum as a matter of course. Venezuela nationalized the oil industry in the 1970s, and it more recently has been trying to lure some of the major oil companies to return to provide assistance.

A history of nationalizations also can teach us a different lesson about what to expect in a given country. Many nations, particularly in Latin America, have learned that excess expropriations have led to a monstrous, unproductive public sector that draws on the country's currency reserves. Mexico is in a curious position. In September 1982, because of its critical economic circumstances involving a run on the banks, the Lopez Portillo government nationalized the banks and, with them, 45 percent of the bank-owned private companies. This administration's realization of the negative effects of government ownership could tend to prevent further nationalization in the near term. Over the intermediate and longer terms, however, the government may have to nationalize anyway to appease an increasingly bellicose domestic left.

A more clearcut example of a country's having developed an aversion to nationalization from its own historical experience is Peru. Between 1968 and 1975, General Velasco's junta redistributed the country's wealth. Several large MNCs were expropriated, and foreign mining companies were forced to expand their investments (often the alternative to expropriation or repudia-tion of contract is the forced renegotiation of contract to the host country's advantage). In the most recent past, President Belaunde Terry has begun to restore a liberal economy. Even if there were another military coup, it is unlikely that the next junta would be as radical as its precursor in the 1970s. It might seem to be nationalistic, but it would not be likely to rape the private sector or toss out foreign interests.

A country also might try to compensate for its historical image with regard to expropriation. The People's Republic of China wants to repatriate both Taiwan and Hong Kong, yet it must show the free world that this is *repatriation without expropriation*. Immediately after the revolution, China granted "autonomous" status to its largest external trading zone of Shanghai; many Shanghainese capitalists stayed behind to manage their enterprises. However, within five years, Shanghai's enterprises had been integrated into the socialist economy. If the new trend in Chinese policy continues, the PRC will demonstrate by its handling of Hong Kong that times have changed and that history will not repeat itself. The approach to the reintegration of Hong Kong will serve as a model to reassure defensive Taiwanese businessmen and the international business community in general.

Thus, the history of nationalization/expropriation and even default as a political act in a given country can provide some tentative indications about the political security of our own investments. We must be certain to examine the whole spectrum of the political elite, including the way a people reacts to its own history of nationalization/expropriation. Even in Peru where there is an almost overwhelming horror at the economic disaster of the 1970s, some elements of the younger military officer corps might allow their populist leanings to cloud their judgment if they came to power. Even in China, if ever the ideologues resurface to challenge the modernizers, an ideological regression might be possible, which could lead to repudiation of contract and expropriation, with or without compensation.

A country's decision to default on external debt can in part be political. Present actions are a guide to future actions, and past actions indicate how a given political group might act in a looming economic crisis. When the Lopez Portillo government in Mexico sought to enlist the support of Brazil and Venezuela in a collective default, that gesture indicated something to us about the political impact of Mexican nationalism. On the other hand, the PRC demonstrated its creditworthiness and aversion to default when it repaid loans from the Soviet Union after the Sino-Soviet dispute erupted in 1960. Like the adolescent child asserting itself against the father, China proved its autonomy and integrity to its erstwhile benefactor. And since the "Four Modernizations" were undertaken, the PRC only very slowly and cautiously has begun to draw down on the large commercial credit lines that have been made available to it.

Corruption

In many societies, corruption has been institutionalized as a means of redistributing wealth or of compensating for low salaries of government employees. In premodern China, scholar-gentry who ascended to official positions were given prebends (state-gained properties) as compensation for their service to the Confucian state. In turn, they took care of even the poorest in their large, extended families. In Indonesia, active military officers are allowed to hold positions in business, in part to ensure their loyalty but also to supplement their low salaries and militate against possible excessive corruption. Only if we arrogantly project our own Calvinist values on other cultures can we regard any of these practices as reprehensible. Even bribes and "facilitators" theoretically ought to be treated as the way some societies work. Only when the level of official corruption surpasses the threshold of tolerance of a country's own people does venality become a risk to the stability of the political system. This development has caused some disturbance in countries where the level of corruption among a narrow elite has risen in direct proportion to newly found oil wealth.

As people become more politically aware, they become more critical of unbounded corruption. In Thailand, for example, corruption has become a popular rallying point. In one Latin American country, narcotics-related corruption pervades the political system at all levels and in the legislature, judiciary, and political parties. This corrosive corruption undermines the legitimacy of political institutions, particularly in the eyes of university students and among the broader professional and middle class. In countries with a history of military coups, a high level of official misbehavior, compounded by other social and economic problems, can be an invitation for the military to reemerge from the barracks. Even in societies where official corruption is acceptable, it becomes a problem of political risk when it exceeds the bounds of propriety.

Secular and Sacred Ideologies

When either a secular ideology or a religion becomes a political force, it can become an organizing ethos for challenging the system—a sort of cement that can hold a revolutionary entity together. The very political and structured organization of the Shia Muslim sect and its eschatological appeal provided a cause, a goal, and a psychological identity for the Iranian revolution.

Political religion (both secular and church-related) can perform similar functions for smaller-scale social protests and civil disobedience, both of which at worst can target business installations and/or disrupt operations, and at best can be alarming to the members of families of expatriate employees in a given country. In the 1960s in South Viet Nam, militant Cao Dai Buddhists organized demonstrations that had a very negative and psychologically destabilizing effect and indirectly increased the effectiveness of communist activities. In Indonesia, outbreaks of civil disorder increasingly have been spurred by Islamic militants. It is possible to hypothesize that in Brazil, given a further deterioration of economic conditions combined with a higher level of politicization of the Workers Party and the working class as a whole and *supported by the church* (which would provide a veil of legitimacy), very disruptive demonstrations could ensue.

In this century, Marxism-Leninism has been the most common revolutionary ideology in the developing world. Democracy *cum* capitalism does not provide a cogent thought system that can easily be communicated to lower echelons of the leadership or to the masses. Marxism, the natural panacea, offers a centrally planned program of postrevolutionary economic development for the deprived. As many scholars have noted, it also serves as a stick with which to beat the Western world and therefore is well suited to national liberation movements of various kinds. In today's world, Marxism-Leninism and militant forms of Islam are the two ideologies that most frequently serve as focal points for political unrest in developing countries. Sometimes some curious hybrids can emerge. In Burma, the religion is Buddhism and the anti-establishment ideology is secular communism. The Buddhists show signs of restlessness under state jurisdiction. The Burmese Communist Party (BCP) is illegal and is currently fighting a guerrilla war against the state army and against the ethnic liberation armies who get in their way. In the event of general political unrest, both the BCP and the monks could join forces to arouse the masses through their separate ideological appeals.

An ideology—a denunciation of the political economic status quo, a set of goals or objectives, a presentation of the means to achieve those ends, and the promise of a utopia at the end of a rainbow—is an essential force for binding together an anti-establishment movement bent on either revolution or militant social protest demonstrations. In societies where the economically disenfranchised and most politically frustrated people have been displaced from their villages and are leading isolated and psychologically dislocated lives in dense urban ghettos, or where traditional ethnic and religious differences have made persons naturally mistrustful of one another, political religion is an indispensable tool for organizing against the existing political order and social hierarchy.

Demographic Patterns

The examination of population growth and distribution trends can pinpoint other sources of tension within a social system. A prime example of the burdensome effect of population growth on the economic complexion of a country is Kenya. Now exceeding its own yearly increase in GDP, Kenya's annual population growth rate is more than 4 percent—perhaps the highest in the world. More than half the population is under the age of 15. Eighty percent of Kenya's people are for the most part concentrated on the 20 percent of the land considered potentially arable. The population will double to 35 million by the year 2000. Because procreation is an important symbol of masculinity in Kenyan society, politicians are afraid to address the issue of population control.

Unemployment and Rural to Urban Migration. Land subdivision, drought, the pressures of subsistence living in the countryside, and the appeal of what seems from afar to be a more comfortable life in the cities have led to a constant stream of refugees from the countryside to the urban centers. This problem is shared by most developing countries to a greater or lesser extent. First, an extreme rural to urban imbalance can make inroads on the country's agricultural productivity, sometimes transforming a net exporter of food into a country that is no longer self-sufficient in feeding itself. Second, rural-to-urgan migration is socially and psychologically dislocating. If, as in Algeria, whole families migrate together, the social problem is not as grave. But more often, family members are separated from one another, and the new arrivals in the city are alienated, alone, and emotionally disoriented. Frustrated by urban living conditions that do not measure up to their earlier fantasies, they can easily fall prey to anti-systemic groups that offer friendship and identity through an appropriate ideology that reflects the cleavage between the "haves" and the "have nots." Third, the population flow from the outlying areas to the high-density cities puts pressure on the system to provide adequate housing and social services (most often it simply does not) and to absorb the new manpower into the employment force. Throughout the developing world, unemployment and underemployment in the cities are on the ascendant because of this phenomenon and because of the world reces- sion. In Kenya, unemployment and underemployment approach 30 percent of the workforce. At the same time, the government cannot afford to increase its public spending, nor can industry expand at a rate fast enough to absorb this manpower. Large numbers of idle, unemployed men can easily be ignited into civil violence.

Migration from Beyond the Borders. Some countries have the additional problems of immigration from neighboring countries, where either economic and social conditions are worse or internal war has made life unenduringly insecure and unstable. A heavy flow of migrant workers exists in the Middle East between the poorer countries and the oil-rich states. In Mexico—already suffering from a serious population problem—the influx of Guatamalan refu- gees on the southern border has put enormous pressure on the system. If social violence in Central America were to escalate, this problem would be compounded. (This seems to constitute one very practical reason why Mexico has been trying to persuade the U.S. government not to increase its involvement in Central America and thereby encourage increased fighting there.)

Age Demographics: Youth and Politics. Many countries in the developing world experienced a bulge in the rate of population growth in the 1960s. Even if the rate has declined since that time through deliberate efforts at birth control, a large proportion of the total population has already reached a working age. In Colombia, although the population growth rate has declined from 3 percent in the 1960s to 2.4 percent, more and more young people will be moving into the workforce for another decade. Still other countries which have not limited population growth have an even more disproportionate number of youth who are seeking or soon will be seeking work. In the more-advanced less developed countries (LDCs), where the educational system (secondary- and university-level) is now well developed, young graduates are looking for positions commensurate with their training. In many cases, the bureaucracies are already swollen and the industrial base has not developed at a sufficient pace to absorb these young people. Although these youth may be able to express themselves through the vote, their participation in the political process is limited. In so many cultures, a gerontocracy prevails in the formal and informal political structures of societies, and adults are conditioned to it. Members of the younger generation have been exposed to modern ideas and have reached an age when they are anxious to prove themselves in adult roles.

Educated youth in China, frustrated politically and alert to the risks of making too great a political commitment, are seeking to pour their energies into economic pursuits.[1] But youth in many countries are both economically and politically disenfranchised. Armed with an education and ability to communicate, and susceptible to new ideals and ideologies ranging from communism to the Koran, they are both potential leaders and recruits for dissident movements. At best, large numbers of frustrated youth in the cities (educated and uneducated alike) are prone to spark outbursts of civil unrest. This is a very real political risk that can be monitored by operations executives on site.

Labor Agitation and Worker Participation in Management

An Activist Labor Force. The political risk inherent in excessive agitation on the part of organized labor should be obvious. Work stoppages and strikes can paralyze local operations; moreover, if such actions have political overtones, they might become part of a much larger, nationwide social movement that could threaten the private sector or international business sector in general. It is important for the political risk analyst to learn about national confederations of unions, their links with the major political parties or the governing elite, and how effectively they can control their member unions at the grassroots level. (Like our own AFL–CIO or Teamsters, some of the federations are not equally effective at gathering input at the lower level and aggregating and articulating those demands before the higher political level, or in manipulating and controlling their members.) Only a few years ago in Tunisia, the UGTT was a militant movement whose leaders were jailed. It now seems to be evolving into an ally—if not an instrument—of the government. In Venezuela, where once the powerful CTV had great influence over the Accion Democratica (AD) party, President Jaime Lusinchi and the AD no longer seem to ascribe as much priority to labor's interests. As a result, either the union could ossify or there could be a resurgence of strikes. In any case, the advantage of one large labor confederation is that it is usually either controllable or already part of the established system.

Still another factor that might invite further analysis of the dynamics of organized labor is the extent to which multiple labor federations might be utilized by competing parties and politicians, or the extent to which unions themselves might compete for power and constituencies. As in the earlier Peronist movement in Argentina, such labor federations occasionally can be manipulated by anti-systemic political parties to throw their massive weight against the established order; demonstrations and general strikes can ensue to disrupt operations by paralyzing urban services. When politics and rivalry within the labor movement become interwoven, the effect of the contest can have a direct impact on business operations. An example is the contest in Spain between the communist-led union, Comisiones Obreras, and the social-ist-controlled UGT. The few communists who won seats in the 1982 election will want to retain and expand their hold on labor; Felipe Gonzalez's ruling socialist party will tinker with various formulas to maintain a standing with labor and to strengthen its own union's standing vis-à-vis the communists' union. This rivalry could instigate more overt demonstrations and increasing pressure for each to extract more from management.

Much less predictable is a situation in which the larger federations have become inactive or where there are no national unions at all. Under such circumstances, local unions can develop more autonomy; they are less hierarchical, more informal, and more united in purpose. In Morocco the large UMT is controlled by the government, and the more militant CDT seems to have been coerced into at least temporary passivity. In this atmosphere, scattered and localized wildcat strikes occur among taxi drivers, teachers, and some other groups. When the austerity measures become still more stringent, a greater number of local unions on both the left and right of the political spectrum are apt to protest. The more militant behavior probably would come from the transport workers, port workers, and secondary school teachers. It is important to note that workers' strikes at mines or other extractive and infrastructural projects can be isolated and policed fairly easily.

Worker Participation in Management. A trend is taking place among the political elites of both developed and developing countries, which either seeks to appease working person constituencies by substituting worker participation in the management process for having to meet wage demands, or, in the interest of greater social justice, hopes to complement the redistribution of wealth with a blurring of the distinction between management and labor.

The European Community (EC), or Common Market, is currently considering a series of directives that, if passed into law, would not only expand mandatory consultations between management and employees, but would also set new guidelines regarding relationships between parents and subsidiaries in MNCs and would substantially increase the amount of information that companies would have to disclose about their operations. The Vredeling Proposal has attracted the most public attention in recent years. Under such a directive, companies would be required to provide employees with information regarding local and worldwide plans. Reporting would be statutory, and penalties would be enforced for non-compliance.

Among the market economies of the developing countries, the staunchest advocate of worker participation in the management process seems to have been the Venezuelan CTV. Multinational corporations must closely monitor any universalized comanagement schemes in countries with powerful labor unions. As economic conditions have become harsher in Mexico, one specialist on the country has suggested that the de la Madrid government might try to forestall further wage increases by giving organized labor a greater role in management, in effect selectively coopting potential dissidents from the floor level of the factory to participate in management decision-making.[2] Because the single ruling party exercises control by drawing troublemakers and "young Turks" who have some sort of following into its own ranks, this pattern already is an integral part of the Mexican political culture.

Cultural, Regional, and Traditional/Modern Differences

Clashes between regions, cultures, and the traditional and modern sectors of societies are often interrelated. To multinational corporations and international banks they pose such common political risks as lack of coordination and communication between center and regional institutions (e.g., between central banks and regional banks), disagreements over jurisdictions, the inability of the center to enforce law and order over a region, regional separatist movements, and even civil war. Further problems can arise from a clash between the traditional and modern sectors of a society and from difficulties in integrating a diversity of cultures and ethnotribal groups. The foreign businessman may have to adapt to different styles of doing business or brace himself for social disturbances that might develop as people feel that the dominant culture, or even modernity itself, is overtaking them and threatening their identities.

Problems involving cultural, regional, and traditional versus modern differences are prevalent in certain Third World countries where they are caused by (a) the artificial borders and linguistic/cultural overlays imposed earlier by colonizing powers; (b) the efforts of newly emergent countries to create strong nation-states out of diverse groups; and (c) the attempt of these diverse groups to maintain their traditional ethnic or religious identities in the face of modern institutions and laws. These problems commonly occur in countries in Africa, the Middle East, and South and Southeast Asia. Nevertheless, regional rivalries and assertions of autonomy per se are simply a resistance to the more generalized process of nation-building and national integration.

Regionalism. An appreciation of the nature of regionalism is a most important aspect of doing business in a given country, developing or developed. First, the businessman must obtain approval for a range of things from licenses to location. (The businessman wishing to spud an oil well off Newfoundland may find himself more directly obstructed than would an oil man operating in the Cabinda enclave in Angola; the latter might be surrounded by Cabinda Liberation guerrillas, but the former would have to deal with the active injunction of the central government.) If the central government offers commercial incentives to invest in an outlying area, the businessman must weigh these incentives against the inconveniences of poor infrastructure, poor living conditions, and the like.

In other cases, a conflict might erupt between central authority, provincial or state authority, and local authority. Sometimes, as in the case of a developed country like Australia, disagreements are based on a legal or regulatory pretext. In Australia, a hydroelectric company being built by Tasmania was blocked by the Australian government, which used provisions of an international convention on protecting wilderness as grounds for halting the project; the country's high court upheld that action. In Nigeria, because the state governments often stray too far from the central government's development plan, payment guarantees should be obtained from the Central Bank. Such micro-risk analysis borders closely on a market conditions study, and the staff analyst should undertake this work in cooperation with the marketing and field operations officers of his company.

The analyst must be aware that differences between center and region might involve a range of complex and inconsistent procedures that might even impinge on the viability of the contract itself. In the People's Republic of China, for example, as many as three layers of bureaucracy may be involved as well as the Party, which is the key decision-making locus at every level. (Kim Woodard's country study elaborates on this point.) In this case, the risk analyst must assist the concerned operations persons to identify an appropriate local agent or to find a way to bypass the bureaucratic obstacles. In Chinese society, cultivating a personal relationship *(Guanxi)* with the right individuals at the highest possible level (even above the relevant ministry itself) may do wonders!

If a central government cannot easily communicate its directives and laws to the state level and then to the local level, the ensuing political paralysis could indirectly affect business operations. In pre-coup Nigeria, in spite of the fact that power had been diffused among 19 states rather than the four old regional divisions which had permitted the major tribes to form political blocs, the lack of coordination between the president and the state governors and the federal and state governments still had a crippling effect.

In some countries in the Middle East and Africa, nation-states are still so fragmented into their traditional regional or tribal units that the central government is limited in its power to exercise law and order. This factor is an important consideration for businesses contemplating a project in such a "frontier" milieu. In southeast Turkey, for example, where the oil fields and many large-scale infrastructure projects are located, the Kurdish population makes its own law and order. Banditry and killings are common, and the local police arrest whomever they please and treat them as they like. The central government can do little to intervene in this Turkish "wild west."

Finally, regionalism in its extreme form can lead to wide-scale violence and civil war. The Ibo secessionist movement in eastern Nigeria in 1969–1970 mixed tribal autonomy with economically motivated regional separation. The latent conflict now in Nigeria between the Hausa-Fulani in the North and Yoruba in the South is a mix of regional economic imperatives, religious differences (Muslim and Christian), and tribalism.

Cultural and Traditional/Parochial Sources of Tension. Cultural heterogeneity remains a source of tension in many countries seeking to forge an almost contrived unity from an earlier diversity of languages and customs that may have developed during the colonial era. In Nigeria, the Ibo tribal structure was already a contrived product of the colonial era when it launched the Biafran secessionist movement in the late 1960s. Yet, comprised of many smaller communities with similar cultures, the "Ibo" perceived itself as a subnational, culturally interrelated entity. Hence, it opposed the Hausa-Fulani–dominated central government. In Cameroon a few years ago, former President Ahidjo adroitly deflected a potential conflict between the northern and southern regions onto the rivalry between the anglophones (English-speaking people) and the majority francophones (French-speaking people). The more recent Biya government seems to have aggravated both sources of tension. In 1984, the administration changed the school curriculum at the University of Yaoundé (the national university) without consulting the anglophone students; almost concurrently in Bamenda, in the northwest, a francophone policeman unjustly shot an anglophone youth, and local violence ensued. Against a backdrop of deteriorating economic conditions, such tensions can threaten general political and social stability. In Burma, some 26 armed, dissident ethnic groups vie for autonomous control of their territories and absorb the energies of the central government in the fighting.

Some countries have found ways to cope with such problems, and the analyst must weigh the problems against the efficacy of the procedures for alleviating them. One answer is tolerance. The PRC usually has been tolerant of the cultures and customs of its minorities. A different approach has been to use coercion against ethnic assertiveness or to cope with the matter by employing a "carrot and stick" approach. The analyst must evaluate how well these methods of control have worked. Berbers in the Kabyle (eastern Algeria) in 1981 rose up against the trend toward Arabization of the educational system. The prospect of the government's substituting Arabic for the French language in the local schools threatened the Berbers' economic mobility (i.e., the pursuit of jobs in France, where 800,000 Berbers already have found work) and their cultural identity. The government reacted quickly to the unrest by suppressing it and then by instituting a faculty of language and culture at the local university. A volatile situation was successfully defused.

Where the idea of the nation-state is still new, the conflict between central government and the modern elements of society, on the one hand, and the local ethnic or tribal political structures and practices, on the other, can lead to problems of control and to paralysis of the decision-making function. In our opinion, the civilian government in Nigeria was particularly vulnerable in this regard. The creation of 19 states that cut across the former major tribal boundaries had militated against a recurrence of civil war along tribal lines. Yet the strength of some 200 traditional cultural groups persists and makes the absorption of the groups into larger political entities a long and difficult process. For example, serious riots erupted in the northern state of Kano in July 1981 because the governor had taken steps to discredit and reduce the power of the chief emir, or religious head of state. State, not federal, buildings were symbolically set afire. More recently, conflict between fanatical Muslims and others in Kano and elsewhere in the north have created a volatile political situation in the region. Concurrent outbreaks of these sorts in combination with other types of unrest, against a backdrop of a deteriorating economy, could wreck havoc on the system and indirectly disrupt business operations.

Civil Disorder: Violence and Terrorism

The analyst must consider the prospects for organized mass violence (through unions, associations, parties or student vanguards), anomic outbursts of social violence (such as the spontaneous crowd hysteria of overturning trains and buses), or a general state of lawlessness. If a society is given to organized violence, which under certain circumstances might escalate and spread, executives should be made aware of the fact. In Colombia, for instance, corporations must monitor two countervailing trends: the spread of guerrilla activity and the gradual integration of the middle class into the political system. If successful, the latter would broaden the base of the existing political elite and could deprive the urban guerrillas at least of potential recruits.

Even if it is well short of a social revolution, civil disorder, particularly when it spreads from city to city, can disrupt international business operations and pose obvious hazards for expatriate personnel. Many countries in the Third World have histories of civil unrest. This factor alone should not be a deterrent to investing in a country or expanding operations there, but the analyst and planner should consider five variables that will help predict what to expect:

1. the history of civil violence in a given country (frequency, causes, pattern of locations);
2. the extent of the deterioration of economic, social and human rights conditions, and whether a boiling point is approaching;
3. organizations (religious, political, student, labor) that might spearhead or manipulate demonstrations or riots;

4. the likelihood of an outbreak's being easily contained by the police or military through coercion or threat thereof; and
5. the focus of acts of civil disorder: would they target foreigners and foreign businesses, and why?

Outbreaks of civil unrest are numerous and in many ways so redundant that it is unnecessary to go through a litany of them. The situation in Egypt provides an historical lesson through its cost-of-living riots in 1977 and the economic disaster that preceded them. The possibility exists for similar outbreaks by the late 1980s if the present economy continues to deteriorate and/or food subsidies are lifted. (The latter is unlikely to be undertaken too precipitously after the violent reaction that followed the lifting of subsidies in Tunisia and Morocco in winter 1983–1984.) An assessment of the way in which Mubarak has consolidated his power vis-à-vis the military and strengthened his position before the Egyptian people, as well as an appreciation of the deference toward authority in Egyptian society, suggests that the Mubarak government would have little difficulty in bringing civil disorder under control. An understanding of the mechanisms of control and their efficacy in a country is as important for the analyst or planner as the ability to identify potential sources of civil disorder and to predict volatility.

Not only is the *possibility* of a given type of civil disorder predictable, but careful observation also can anticipate the *timing* of the event. In the months preceding the food riots in January 1984 in the Rif Mountains in Morocco, a first reduction in food price subsidies was undertaken. On December 17, King Hassan II appeared on television ostensibly to talk about a new census that would lead to a more equitable distribution of wealth between rich and poor; he implicitly was letting the people know they were in for harder times under a draft budget then under consideration. At the same time, an exit tax was implemented that penalized the migrant workers in the north; a crackdown on contraband upset the smuggling operations among the poorer people of the region; the nucleus of the nation's police force was called up to provide security for the Islamic Conference meeting the king was hosting in Marrakech, thereby limiting their distribution throughout the country; and the king declared a national holiday and let the young people out of school. After the proper background analysis and briefing, a good operations executive could have followed easily the denouement of the events leading up to the popular outburst. A triumvirate of risk analyst (at headquarters or in a Washington Office), on-site operational executive or country/regional manager, and the political and economic officers in the U.S. Embassy of the host country could have forecast the limited unrest.

We should emphasize again that excessive use of state violence to deal with social violence and unrest can be the undoing of a political system. Indeed, the frequent use of force to suppress dissidence and protest can radicalize citizens who would otherwise be waverers or settle for the status quo. It is a fair measure of the weak underpinnings of a political system. The successful exercise of control is not the same as repetitive coercion.

Terrorism. Still another variant of social/political violence is terrorism. Consulting agencies in the United States and Europe specialize in monitoring acts of terrorism that range from blowing up installations, to kidnapping businessmen, to murders and political executions. Often, as in Colombia, crime or banditry, kidnapping for ransom, violence connected with the illicit drug traffic, and political protest are interwoven. The purpose of political kidnappings can be (a) to gain the release of colleagues from prison, (b) to obtain a material ransom, and (c) simply to make a political statement by the execution of the victim. We live in a world of increasing terrorism, but businessmen cannot hide from it. Nor can they create an effective image for themselves and their companies by going to work in a host country with a gun turret on the top of their cars. Since governments increasingly will refuse to meet political demands to rescue kidnap victims, and since host governments often forbid private foreign corporations to make a transfer of money in kidnapping cases, a multinational corporation or international bank can best protect its expatriate personnel by *monitoring* terrorism and by *preparing* for emergency situations in host countries. Concrete plans can provide guidance to personnel and their families for circumspection, evading would-be perpetrators on site, and responding systematically to a crisis situation; at company headquarters, a crisis action network of communications can be established.

In examining countries for both incidence of terrorism and impact on his company's interests, the political risk analyst must look for patterns that indicate *type* of activities, *location* of prevalent acts of terrorism, and the nature of the *targets*. In Peru, for example, much is written of the notorious Sendero Luminoso guerrillas. Yet they tend to choose only physical targets for maximum propaganda impact: they attack dams and other infrastructural projects to demonstrate symbolically their strength without alienating the people. They are located primarily in the southern Andes, and much of the large foreign infrastructural and petroleum development projects are in the outlying areas. Thus, in Peru, physical installations more than personnel are in jeopardy, but safety can be increased in choosing the right location. In contrast, Colombia has a higher level of kidnapping, foreigners and foreign installations sometimes are affected, and many rural areas—from Caqueta to the Magdalena Medio—are unsafe. The number of kidnappings rose from 17 in 1981, to 32 in 1982, to 20 incidents in the first three months of 1983. Even as President Betancur was signing peace agreements with key guerrilla leaders, kidnappings and executions were continuing. And even if political elements could be extirpated from the cities, widespread urban crime would continue to endanger foreigners living in Bogota who worry about the walk from their apartment in the luxurious high ground above the city to their cars in the parking lot.

Military Unrest

Countries with frequent military coups are often considered unstable. In a sense, this is untrue. In cultures where political change is routinely wrought by military takeover, there is in fact stability in instability. Moreover, military interventions often restore order by deterring or reducing social unrest that could hamper the foreign businessman. The foreign businessman or international banker need be concerned only with the impact of such a changeover on business as usual. Will the new military regime leave the private sector alone and not change the rules of the game? Will it meet the previous government's external financial obligations? In general, a military government will continue to follow a tradition of conservative politics in such situations. The businessman need be concerned only about the uncertainty and temporary paralysis that such a regime change might engender and whether his particular project(s) might be too controversial and too closely linked to the previous leadership.

Can a military coup be anticipated? Not too many years ago we questioned an expert on the likelihood of a military coup in Ghana. At the time, the civilian government of Dr. Hilla Limann was facing severe economic problems. The expert, who had in fact inadvertently allowed himself to become an advocate for democratic government in Ghana, said he considered a coup highly unlikely because no consensus for such a takeover had developed. Of course, no polls were taken when Limann was replaced by Flight Lieutenant Rawlings. A general rule is that where there is a history of military control, the military might be prepared to rise again under certain circumstances.

An analyst has to ask himself whether the military, or a part of it, thinks of itself as having political responsibilities; what general political, social, and economic circumstances would arouse its indignation? Does it picture itself as an enforcer of morality and, like Nigerian Col. Buhari's New Year's Eve coup of 1983–1984, would its mission in good part be to clean the Augean stables and to wash away corruption? In the Nigerian coup, crushing economic circumstances, official corruption, and *anxiety over the outbreak of social unrest* apparently prompted the coup; the anti-corruption issue became the banner of the intervention. Despite the Nigerian military's historical image of itself as a political instrument, no academic specialist on Nigeria seems to have predicted this outcome. Why? Because the tendency is to be afraid to accept major social or political change before it occurs. Yet a political risk analyst cannot afford to allow his judgment to be anchored in the status quo.

Further analysis of the military, even in societies like Tunisia where the military does not perceive itself as any more political than, perhaps, in France or the United States, takes on particular importance in a time of political instability when the legitimacy of the civilian government might be called into question. If the alternative to social chaos is military intervention, nuances in the military's self-perception are important. Its demographics and elite composition should be examined. The Moroccan military has generational differences. The senior officers never developed a sense of separate identity since Morocco's independence; the younger officers are more inclined to question the political order. They are also more likely to be of urban and Arab origin than the preceding generation, better educated, and drawn from the middle class in the coastal cities. They tend to be more politicized and might crave a political identity. Many even have turned to fundamentalist Islam and might use it as a legitimating symbol in the event of a coup. In contrast, in Kenya or in Venezuela a military coup is unlikely, because the military is drawn into the existing political process. (In Kenya, Kikuyo officers often marry the daughters of politicians.) And even if a coup were undertaken, it would not be likely to be other than politically conservative.

If a civilian government has become more unsteady, has the military been given a broader role in policing the people? In Peru, where Belaunde gave the military a broader role by implementing emergency rules in Lima in spring 1983, he might have set an unfortunate precedent. Soldiers rather than police enforced the curfew. Nothing may come of this phenomenon, but to avoid the threat of a coup the object is to professionalize, not politicize, a military force.

In anticipating a coup, it is also important to ask some fairly obvious questions. Are the troops happy? Do they have enough prestige, mobility (particularly junior to senior officer levels), pay, and other benefits? In Indonesia, both active and retired military officers are encouraged to take civilian and even corporate jobs. In China, the military—perhaps the one major potential source of instability—are being courted and restored to prominence at the same time as they are being professionalized. In Algeria (a highly militarized society), not only is the president a product of the military, but the army is represented in the party, state, and judiciary.

Finally, we must ask ourselves: if a coup, what then? In most cases, as we have discussed above, the most likely disruption would derive from the atmosphere of uncertainty surrounding the military takeover. A bit more elite analysis of the military is required. Information may exist on dissidence within the armed forces. There may be rivalry between field command and headquarters about reconciliation with communist insurgents, or some of the younger officers in a given country may embrace a militant form of Islam. A most important factor to consider in examining the ranks of the military in Third World countries is that elements within the armed forces might have poor, rural origins and a populist orientation that would incline them to be hostile to multinationals and international creditors if they came to power.

External Territorial Disputes

Territorial disputes have taken on new importance since the Falklands/Malvinas war in Argentina. Some country, perhaps to draw attention away from domestic ills, might ignite a smoldering feud with a neighbor. A close examination of the political rhetoric and the nature of domestic problems on both sides can help the analyst gauge the importance of this dimension of political risk. Most border disputes in the Third World have their source in colonial times when boundaries were imposed on them. What are the substance and salience of each nation's commitment to regain or retain the territory in question? Have developments occurred to defuse the emotional content of the contest? For example, by 1984 Guinea and Guinea-Bisseau had taken their dispute to the Hague for adjudication, and Nigeria and Cameroon, which in the past had argued hotly over supposedly oil-rich border areas, were enjoying cordial relations because of the Cameroon's support of the New Year's Eve coup in Nigeria.

In regions where local wars frequently erupt (such as the cluster of states surrounding Israel), a foreign company must be careful about operating in contested areas or major cities or strategic locations (i.e., where there are concentrations of heavy infrastructure). Thus, although hostilities ranging from skirmishes to war nearly always seem to be imminent between Israel and Syria, a company building a pipeline in remote western Syria is unlikely to be affected.

External territorial conflict also can be destabilizing to the domestic situation in a given country. King Hassan II of Morocco is fighting a war in the Western Sahara which his whole country applauds, despite its drain on the country's economic resources; further, if Hassan were to quit now and compromise with the Polisario, his own people might force him from his throne. In Syria, another less-than-victorious war with Israel could force Assad out of power and leave a leadership vacuum which, given a situation in which the military is preoccupied with fighting or licking its wounds, could be filled by the Muslim Brotherhood or elements sympathetic to it; such an outcome could be potentially more threatening to a Western business presence in Damascus than war itself.

Still another consideration for international planners—particularly in the extractive industries—is the inadvisability of locating in an area disputed by two or more countries. In such contests, the U.S. government usually warns in advance that it cannot be accountable for the safety of its citizens. In an area that was being offered as an oil concession off South Korea, sovereignty over the terrain is claimed not only by South Korea, but by North Korea, Taiwan, and the PRC. The PRC once shelled the boats of a previous American concessionaire.

Elites and Their Relative Influence

In examining the political stability of a country and/or the ways policies may evolve to the advantage or detriment of the international bank and multinational, the importance of identifying the key actors or groups of actors within the political and social elites and where they stand on critical issues is paramount and does not need emphasis here. The reader will see examples of it in the country studies (Mr. Coronel's exploration of political actors in Venezuela is especially impressive) and will realize that it is equally as relevant in examining developed countries as well as in assessing Third World countries. (In fact, this dimension of analysis may be more important in assessing the former because it will help to identify not the obvious events like social disorder and revolution, but the likelihood of more subtle changes in policies toward investment and trade, differences in economic philosophy, and alterations in state-private, center-local relations.) The Frost and Sullivan technique described by Coplin and O'Leary in Chapter 12 focuses almost exclusively on this dimension of analysis. Coplin and O'Leary quite rightly ask how important these actors are relative to one another and how committed they are to specific issues.

A still more refined approach would take a micro look at divergencies within one group of actors itself. Thus, within one country's military force, we may not only want to know if there is a conflict between junior and senior officers, but also how their origins and worldviews differ. Also, how well entrenched in the senior command are those officers who are less desirable from a foreign business standpoint? In the Thai army, Gen. Chawalit, who encouraged the left-leaning, so-called "Democratic Soldiers" coup in April 1981, is still a key figure in the army, still rigid in his opposition to monopolies and multinational corporations, and could well be a prime mover among the more idealistic soldiers in the future should economic and social circumstances warrant military intervention.

Among the civilians, we would look not just at the different political parties or interest groups, but at the factions within them. (a) Are these factions divisive? In Syria, one might try to examine how well-organized or fragmented is the political opposition Muslim Brotherhood. (b) Can all factions be identified? Not all are represented by a formal group. Allegiances also vary within a large group, and there are cross-cutting alliances between groups. One can make the argument that Indonesia is controlled by an interlocking directorate of elite groups, which run the gamut from the president's inner circle to the more vociferous political dissidents. Everyone seems to know everyone else personally, and the system seems to be virtually all-inclusive. To prepare for a long-term stay in such a market, a company must learn who is who, who has "stabbed whom in the back," with what party and with what faction an Indonesian friend is likely to be affiliated, how his group might lend positive support to one's enterprise and, finally, how well situated his political faction would be in the event of a leadership succession crisis. Such information probably can be obtained on site. Such an inquiry can be carried out openly as the logical and sophisticated extension of a normal check of market conditions and business associates; it can even be integrated into a public relations effort to get to know one's local principals better.

Nationalism and National Goals

In the process of nation-building, the inculcation of a shared value of nationalism among all the people within a country's boundaries is necessary for the cohesiveness of the nation-state, yet some of the permutations of this value historically have been dangerous and destabilizing to the international community (either regional or on a wider scale).

International business must be wary also of xenophobia, an historical hostility to foreigners among the people in some countries. Often, this nationalistic or ethnocentric resentment of outsiders takes the form of a proclivity to blame foreign business interests or Western materialism for corroding the traditional culture or damaging the economy.

Whether it involves an adventurous military occupation (such as the Falklands/Malvinas Islands by Argentina) or a politically explosive domestic economic crisis that is alienating the people's support for the polity, nationalism often can be effectively manipulated by the political leadership for the sake of self-preservation. If the leadership feels that its message will resonate with a xenophobic strain in the ingrained nationalism of the people, it will blame foreign investors or the high interest loans of capitalist banks. The Mexican leadership, in the last phase of Lopez Portillo's term, actually tried to turn its back on its external debt problem by manipulating what it perceived to be a shared "Yanqui go home" attitude on the part of two other debt-burdened Latin American countries. But they refused, and it was only then that Mexico began to face its problem seriously in negotiations with the International Monetary Fund (IMF).

Mexico's manifestation of a sort of *extra-national communalism* suggests that, in a shrinking world, strictly nationalistic sentiments can be stretched beyond borders to include regional loyalties, particularly in the Third World. Thus, Mexico will not betray Castro rhetorically to the United States, and Nigeria in good economic times was able to "put the squeeze" on British Petroleum because of its interests in the apartheid nation of South Africa. In the Third World in general, however, this is the weakest (and least amenable to mobilization) emotionalism. It is difficult enough for the average villager in a developing country to identify with the concept of nation-state. Yet the villager in a more modern nation-state—Morocco, for example—can become fired with fury over a squabble over national boundaries. Loyalties beyond the nation-state are thinner. While U.S. businessmen were treated badly throughout most of Latin America for the U.S. position during the Falklands/Malvinas interlude, no serious consequences resulted. The question is often raised whether Nigeria is serious about not wanting to do business with enterprises that have interests in South Africa (the implication being that these companies indirectly support apartheid). In times of internal weakness and dependency on Western economic assistance, the Nigerian political leadership is not apt to do more than pay lip service to the issue, even though it may be part of Nigeria's national ideology. In periods of economic and political strength, the Nigerian leadership could use the issue both to demonstrate its assertiveness to its people and to toy with uncooperative foreign business interests. But the issue is not important enough that the Nigerian small businessman or farmer would make material sacrifices to stand behind the black people's struggle in South Africa. In other words, the government could not afford to oust all multinationals and banks with interests in South Africa.

The Reform Versus Retrenchment Pattern

Perhaps no force can be more subversive to the legitimacy of a political system and more of a catalyst to mob violence and even social revolution than the introduction of popular reform measures—political, social, or economic—and then the reversal of these concessions. The old hypothesis that Alexander's freeing of the serfs may have set the Russian revolution in motion certainly seems to have withstood the criticism of countless social scientists. We already have discussed rising economic frustrations. What about those political and social expectations which have been encouraged and then thwarted?

As the citizen's mobility and access to the political system improves, his level of self- and political awareness usually increases. As he perceives that his horizons can be expanded, he realizes he can take more control of his destiny and can cooperate in striving to fulfill common needs with other people. In Brazil, retrenchment in the *abertura* (the opening of the political system which was initiated by President Figuereido), combined with severe economic crisis, could be the undoing of democracy.

It is easy to identify the "have nots" in a society. But how does one distinguish them from the "have not, used to have less, but expected mores"? First, one has to identify a marked effort on the part of the state to improve the lot of a certain constituency. Second, one has to discover to what extent the political leadership has developed a consensus among the elite to sustain the continuity of such reform from one administration to another. Third, one must develop a sense of the constituency's expectations from such change, its strengths and organizational potential and how defiantly it might react to a reversal.

Although our primary concerns in examining this variable are civil disorder and social revolution and their indirect impact on foreign business operations, it is possible to conceive of cases in which international business commitments are interwoven into the very process of reform and retrenchment in the host country. Speaking only hypothetically, China's related policies of Four Modernizations and Open Door *(kai-fang)* to the West could run afoul of economic setbacks; China then could blame the West, assail the international economic order for its domestic woes, turn inward again and expel the foreigners—all to avoid internal rebellion deriving from the unfulfilled expectations which the post-Mao era had created.

Social Revolution and Living with the Winners

The seemingly ultimate question is whether a social upheaval looms—a successful rebellion that would bring in a new set of elite groups and perhaps even alter the rules of the game altogether. Such revolutions depend for their success on some of the factors discussed in the preceding pages, as well as others yet to be discussed, coming together in just the right combination and with the appropriate catalyst to bring about combustion and the rise of a new social elite.

At what point does a rebellion become a revolution? Only the best intelligence can predict that a rebellious movement is gathering enough momentum or forming a coalition with other anti-systemic groups to topple a political system. Only the most objective analysis of the coordination between capital and villages can indicate whether the central government is decaying and its influence deteriorating. A simple paradigm, comprised of the existence of a rebellious organization or coalition, a binding revolutionary ideology, and the delegitimation of the central government, may not necessarily be sufficient. External interference and unknowns also can affect the outcome. As we approach the culmination of a revolutionary movement—let us say, well after the theater was set ablaze in Iran in 1978—what at first might have seemed to be a rebellion becomes a more predictably successful revolution. But there is often very little a corporate, or bank, executive can do about recovering assets from the host country. Indeed, while the existing regime still has a chance, the investor/creditor is inclined to tie his fortunes to the regime that welcomed him. After all, many revolts are launched; few succeed. A survey of companies with investments or trade exposures in Iran prior to 1979 indicates that more than 75 percent lost all but a small percentage of their assets in the Iranian revolution.

A national liberation struggle, like the war for black rule in Zimbabwe (then Rhodesia), poses a particular problem for the corporate strategist. In revolution-torn Zimbabwe, only a radical would have been so bold as to support Mugabe or the pro-Soviet Nkomo, and only a blind conservative would have identified too closely with Smith or Muzorewa. The pragmatic and conservative businessman had only one choice:

> to ensure that his losses would not be disastrous and equally that he was positioned to take advantage of opportunities if they occurred. Because of the uncertainty, he would not align himself with any individual or party. But he would recognize that the old order was finished and would carefully but visibly cut any strong existing ties to the associates of Smith and Muzorewa, taking care to do so in a way that would not lead to government reaction in the short run.[3]

If a bank or multinational already has substantial interests at stake during the course of an apparent revolutionary movement, a concerted effort should be made to analyze the character of the movement and consider one's options in the country. On-site operations executives have acquired a reputation for being politically myopic. But an open mind and intellectual curiosity, as well as a willingness to mix with local people and to listen, should be additional criteria for recruiting executives for potentially sensitive posts. Key factors to observe in assessing the denouement of a revolutionary movement as it might affect future business interests are:

1. *The nature of the personalities of the revolutionary leaders.* What is their social background? Are they likely to embrace a very populist worldview because of their origins?
2. *Factionalism.* Are there cleavages within the revolutionary elite, and can one position oneself appropriately? Is it best to address the impending revolutionary government as a collective entity?
3. *The nature of the ideology.* Does the ideology promise the realization of some apocalyptic vision upon accession to political power? Is it an adaptation of some external ideology, like Marxism-Leninism? Is it being used primarily to hold a broad-based revolutionary organization together? Is there room within its theoretical bounds for the sorts of tactical, or even strategic, flexibility that would permit private investment to continue after the revolution's victory?
4. *The question of external assistance.* In a complex revolution/civil war, such as in Zimbabwe or Angola where different revolutionary groups

have been at odds with one another, is the struggle inviting external interference by a superpower or a regional power? A given faction should not be labeled "pro-Soviet" or "pro-Chinese." The recipient of aid may repay with rhetorical fealty; but the exploited may well be the exploiter and, if necessary, allegiances can change. In Zimbabwe, Robert Mugabe, called "pro-Chinese" and a "Maoist" in the 1960s and 1970s, still shares a cordial relationship with the PRC, but then China has changed markedly; it was Mugabe's ZANU party-dominated government, not the Chinese, that first encouraged a mixed, private-public economy.

Given the likelihood that revolutionary movements from time to time will ascend to power, a foreign company or bank can roll with the punches. Gulf Oil is still ensconced in Angola ten years after independence and civil war. And Marxist-Leninist social revolutions do evolve—a basically foreign ideology that serves a revolutionary movement well as an organizing set of principles may have to be altered to cope with the harsh realities of the aftermath of victory.

THE POLITICAL CULTURAL DIMENSION

One very important facet of political risk analysis is the recognition that every nation has its own unique cultural characteristics, the more salient of which may affect political attitudes and behavior and may even constitute constraints against social disorder and upheaval. For this analysis, the political science term "political culture" serves best to describe this dimension. Sidney Verba defines this approach thus: "The political culture of a society consists of the system of empirical beliefs, expressive symbols, and values which defines the situation in which a political action takes place."[4] Defining the term further, Lucian Pye states: "Each generation must receive its politics from the previous one [and] react against that process to find its own politics."[5] In other words, political culture is a country's subjective orientation to politics that develops psychodynamically over generations.

Often, an appreciation of the special characteristics that influence one nation's particular political orientation can have a direct, positive impact on doing business there. The strategic planner or international business development executive can draw on these elements to formulate a marketing approach to that country or to position his organization comfortably for a long stay in that particular market. Let us examine the ways in which a country's political culture might affect the stability of the broader political environment for international business operations.

Constraints Against Upheavals and Image of the World

Any society has certain values, orientations, and organizational characteristics that lend themselves to top-down manipulation for the purpose of control. Often, these psychological levers of political and social control outweigh the apparent political risks, and the analyst should be as attentive to one side of the equation as to the other. Some societies have psychosocial safety valves, such as an entrepreneurially prevalent "minority," against which the government can deflect hostilities that ought to be directed against the system itself.

In societies like Indonesia and Algeria, social control and manipulation by the political leadership seem to coincide with a deep attitude of deference toward authority on the part of the people. In Algeria, the regime will respond to a mass demonstration first by dispatching the military to the scene to knock heads and make arrests and then by taking steps to pacify the interest groups in question. The military barracks are omnipresent throughout Algiers and outlying towns, and create a peculiarly somber atmosphere. In Indonesia, the authoritarian approach of the Suharto government always has been effective; however, ironically, because it has compromised too much in its treatment of the Islamic fundamentalists, it might face tougher problems ahead. Other societies seem inclined to accept the oppression of authoritarian regimes as preferable alternatives to earlier periods of political chaos, gang or guerrilla terrorism, and general social uncertainty.

Often, a combination of political cultural orientation and social structure works against mass upheavals. For instance, a dense urban population, comprised of somewhat educated people who are unable to find proper employment, is expected to be a constituency eager for a social protest movement. Yet, though circumstances conform to this paradigm in Algeria, they are offset by the migration of whole extended families to the city at one time. The preservation of the rural family unit ameliorates the psychological trauma of leaving home for a "better life in the city."

In Mexico a plethora of complex social and political conditions exists that in another milieu could portend a political cataclysm. These include the following: an extremely uneven distribution of wealth between the cities and countryside, a high debt burden coupled with near-zero economic growth, an adult workforce only 50 percent of which is adequately employed, an acute population growth problem, an inordinate number of politically aware young people entering an overburdened job market, an outmoded land tenure system, extreme rural-to-urban migration, and a frightening density of population in the main cities. Add to these factors severe economic jolts, which stem in part from worldwide conditions, and one can imagine hordes of political risk consultants clamoring at the doors of major corporations, offering a diagnostic work-up and a series of prescriptions for "another Iran."

Mexico, however, is in little danger of either social revolution or military takeover for a number of sound political and economic reasons. The facets on which we will focus here are social and political cultural:

1. Mexico's social structure in general and its political system in particular are characterized by patron-client relationships through which political dissidents are coopted into the system and which assures top-down control. The people seem to respect power and a central authority. Each person in a position of authority is limited by authoritative and paternalistic powers

above him. The patron-client relationship is so well developed that in most instances local grievances involving everything from health clinics to sewerage are settled by appeal to the local political authority. More vocal critics of the system at the grassroots level are usually coopted into it.

2. An apparently low level of interpersonal trust tends to militate against the formation of collective groupings that might pit themselves against the macro-system.

3. Family consciousness is strong and normally will take precedence over other social and political obligations—a factor which also works against a person's taking the risk of joining or forming a political organization that is apt to get his family into trouble. Also, as in Algeria, the existence of large, extended families in urban areas tends to dispel feelings of displacement or anomie that might otherwise contribute to anti-social behavior in political form.

Image of the World. A people's image of itself, its memory of events, fundamental attitudes, and unconscious fears can be relayed from one generation to another and can be reflected in its view of the outside world. This perception may be revealed in the speeches and writings of its preeminent personalities—past and present—and in the efforts of political leaders to manipulate certain sentiments among the people. Some insight into a country's perspective on its purpose and how it fits into the outside world can help the foreign businessperson understand how and why he/she might be perceived a certain way. Can the American operations executive, for example, who is seeking to make headway in a francophone African country, adapt to the prejudices against him and exploit the weaknesses of competitors who are nationals of other countries?

From the standpoint of political risk, what is the propensity of a country to xenophobia or to more specifically directed hostility toward a major economic power? As Gustavo Coronel points out in his case study, the Venezuelan people have a deep-seated resentment of the United States because of its historical support for authoritarian governments in Venezuela, and thus are particularly sensitive to American intrusiveness in Latin American affairs.

Could a national leader, under adverse economic conditions, point a finger at a foreign country or company and evoke a special emotional, popular reaction that would divert attention away from the government in power? Could a Third World nation—at one time wedded to the West in a colonial or neo-colonial relationship—have a national compensation neurosis? In China, to cite one possible example, there may be an historical memory, perpetuated by political elites over the generations, of the depredations wrought by Western imperialist countries in the nineteenth century. Are the United States, European countries, and the Japanese now being made to compensate for past misbehavior by an unusually demanding sort of technology transfer? Or, to go back in history even further, are the barbarians expected to pay *tribute* to the middle kingdom before getting on with their normal commerce? At the same time, Westerners put themselves at a disadvantage with the

Chinese by virtue of standing in awe of China. The above are merely musings—but important musings nonetheless.

U.S. GOVERNMENT CONSTRAINTS ON DOING BUSINESS ABROAD

Heretofore, we have examined political risks that derive from the environment of the host country. Often, the political relations between our government and that of the host country have a direct influence on opportunities and conditions for doing business. A company that operates in a country where its own government cannot protect its nationals is taking on an added risk. The corporation should first determine whether opportunity outweighs risk and/or whether it has the leverage on its own to secure its position in the country in question.

A diplomatic reversal can constitute even more of a trauma than the absence of normalized relations in the first place. Whereas the opening or upgrading of diplomatic relations between the home country and country x can lead to an investment treaty, trade initiatives, and even a honeymoon period in bilateral business relations, the deterioration of diplomatic relations can severely impair business with the host country. A U.S. multinational is particularly vulnerable to hostility and abuse, sometimes expressed in violent acts of terrorism against installations because they seem to stand symbolically for the politics and economics of the home government. Robert Ebel notes:

> Contracts can not be equated with diplomatic relations, which can be turned on and off as circumstances dictate. A corporation can not pull out, leaving behind an "Interests Section" to look after matters . . . A corporation either attempts to live up to the terms of a contract, or it leaves. Generally, a corporation will do what it can to protect its current and future income and will stay on unless forced out by threat of life.[6]

A corporation can ill afford the damages to its reputation, not to mention the loss of its investments or assets, of withdrawing from the country in question. At the same time, it stands naked in the chill of the host country's political climate and frequently suffers from the related punitive measures of its own government (such as the U.S. government's refusal to grant visas for needed personnel in existing operations in Libya).

Trade Sanctions/Embargoes/East-West Trade

It is quite understandable that the climate of diplomatic relations between two countries can have an indirectly salutary or adverse effect on bilateral commerce. But for international businessmen the most noisome aspect of international relations concerns the manipulation of trade to augment foreign policy objectives. Indeed, sometimes the political disincentives to doing business abroad derive not from the elements of instability in the countries in question, but from one's own government's manipulation of trade for political purposes.

The United States, in particular, always has controlled exports for national security, foreign policy, and short supply reasons. The United States also is notorious for using embargoes or exercising restrictions on dual technology solely for punctuating a particular policy message to the government of the country in question. When another government acts in a way that the U.S. finds threatening, or even at odds with our national policy, we frequently resort to trade sanctions against it. In effect, we punish that foreign government by not permitting it to purchase those goods and services we regard as important to it. Unfortunately, seldom is one country the sole source of supply available to the purchaser, and our companies suffer in the process.

Short of actual embargoes but just as harmful to U.S.–based multinationals, export controls imposed for foreign policy purposes can be employed as sanctions over such issues as South African apartheid, human rights, nuclear non-proliferation, transnational aggression, terrorism, or East-West tensions (always depicted as necessary for our national security). Again, the U.S. private sector pays the price.

The proclivity of large, supplier nations—particularly the United States—to utilize trade controls sanctions against other countries makes it necessary for us to look for trends in our own government's foreign policy instead of merely casting our gaze outward toward the host country in question. Recently, both the Carter and Reagan administrations have had their own sets of trade sanctions, predictable on the basis of foreign policy goals and values articulated publicly. In our strategic planning, we can do our best to ready ourselves for this loss of markets by identifying those which seem to be most vulnerable in the context of international politics.

The U.S. Foreign Corrupt Practices Act

In 1978, in the spirit of continuing to make the United States a standard bearer for the rest of the world, Congress passed the Foreign Corrupt Practices Act, which was designed to prohibit corporate bribery of foreign government officials. Putting aside the philosophical question whether one nation should impose its values on another, the language of the act puts the American businessman in jeopardy whenever he attempts to do business in a Third World country where some degree of what we call corruption has become an institutionalized social and political practice. What we regard as corruption often is just "the way things are done" in country x, and the language of the Foreign Corrupt Practices Act places too much of a burden on the U.S. businessman to become enough of an insider both to understand and, if necessary, set straight local business practices.

Let us focus on just one particular aspect of the Act. Under the bribery provision, a company may be liable in accordance with the "reason to know" standard if an agent pays a bribe, even if the company had no knowledge of the agent's actions or intent. Moreover, there are no standards for what constitutes a "reason to know." Suppose a certain corporation is seeking an oil concession in the Middle East. To accomplish his objective, the corporate representative must hire an agent in the country in question. Through his connections, that agent makes it possible for him to meet with the appropriate officials to negotiate a concession. The agent then collects his commission. It is known that pay-offs are commonplace in this particular country. Does the representative have "reason to know" that the agent's fee will be shared with government officials? In effect, was he paying the appropriate officials for meeting with him, and did he have reason to know that this might be the case? If so, he is guilty of violating the Foreign Corrupt Practices Act and is subject to fine and imprisonment.

In effect, the act inhibits the American businessman from seeking to penetrate certain markets. Many companies have ignored opportunities in Nigeria or Indonesia for this reason; others have approached too cautiously and inadvertently yielded the ground to their competitors. Should the businessman ask for a letter from his local agent or principals in which they disavow the intention of using bribery, or will he be offending and alienating them in the asking?

In general, this act is a real hindrance to American business overseas. Not only is its language ambiguous, but its purpose is questionable and even self-defeating. What we regard as venality is just a way of distributing wealth or compensating underpaid bureaucrats and officials in many cultures.

Anti-Boycott Restrictions

In yet another way the U.S. government obstructs business operations overseas. The Export-Administration Act expressly prohibits U.S. entities from refusing to do business with a boycotted firm or in a boycotted country, when that boycott is fostered or imposed by any country against a country friendly to the U.S. Of course, the allusion is specifically to the Arab boycott of Israel. As Hermann Eilts indicated in his chapter on Saudi Arabia, Americans, like the U.S. government itself, are now caught in the middle of this interminable dispute. Relevant statutes enumerate in great detail what U.S. firms can and cannot do under this boycott, all accompanied by very detailed reporting requirements. As an example, a company may be charged for failing even to report a boycott request, let alone complying with such a request.

Suffice it to say that the reporting burden alone would deter many smaller firms from entering the marketplace, and for larger firms it means maintaining a separate staff to follow boycott-related developments in order to ensure compliance.

The Act of State Doctrine

The Act of State Doctrine is largely unique to the United States. Born in more gentlemanly times two centuries ago, it means in essence that the legality of any action by any foreign state committed within its own territory cannot be challenged in our courts. An aggrieved U.S. company is offered sympathy and nothing else, hence the greater need in the United States for the political risk analyst to alert his firm to potential governmental actions that could have a negative impact on assets or operations.

Thus, the U.S. government can be the private sector's worst enemy in dealing with certain foreign countries. In a sense, in many areas of the world, U.S. businesspersons may be at counterpoint with their own government. Objectives do differ. Making money is not necessarily consistent with national geopolitical goals. The activities of several U.S. oil companies in Angola constitute an example of being somewhat at odds with the U.S. government. And when the U.S. government fails to recognize a particular country, it makes operating in that country more uncertain and frightening for U.S. corporations and personnel. An individual will think twice before taking his family to the People's Democratic Republic of Yemen, for example, when one of the last Americans there—a stamp collector—was arrested and interned for several years. Further, because our government assumes a neutral posture in all territorial disputes, certain operations in contested areas will not be protected by the U.S. government. And if a contract is repudiated in the middle of a deal, the U.S. government will not consider the matter in its courts. Finally, if the U.S. government wants to put pressure on a given country in which U.S. corporations are operating, it may implement economic sanctions that disrupt their in-country operations or put them out of business altogether.

NOTES

1. See *Christian Science Monitor,* August 28, 1984, pp. 16–17.
2. Conversations with an authoritative source, Council on Foreign Relations, New York, 1984.
3. William H. Overholt, *Political Risk* (London: Euromoney Publications, 1982), p. 20.
4. Lucian W. Pye and Sidney Verba, eds., *Political Culture and Political Development* (Princeton: Princeton University Press, 1965), p. 513.
5. Ibid., p. 7.
6. Robert E. Ebel, "The Magic of Political Risk Analysis," in Mark B. Winchester, ed., *The International Essays for Business Decision Makers* Vol. 5 (1982), 300.

chapter three

Assessing the Economic Side of the Equation

FINANCIAL AND COMMERCIAL VARIABLES

As has been stated, the risks involved in financial transactions, particularly in developing countries, are at once political and economic. Political and economic risk are intertwined and, in reality, cannot be separated. Having recognized this phenomenon, however, we must make an analytical distinction between the two categories. Political risk involves the possibility of financial loss due to government actions such as expropriation, the imposition of crippling legal restrictions, a freeze of assets, insistence on divestment, or disruptions from various types of popular agitation and civil disorders. Financial risk, on the other hand, entails currency and related problems such as devaluation, inconvertibility, delays in payment, rescheduling of external debt, default, and deposit blockages. Although the causes of the two sets of risks cannot always be separated into political/social or macroeconomic variables, we can analyze the salient economic indicators.

Although it is impossible to foresee with absolute certainty what risks are entailed by investment in a particular country, it is possible for the treasurer or finance department, with the assistance of the political risk department, to develop an accurate, up-to-the-minute assessment of those factors—foreign exchange fluctuation and control, devaluation, and payment delays—that bear most closely on investment and to maintain and update these analyses at short intervals. This part of the country risk evaluation, if scrupulously researched and carefully organized, can be presented in a concise, comprehensive form. To demonstrate this approach in formulating such assessments, country x will be used as a case study.

When an organization lends foreign exchange to an entity in another country or expects to earn foreign exchange from operations in that country, it must rely on the ability of that nation's economy to generate sufficient foreign exchange not only to carry out its day-to-day operations, but also to repay loans denominated in foreign currencies. Therefore, while it is important to consider the country's overall economic performance, the international transactions of the economy have the most direct bearing on whether a

Special acknowledgment is made here to Dr. Fariborz Ghadar for his substantive contribution to this chapter.

multinational doing business in that country will be able to realize a return on its outlay. The financial risk evaluation of country x, therefore, begins with a summary that quickly establishes the details of this context and isolates the key factors involved.

Summary: The general long-term deterioration of the current account since 1972 and the large amounts of maturing short-term debt are two of the most pressing problems facing this economy. In general terms, the current account deficit can be attributed to the two-year slump in world commodity prices. This slump is the result of the world recession and the historical overvaluation of the currency relative to the currencies of its major trading partners. Country x must take corrective measures to improve its current account position. Failure to do this may adversely affect the country's long-term development plans because of shortages of foreign exchange. Consequently, in the next six months, the government must accelerate its efforts to devalue the currency and will maintain or increase foreign exchange restrictions in an effort to improve the economy and avoid payment delays.

After establishing this profile of the country's international economic standing, noting the pressing need for devaluation and the likely effect of devaluation on foreign exchange restrictions and debt repayment capability, analysis should concentrate at least on the following six indicators of international performance:

1. Current account
2. Debt service ratio
3. Reserves-to-import ratio
4. Export composition
5. Currency competitiveness
6. Import incompressibility.

These indicators reliably measure a country's ability to generate the foreign exchange necessary to service foreign investment and to repay international loans because they produce a comprehensive and interrelated picture of the economy. These indicators can also be used to provide common ground for assessing the comparative risks of investment in one country or another. It should be stressed that the information used in calculating these parameters must be current. The volatility of developing nations as well as that of the international marketplace requires that economic developments be closely followed, that reports on these countries be updated quarterly, if not more often, and that special attention be focused on the semiannual and quarterly trends of the previous two years. Old data may be useless or worse because it may mislead as well as misinform. Therefore, information from commonly available references such as the *World Bank Debt Tables* and *International Financial Statistics* must be supplemented by the most current available data gathered from private, independent experts and, in particular, from field representatives of subsidiaries. Furthermore, this data must be verified by at least two sources to ensure that it is reliable and unbiased. Current data is useless if it is not totally objective.

The definition, implications, and significance of each of the six key parameters chosen are discussed below, and are followed by the appropriate data for country x to illustrate the concise and usable format in which such data can be framed.

1. Current account. The current account position of a country is the net balance (exports less imports) on all transactions of merchandise goods, services, and unilateral transfers with all other countries within a specified time period. Consequently, it is a measure of the foreign exchange flow into or out of a country. Generally, in developing countries, a current account deficit over exports of 10 to 20 percent is cautionary; above 20 percent it is alarming. Persistent deficits affect exchange rates and can result in the imposition of currency controls and import restrictions, which could hamper the operations of multinational corporations. The data show that country x's current account position has been at an alarming level since 1981 (see Table 3.1).

2. Debt service ratio. The debt service ratio is the percent of total exports required to finance annual interest and principal repayments on external debt. It indicates the portion of a country's foreign exchange earnings that must go to repay loans. Foreign exchange used to repay foreign debt is unavailable to other areas of the economy. Different analyses use different figures for computing the debt service ratio. In general, ratios based on both public and private debt are most accurate. While short-term debt (less than a year) is not often included in debt service calculations, it must be ascertained that this

Table 3.1   Country X Current Account (in millions of U.S. $)

	Exports FOB	Imports FOB	Transfers Net S-T	Curr. Acct. Balance	Curr. Acct./ Exports %
1977	3514.00	3133.00	59.00	440.00	12.5213
1978	4130.00	3881.00	73.00	322.00	7.7966
1979	4851.00	4461.00	100.00	490.00	10.1010
1980	5862.00	6186.00	165.00	−159.00	−2.7124
1981	5014.00	7152.00	243.00	−1895.00	−37.7942
1982 1st half	2571.00	3712.00	124.00	−2034.00 (a)	−39.5566
1982 2nd half	2421.00	3795.00	124.00	−2500.00 (a)	−51.6316
1982	4992.00	7507.00	248.00	−2267.00	−45.4127
1983 1st quarter	1204.00 (e)	1720.00 (e)	62.50 (e)	−1814.00 (a)	−37.6661
1983 2nd quarter	1355.00 (e)	1648.00 (e)	62.50 (e)	−922.00 (a)	−17.0111
1983 3rd quarter	1304.00 (e)	1863.00 (e)	62.50 (e)	−1986.00 (a)	−38.0752
1983 4th quarter	1154.00 (e)	1936.00 (e)	62.50 (e)	−2878.00 (a)	−62.3484
1983	5017.00 (e)	7167.00 (e)	250.00 (e)	−1900.00 (e)	−37.8712

(e) = estimate.
(a) = annualized.
Note: All 1977–82 data from November 1983 IFS.

Table 3.2 Country X Debt Service Ratios: Public, and Public and Private

	Debt Service Ratio—Public Only (millions US $)					Debt Service Ratio—Public and Private (millions US $)				
	Principal payments	Interest payments	Total debt service	Exports	Debt Service ratio	Principal payments	Interest payments	Total Debt service	Exports	Debt Service ratio
1977	175.50	137.10	312.60	3556.00	8.79	234.10	161.00	395.10	3556.00	11.11
1978	224.80	168.20	393.00	4174.00	9.42	287.30	198.80	486.10	4174.00	11.65
1979	430.10	227.10	657.20	4952.00	13.27	472.20	270.10	742.30	4952.00	14.99
1980	263.10	282.20	545.30	5655.00	9.64	316.20	296.70	612.90	5655.00	10.84
1981	308.70	416.90	725.60	4953.00	14.65	581.70	564.10	1145.80	4953.00	23.13
1982 1st half	164.55	263.20	427.75	2571.00	16.64	N.A.	N.A.	674.50	2571.00	26.23
1982 2nd half	164.55	263.20	427.75	2421.00	17.67	N.A.	N.A.	674.50	2421.00	27.86
1982	329.10	526.40	855.50	4992.00	17.14	N.A.	N.A.	1349.00	4992.00	27.02
1983 1st quarter	101.15	140.05	241.20	1204.00 (e)	20.03	N.A.	N.A.	477.00	1204.00 (e)	39.62
1983 2nd quarter	101.15	140.05	241.20	1355.00 (e)	17.80	N.A.	N.A.	477.00	1355.00 (e)	35.20
1983 3rd quarter	101.15	140.05	241.20	1304.00 (e)	18.50	N.A.	N.A.	477.00	1304.00 (e)	36.58
1983 4th quarter	101.15	140.05	241.20	1154.00 (e)	20.90	N.A.	N.A.	477.00	1154.00 (e)	41.33
1983	404.60	560.20	964.80	5017.00 (e)	19.23	N.A.	N.A.	1908.00	5017.00 (e)	38.03

(e) = estimate.
N.A. = not available.
Note: 1977–81 Total debt service and exports from World Debt Tables.
1982 and 1983 public debt service figures are World Debt Table projections.
1982 and 1983 public and private debt service figures are Morgan Guaranty projections adjusted for short-term rollover debt. Without this adjustment the debt service figures would be 95% for 1982 and 98% for 1983. 1982 exports are from IFS.

type of debt does not rise too rapidly as a percentage of total borrowing. A debt service ratio of 20 to 30 percent is cautionary; above 30 percent it is alarming. Everything else being equal, an alarming debt service index indicates the need for a more restrictive foreign exchange policy. The data demonstrate that country x's combined public and private debt service ratio reached a precarious level in 1983, while its public sector debt service ratio continued to approach the cautionary level in 1983 (see Table 3.2).

3. <u>Reserve-to-import ratio</u>. International reserves consist of a country's holdings of gold, its special drawing rights (SDRs), and its foreign exchange and reserve position in the IMF. The reserves are used to protect a country from fluctuations in foreign exchange earnings. International reserves divided by imports of goods and services produce the reserve-to-import ratio. This percentage, in turn, is expressed as the number of months the reserves on hand could cover current imports. A ratio of two to three months is considered cautionary; less than two months is considered alarming. The ratio is used to measure a country's ability to weather temporary balance-of-payments difficulties. A country's foreign exchange reserve can be used to finance imports and debt payments during periods of reduced export earnings or high import demand. In general, an alarming indicator shows a loss of flexibility to cope with foreign exchange fluctuations and a need for immediate action if cross-border flow conditions deteriorate. Because the diversity of export and import baskets affect the need for reserves, this factor must be considered when interpreting this ratio. The data show that country x's reserves-to-imports ratio remained at the satisfactory level in 1983, while continuing a four-year decline (see Table 3.3).

4. <u>Export composition</u>. Export composition is the degree of concentration of each commodity in the overall export picture of a country. It measures vulnerability due to dependence on one commodity or a narrow range of commodities. The export composition factor measures what percentage of a nation's export revenue the commodity accounts for and how dependent a given economy is on commodities in general. Dependence on one commodity for 30 to 50 percent of the economy's foreign exchange would be cautionary, while more than 50 percent is considered alarming.

5. <u>Currency competitiveness</u>. Currency competitiveness measures the extent to which local inflation has been offset by the exchange rate movements. It is the inflation index divided by the exchange index. A high domestic inflation rate eventually will render a country's exports noncompetitive in the world market and imports less costly than domestic goods. This situation is disastrous for domestic producers and causes large current account deficits. The normal remedy is to devalue the local currency, thereby reversing the trend. The theoretical extent of devaluation needed to achieve currency competitiveness can be tentatively projected. An index of 1.3 to 1.5 is cautionary; an index above 1.5 is alarming. It is difficult to project a completely reliable range for this factor, however. In the case of country x, the data show that country's currency competitiveness to have hovered at the cautionary level for the last four years (see Table 3.4).

Table 3.3   Country X Reserves/Imports (in millions U.S. $ end of period, except imports)

	Reserves less gold	Gold—million Troy ounces	Gold—mkt price edp London	Gold reserves	Total res. incl. gold	Imports	Res. as % of imports	Res. in mos of imports
1977	1747.00	1.7310	160.60	278.00	2025.00	3133.00	64.63	7.76
1978	2366.00	1.9610	208.20	408.28	2774.28	3881.00	71.48	6.58
1979	3844.00	2.3170	455.20	1054.70	4898.70	4461.00	109.81	13.18
1980	4831.00	2.7870	595.20	1658.82	6489.82	6186.00	104.91	12.59
1981	4801.00	3.3550	410.70	1377.90	6178.90	7152.00	86.39	10.37
1982 1st half	4301.00	3.5790	314.90	1127.03	5428.03	7424.00 (a)	73.11	8.77
1982 2nd half	3861.00	3.8170	444.00	1694.75	5555.75	7590.00 (a)	73.20	8.78
1982	3861.00	3.8170	444.00	1694.75	5555.75	7507.00	74.01	8.88
1983 1st quarter	3157.00	3.9250	419.90	1651.05	4808.05	6880.00 (a)	69.88	8.39
1983 2nd quarter	2774.00	4.0250	413.00	1662.33	4436.33	6592.00 (a)	67.30	8.08
1983 3rd quarter	2015.00	4.1450	405.30	1679.97	3694.97	7452.00 (a)	49.58	5.95
1983 4th quarter	2000.00 (e)	4.2000 (e)	385.00 (e)	1617.00	3617.00	7744.00 (a)	46.71	5.60
1983	2000.00 (e)	4.2000 (e)	385.00 (e)	1617.00	3617.00	7167.00 (e)	50.47	6.06

(e) = estimate.
(a) = annualized.
Note: All reserve data from November 1983 IFS.

Table 3.4 Country X Currency Competitiveness: Change in Inflation/ Exchange Rate

	Consumer Price Index—Country X 1975 = 100	Exchange rate	Consumer Price Index—USA 1975 = 100	Ratio
1977	159.40	37.86	115.40	1.20
1978	189.40	41.00	125.90	1.21
1979	258.50	44.00	142.60	1.36
1980	327.70	50.92	160.30	1.32
1981	413.50	59.07	174.60	1.32
1982 1st half	473.90	63.84	180.30	1.36
1982 2nd half	512.96	70.29	181.42	1.33
1982	512.96	70.29	181.42	1.33
1983 1st quarter	536.38	74.19	182.04	1.31
1983 2nd quarter	570.87	78.51	184.94	1.30
1983 3rd quarter	607.97 (e)	83.40	188.22 (e)	1.28
1983 4th quarter	647.49 (e)	89.27 (e)	190.49 (e)	1.26
1983	647.49 (e)	89.27 (e)	190.49 (e)	1.26

(e) = estimate.

Note: All data except estimates from IFS.

 1975 CPI (US and Country X) = 100.

 1975 exchange rate: 32.96P/dollar

 CPI and exchange rate are end of period figures.

6. Import incompressibility. Food and fuel are considered to be essential imports; that is, they are considered vital to the economy of a country. The ratio of food and fuel to the total import of goods and services determines the import incompressibility of a country's economy. The ability of a country to discourage imports by manipulating the exchange rate depends in large part on the composition of its imports. Comparatively high dependence on essential imports reduces the feasibility of devaluation as a means of reducing total imports to more manageable levels, and may lead to the imposition of foreign exchange controls. An indicator between 25 and 35 percent is considered cautionary; an indicator above 35 percent is considered alarming. The data show that country x's import incompressibility has steadily risen from a satisfactory level in 1970 to a cautionary level in 1983 (see Table 3.5).

The data used in calculating these six indicators, the trends which the indicators suggest, and the interrelationships among the data and the trends can be concisely and pointedly assimilated into the country report. In an integrated approach designed to convey a thorough conception of the financial risks that bear on investment in a particular country, the user is encouraged to study and consider the data base, the tabulation of the data in the reports, tables, and graphs, and the discursive assessments and judgments made from the statistical and analytical substructure of the report. The

Table 3.5 Country × Import Incompressibility

	Fuel Imports		Food Imports		Food and Fuel as % of Total Imports
	% of imports	US $ millions	% of imports	US $ millions	
1977	6.80	213.04	9.70	303.90	16.50
1978	7.30	283.31	8.50	329.89	15.80
1979	10.10	450.56	7.10	316.73	17.20
1980	12.20	754.69	9.30	575.30	21.50
1981	13.00	929.76	10.00	715.20	23.00 (e)
1982 1st half	14.00 (a)	1039.36	11.00 (a)	816.64	25.00 (a)
1982 2nd half	14.00 (a)	1062.60	11.00 (a)	834.90	25.00 (a)
1982	14.00 (e)	1050.98	11.00 (e)	825.77	25.00 (e)
1983 1st quarter	15.00 (a)	1032.00	12.00 (a)	825.60	27.00 (a)
1983 2nd quarter	15.00 (a)	988.80	12.00 (a)	791.04	27.00 (a)
1983 3rd quarter	15.00 (a)	1117.80	12.00 (a)	894.24	27.00 (a)
1983 4th quarter	15.00 (a)	1161.60	12.00 (a)	929.28	27.00 (a)
1983	15.00 (e)	1075.05	12.00 (e)	860.04	27.00 (e)

(e) = estimate.
(a) = annualized.
Note: All data except estimates from IMF Supplement on Trade Statistics.

financial risk picture in a given country becomes clarified but is not oversimplified. In the case of country x, for example, in-context analysis of the data and interpretation of the trends of the six key economic indicators lead to a detailed but succinct assessment of the pivotal financial considerations in this case—devaluation, foreign exchange controls, and debt repayment.

This kind of analysis—focusing on the essential problems themselves—is most useful to risk managers and planners. However murky the economic situation of a country may be, it is important—indeed, essential—that the delineation and analysis of its problems be unambiguous and direct. This need for a committed analytical clarity should produce not simplistic blanket descriptions of a country's economic situation, but an open-eyed and tough-minded interpretation of the current facts and the recent historical trends. No risk assessment is foolproof or guaranteed, but to be useful a risk assessment must be as precise and confident as possible within the limits of the predictability of economic events. The conclusion of a country report should generalize and conjecture from a firm base of specific facts and trends, both economic and political.

Equipped with the knowledge that such country reports provide, those concerned with foreign investment in the developing world can approach individual transactions with a clearly defined understanding of the essential financial characteristics of a country's economy and an understanding supported by up-to-the-minute and reliable data. This information can facilitate foreknowledge of problems associated with such operations as the year-end translation of funds. Major devaluations, currency controls, significant debt rescheduling, and delays in payment all can be anticipated. In addition, this type of approach, based on risk indicators, can provide the basis for a compromise between centralized and decentralized control of foreign exchange operations. It provides the local manager with the leeway to borrow and lend as well as to cover exposed positions at corporate rates, while enabling the centralized treasury to foresee the net local position of its subsidiaries in order to decide if it needs to obtain a forward exchange contract from a commercial bank. This system is particularly beneficial to the non-bank multinational because it encourages local initiative while leaving the management of foreign exchange controls to the centralized treasury. Service companies, which depend on the foreign exchange earnings of the country to provide funds, will derive special benefits from this approach. This method of financial risk analysis is very useful for companies whose projects have long gestation periods and where project financing depends on future local earnings to either repay the loan involved or to compensate the parent multinational company.

COMMERCIAL DISINCENTIVES

Each business opportunity also should be studied in terms of its commercial environment or market conditions. Although commercial factors do not seem to fall within the purview of political risk per se, they are an integral part of the business environment. Commercial features are more like disincentives than risks, but they can facilitate or erode a business deal. More important for our understanding of the scope of political risk analysis is the awareness that political factors can have commercial consequences. Spain is an example. To appease the left wing of its socialist party (PSOE) and secure its support for joining NATO, the Felipe Gonzalez administration canceled contracts for five of ten U.S. Eximbank–financed nuclear power facilities. In this case, political considerations clearly determined commercial behavior. Similarly, commercial behavior can affect the political climate. In Venezuela a few years ago, just as political attitudes were softening toward foreign intervention, an American construction company—with more than the usually permitted share of local equity ownership—advertised its enterprise as its own, reactivated Venezuelan nationalism and, in turn, reenforced the formalized restraints on foreign ownership.

Although it is important to recognize the relevancy of commercial variables and their interdependence with macroeconomic/financial and political/social characteristics, this sphere is best left to the marketing executives for detailed analysis. For the purpose of establishing a formula for assessing a country's risk environment, let us enumerate the broader aspects of commercial risk that ought to be considered. These include *restrictions on capital flows,* such as import controls and deliberately engineered problems in currency transfer on both sides through the Central Bank; *limitations on foreign investment,* including prescribed limits and guidelines for equity ownership, expansion, and divestment (these may vary with a change in the host government's administration or with a change in political atmosphere); *limits on the employment of expatriate personnel* (a real impediment when a project requires skilled labor not readily available in the host country); *limits on the local availability of skilled or unskilled labor* (in some countries, even the slightly skilled workers may have migrated to other countries for more lucrative jobs); *bureaucratic inefficiency and corruption,* which in some cases can bog down business deals and operations to such an extent that they make the Ethiopian government's management of the distribution of food and aid to its starving seem smooth; *contract repudiation*; *arbitrary action against performance guarantee bonds*; *punitive corporate or personal income taxation* (in Tunisia expatriates are taxed so highly that a company's use of its own managerial personnel is restricted de facto); *the official attitude toward contract arbitration*; and the impediment of a *weak physical infrastructure* (in Guinea, for example, with less than 700 miles of paved roads, any project necessarily would incur a heavy front-end cost just to create the proper environment, transportation and communications to get under way).

THE POLITICAL-ECONOMIC INTERFACE

Although analytical distinctions must be made, it takes little imagination to suppose that politics, political culture, economy, and commercial conditions are all interrelated. Nevertheless, how often one hears the comment that because there is little one can do to control the vagaries of a nation's politics, one ought to focus on financial variables alone. The reality is that in many cases if the analyst or strategic planner does not consider political variables, he may go awry in his financial predictions. Hence, although all pertinent financial indicators suggest the need for an expeditious maxi-devaluation in Colombia (a country with a severe balance-of-payments problem and a fast leak in its hard currency and gold reserves), one must take into account that a maxi-devaluation in 1962 had disastrous political consequences and that the memory of the event caused Colombian leaders in 1967 to change their minds about a commitment to the IMF to devalue. In Mexico, one of the factors that would have militated against a major devaluation in 1985 would have been a political cultural linkage of such a step with a compromise of national pride. And in Indonesia, where gradual devaluation might normally be expected over the next few years, President Suharto's "political style" leads us to predict that when a devaluation is implemented, it will be done in one swoop.

It is also important to look at a longer-range, attitudinal history of the country in question. For example, in spite of its current guarantee concerning repatriation of profits, Turkey has had a long history of currency controls. Given another hard currency shortage, would Turkey not revert to an old pattern?

Political considerations are also inexorably linked to the commercial environment, particularly in mixed economies. Consider how many countries, like Egypt or Gabon, use their public sector companies as dumping grounds for political patronage. In doing so, they exacerbate inefficiency of production and bureaucratism. In Kenya, the elimination of economically burdensome parastatal companies would be economically smart but politically stupid. Such a move would undermine the support for the regime of a large segment of the middle class and of the majority Kikuyo tribe who control the state industry.

One last word for the political scientist who, perhaps sitting across the corridor from the international economist in his bank, does not feel the economist has much to tell him about his job. Economic policy and political policy must be seen as part of an integrated whole. In the case of the Cameroon, where the Biya government has cracked down on numerous small smugglers and deprived them of a livelihood, a contingent of politically disaffected people may develop who could well join the anti-government movement of former President Ahidjo and heighten the danger of civil war. In the same country, the economic trauma of severe drought has aggravated north-south political tensions. In Morocco, the economic exigencies of having 16,000 workers employed in Libya and the need to turn to an oil-rich neighbor for economic aid have created the preconditions for what was at first regarded in the West as a political pact between King Hassan and Qaddafi in August 1984. Finally, it has been argued that a rise in economic growth followed by rapid fiscal decline in Latin American countries like Brazil and Peru could lead to a crisis in democracy for those political systems.*

It is not extraordinary that great opportunities are often accompanied by a commensurate amount of risk. As we learn to identify, understand, and cope with the political risks in international environments, we can clear the way for greater and safer undertakings.

---

* Riordan Roett, "Democracy and Debt in South America: A Continent's Dilemma," *Foreign Affairs* 62, no. 3 (1984): 695–720.

part two

COUNTRY CASE STUDIES

chapter four

Doing Business with the USSR and Eastern Europe: The Political Setting

Zvi Gitelman

Those in the West who greeted the Bolshevik revolution with a mixture of skepticism and fear—and they were the majority—comforted themselves with the thought that it was but a passing phase in the tumultuous history of a troubled country. One observer, a supporter of the Provisional Government, called it a "phantom which will disappear as soon as Russia returns to normal conditions."* It was only sixteen years after the Revolution that the United States granted diplomatic recognition to the USSR. Still, as late as the 1950s, after the Soviet Union had survived the traumas of Stalinist destructiveness from within and the onslaught of the German invasion, some still pinned hopes on "our secret allies in Soviet Russia" for the overthrow of the Soviet regime. By now, most Western statesmen and scholars, even those who thoroughly deplore the existence of the "evil empire," acknowledge the power of the USSR and operate on the assumption that its present form of government will be around for the foreseeable future.

In view of the internal and external shocks administered to the Soviet population, the stability of the system is, indeed, remarkable. The Bolshevik regime began as one of a minority (despite the fact that "Bolshevik" means someone of the majority). It lost the only free national election ever held in Russia (January 1918) and fought a three-year civil war to defeat the various, and often conflicting, opponents who challenged it in different parts of the country. The Bolsheviks fought American, British, and French troops who were sent to aid these opponents and rid Russia of Bolshevism, an ideology that threatened to infect the West. After winning the military struggle, Lenin wisely retreated somewhat on the political front and allowed a limited retreat from the positions taken during the heady days of the Revolution and "War Communism."

By 1928, however, Stalin judged that the retreat could no longer be afforded, as social forces inimical to Bolshevism had gathered too much

---

* A. J. Sack, *The Birth of the Russian Democracy* (New York: Russian Information Bureau, 1918), p. 2.

power and posed an economic and political threat. He therefore launched what some have called the "second revolution." The twin programs of agricultural collectivization and forced-draft industrialization were designed not only to modernize the USSR with unprecedented speed and to thereby strengthen her militarily, but also to wipe out the vestiges of capitalism and the remnants of the pre-revolutionary social classes, both of which had been able to survive under the New Economic Policy (1921–29). Whether Stalin's program has even paid off in the agricultural sector is doubtful, but he did succeed in destroying the Soviet peasantry as an autonomous, or potentially autonomous, economic, social, and hence, political, force. Millions of peasants were killed, exiled, and forced off their land. This brutal campaign did create an instantaneously available labor force, which was drawn into industry, and made possible the industrialization of the Five-Year Plans. The massive political purges that followed closely on the heels of collectivization, the crackdown on non-Russian nationalities, and the weakening of the Party and the military by the thorough purging of their ranks might have seemed ingredients for a mass revolt against a dictatorship cruel beyond belief, or at least for a palace coup against a leader seemingly gone wild. Of course, the cataclysmic events of the 1930s only served to strengthen Stalin's hold, and not even the embarrassing war with Finland in 1940 led to any amelioration.

Even Marxist historians who preach the inevitability of the Russian revolution admit that World War I played a significant role in unraveling the fabric of the tsarist system and hastening the "inevitable." One might have thought that World War II would have done the same to the system of the new tsar, Stalin. After all, it was Stalin who was directly responsible for weakening the Soviet armed forces in two years before the war—three of five marshals and 110 of 195 divisional commanders were purged. It was Stalin, too, who ignored repeated intelligence warnings of the Nazi invasion in June 1941. The result was that the Nazis and their allies swiftly captured huge chunks of Soviet territory, whole Soviet armies were surrounded, and hundreds of thousands of Soviet soldiers were captured. Yet the Soviet regime did not collapse, nor was Stalin driven from office. Although the defeats suffered by the Soviets were far greater than those of the tsarist armies, the Soviet army did not melt away, as the Russian one had, and no revolutionary movement appeared within its ranks, although there were substantial defections to an enemy which, blinded by its racial doctrines, did not know how to exploit them fully. Stalin emerged from the war as the invincible hero of the country and of the entire Allied effort. To this day, if one criticizes Stalin in the USSR, an oft-heard reply is, "Yes, he was cruel, but he won the war for us. Besides, the Russian people need a strong hand."

Another time when the system's stability might have been sorely tested was the death of Stalin, which removed what seemed to be the linchpin of the system. Stalin's colleagues delayed announcement of his death, and when they did break the news, they issued an urgent appeal to the nation not to panic and create disorder. This betrayed their own insecurities but, to their surprise, the Soviet people made no attempt to change the political and social order. The system survived de-Stalinization, though Hungary and Poland were severely destabilized by it. The Soviet system also remained stable despite Khrushchev's often-erratic tinkering with it. More recently, it survived Khrushchev's overthrow, a stagnant and inefficient period in Brezhnev's latter years, and then the rapid succession of Andropov and Chernenko.

The point of this brief historical excursus is that the Communist system has been able to withstand tremendous shocks that would have changed profoundly, and even brought down, many other systems. This should give long pause to anyone tempted by the chimera of the imminent demise, or at least radical reform, of the Soviet political system. It also indicates that anyone doing business with the USSR can fairly safely count on the system remaining the way it is, at least in its fundamentals. On the one hand, this attaches a high predictability to dealings with the USSR. On the other, it means that the kinds of changes that might make dealing with the Soviets more attractive are unlikely to occur very soon.

THE POLITICAL CULTURE OF THE SOVIET UNION

The political culture of a country is the particular way in which most of its inhabitants perceive the political world and act in it. One cannot tell how a system operates simply by looking at its formal structures; the Romanian political system of the nineteenth century was closely modeled on the French and Belgian, but because its political culture was so different, political life in Romania bore little resemblance to that in Western Europe. Political culture involves the subjective orientation to politics and, hence, the dynamics of political life.

Several defining characteristics of Soviet political culture affect the prospects for commercial dealings with the USSR and the ways those dealings would be conducted. Perhaps the most salient of these characteristics is authoritarianism. For several hundred years this country has been ruled by one or another form of strong, authoritarian government. The brief period between February and October 1917, between the breakdown of tsarism and the advent of Bolshevism, represents a small, partial blip of relative democracy in an otherwise uninterrupted authoritarian line. Authoritarianism goes beyond the political system, pervading economic, cultural, and social life. Leaving value preferences aside, this is something of a mixed blessing for outsiders dealing with the system. On the one hand, authoritarianism means that there are many constraints on individual action and thought, so that appeals to an individual's reason and initiative may be frequently unsuccessful, because within the system they are irrelevant. On the other hand, once a decision is taken by the relevant authoritative body, it is highly unlikely to be countermanded by popular pressure or even by another official body. A situation that sometimes arises in the United States—where a decision by one branch of government is countermanded by another—cannot arise in the USSR in the normal course of events.

A second feature of Soviet political culture is its emphasis on collectivism. In contrast to the American value of "rugged individualism," the Soviet culture regards individualism as a manifestation of "narrow egotism" and stresses instead the virtue of being a "team player," of being "a part of the collective." A mundane, but real, example will illustrate this difference. American kindergarten teachers who have asked their students to draw a tree will approve drawings of orange or red trees, in whatever shape, patting Johnny on the head for "expressing his individuality" or "using his imagination." A Soviet teacher will regard the same drawings with stern disapprobation and will expect each student to draw the same picture, and all as realistic as possible. Soviet school children wear uniforms and are organized into groups within the classroom, with all members being responsible for the academic performance and personal behavior of each member of the group. Solitude and highly individualistic artistic expression are frowned upon; literature and art portraying these characteristics in a favorable light are discouraged or even banned. One consequence, compounded by the absence of any private ownership, is the absence of an entrepreneurial style. The individual with initiative, or even with a bright idea, is looked upon with suspicion, as is illustrated by Vladimir Dudintsev's novel *Not By Bread Alone*. This should have implications for the ways in which foreign businessmen would go about enlisting support for their ideas and projects and how they would expect to deal with Soviet decision-makers.

Linked to both authoritarianism and collectivism is centralization. Again, this is a tradition that stretches back long before the advent of Communism. Just as the tsarist empire was run strictly from the imperial center, so is the USSR a highly centralized system. The federal structure of the state is effectively countermanded by the Communist Party, which is organized according to the principles of "democratic centralism." Since it is the Party which guides the state, the latter is effectively run from the center. There are small variations from republic to republic in administrative arrangements— the same function might be performed by a ministry in one republic and a state committee or a special commission in another—but subnational bodies, especially those engaged in foreign trade, have very little independent decision-making power. In contrast to Hungary, where individual firms can make deals with foreign firms, all international commercial activity is routed through all-union (central) ministries in Moscow. Again, this can be both beneficial and detrimental to the foreign businessman. Centralization means that one can easily spot the locus of authoritative decision-making and that there is presumably little need to deal with a great number of widely scattered offices in order to reach an agreement. On the other hand, there is a tendency to push decisions up the line because lower bodies have little power and narrow jurisdiction. Soviet analysts complain frequently about this, but it is deeply rooted in tradition. Under Stalin, punishment for error, real or putative, was so severe that decisions were routinely pushed up to higher levels. Molotov once complained that the Politburo, the highest Party body, was being asked to decide small technical questions, such as the size of nails to be used in construction projects. Of course, such absurdities were the rational response to a system in which, if there were problems in those projects, managers would be accused of deliberate sabotage and made to pay the supreme penalty. For about the last 25 years the penalties of failure have been greatly reduced and, at the same time, more latitude has been given to officials down the line. But old habits die hard, and the system remains highly centralized.

A logical concomitant of the state's authoritarian and centralized nature is its paternalism. The state takes care of its citizens but, by the same token, it has the right to guide and control them. Most Soviet citizens have come to feel that the state—any state—should provide free education and medical care, as well as low-cost housing, to its citizens. Soviet emigrés, even the most anti-Communist among them, consider the need to pay for higher education and for medical care as unjust, even inhumane and uncivilized. But most Soviet people have also accepted what they see as the other side of the same coin, the right of the state to "take care" of their intellectual and moral needs. Except for part of the intelligentsia, more affected by Western values and mores, Soviet people find nothing strange about the state deciding which literature, films, and art they should be exposed to and which would only harm them. Just as we have come to expect the government to protect us against water and air pollution, so does the Soviet individual expect the government to guard him against "ideological pollution."

The paternalistic posture further emphasizes the lack of consumer sovereignty. The state determines what is good for the consumer, and it does so in line with ideological preferences and economic decisions about priorities. Thus, the consumer sector has always taken second place to the industrial one. Heavy industry is always favored over light industry, and capital goods receive higher priority than consumer goods. In the post-Stalin era, however, there has been more of an attempt to satisfy consumer demand, partially out of a feeling that the Soviet people had sacrificed long enough, and partly because consumer desires made themselves felt indirectly, and events in Eastern Europe pointed out the potential danger of ignoring such desires. About twenty years ago the decision was made to allow significant private automobile production, despite economic and ideological reasons for preferring public transportation. More recently, Soviet authorities have been more responsive to the desire for more fashionable clothes. This has resulted in a greater assortment of domestic goods and more imports, largely from Eastern Europe and the Third World. In a well-known concession to public taste, the USSR has allowed the manufacture and sale of Pepsi Cola, perhaps in the vain hope that this might reduce alcohol consumption. But the state remains the arbiter of taste and determines what the consumer will get and where it will come from.

A crucial element of any nation's political culture is the subjective perception of its history. This is what defines a nation's "mission," how it perceives its neighbors, and how it sees its place in the world. Both Russia and the Soviet Union have wrestled with the problem of their standing between East and West, straddling Europe and Asia. The well-known "Westernizer-Slavophile" controversy of the nineteenth century has never been fully resolved, neither in the country nor in the emigration. More important, Russians have long felt inferior to the West, while decrying its culture and values. This has made them determined not to admit that inferiority to outsiders, while striving to overcome it. Only in recent years have the Soviets been able to claim plausibly a rough parity with the West in important areas, notably the military and certain areas of production. Time and again we are reminded that the USSR is the world's largest producer of oil, steel, and coal, and that the Soviet military is capable of meeting any challenge. This kind of rhetoric is indulged in by American politicians, *mutatis mutandis,* as well, but it is probably more deeply felt by, and more important to, those who make these claims in the USSR as well as their audience. The reason for this can be seen most dramatically in a speech Stalin made in 1931, offering a persuasive rationale for the sacrifices he was calling on the Soviet people to make in the industrialization drive.

> Those who fall behind get beaten. But we do not want to be beaten. No, we refuse to be beaten! One feature of the history of old Russia was the continual beatings she suffered because of her backwardness. She was beaten by the Mongol Khans. She was beaten by the Turkish beys. She was beaten by the Swedish feudal lords. She was beaten by the Polish and Lithuanian gentry. She was beaten by the British and French capitalists. She was beaten by the Japanese barons. All beat her— because of her backwardness, because of her military backwardness, cultural backwardness, political backwardness, industrial backward-ness, agricultural backwardness. [Speech delivered at the First All-Union Conference of Leading Personnel of Socialist Industry, February 4, 1931]

Stalin struck a responsive chord in appealing to the desire to escape backwardness and gain international respect. Soviet people and their leaders believe that they have now achieved that recognition, and they are deter-mined to preserve and promote it. They are less sure of their standing than nations which have long been acknowledged as world cultural or economic or political-military leaders. Therefore the Soviets are more sensitive to any attempts to challenge their new-found status. This is the reason they are so sensitive to what they see as attempts "to interfere in our internal affairs," such as the Jackson-Vanik amendment or calls for humane treatment of Andrei Sakharov. They do not want to be told what to do, not by their socialist allies—from whom they are reluctant to borrow successful innova-tions because this would not be fitting for the Bloc leader—and certainly not from capitalist rivals.

The Soviets are therefore uncomfortable with what they perceive as a neo-colonial situation in which they import mainly manufactured goods and export mainly raw materials to the West. It is with no great pride that they make agreements with Western and Japanese companies to obtain technology and manufactured goods that are either unavailable in the USSR or of lower quality. This reluctance, and Soviet sensitivity to the fact that they are dependent on the capitalists for some advanced equipment and processes, may well influence the tenor of negotiations with Western suppliers and should be borne in mind when attempting to penetrate the Soviet market.

National sensitivities and ideological predispositions also make the Soviets leery of entering into joint ventures with foreign firms. They have a predilection for as complete control as they can get, including over their socialist allies in Eastern Europe; unlike some of those East Europeans (Poles, Hungarians, Romanians) they are unwilling to share control over an enterprise. Their distrust of others, even those ideologically akin to them, is often remarked upon, as most of the country is still closed to tourists and one is still not allowed to photograph railroad stations, bridges, airports, or even people in military uniform. This fear of foreigners and of allowing information to leak out is deeply rooted in Russian tradition and, by this point, must simply be accepted as a reality in dealing with the USSR. Foreign businessmen will find that seemingly basic economic information is not available. Only since the mid-1950s has a statistical yearbook been published, and reporting is inconsistent and incomplete. For example, when grain imports came to be embarrassingly great, their volume was simply no longer reported in the yearbooks. For about a decade, data on infant mortality have not been reported, as there are indications that it has risen precipitously, perhaps in large part owing to increased alcoholism among pregnant women. Even telephone books are not readily available.

These, then, are some of the cultural characteristics of the Soviet system that have a bearing on the conduct of business and on the attitudes Soviet officials will bring to any dealings with foreigners. It is not easy for Westerners to reconcile themselves to these outlooks and the behavior they result in, but it is futile for individuals to try to change them. Only those who can understand and accept them, at least for the purpose of dealing with the Soviets, can last out what in any case will often be long and arduous transactions.

POLITICS, DEMOGRAPHICS, AND CHANGE

Having surveyed some of the long-term constants of the Russian and Soviet systems, we can now turn our attention to shorter-range considerations. When examining a system in which power flows most distinctly from the top, the logical first focus of attention is the political leadership.

The long Stalinist reign conditioned us to assume that the Soviet system was intrinsically a one-man dictatorship, and that that dictator reigned supreme. Whatever might have been the case in the 1930s and 1940s, it has become clear that in the last 30 years Soviet leaders are engaged in lively elite politics. Khrushchev struggled between 1953 and 1957 before he emerged as what turned out to be only a *primus inter pares,* and between 1957 and 1964, when he was deposed by his own protégés, he had to struggle hard, and not always successfully, to gain acceptance for his programs. The conflicts he engaged in were as much about policy as about personal power. The collective leadership that succeeded Khrushchev gradually evolved into Brezhnev's preeminence, but the purges of Shelest, Voronov, and others showed clearly that people were still dissenting from the leader's policies and that they were not afraid to make their positions known—and to stick to them, even at the cost of their posts. The successors to Brezhnev, and to his successor, Andropov, reflected the factionalism and need for coalition building that are characteristic of post-Stalin politics.

The Soviet leadership has alternated between more-or-less collective leadership (1924–28, 1953–57, 1964–70, 1984–) and one-man leadership. Each mode produces different kinds of decision-making. Under collective leadership, decisions tend to be taken slowly, as a coalition of support for them must be assembled, and they tend to be cautious and conservative, the result of compromise among the factions and personalities who constitute the coalition. At present, for example, one sees very few bold initiatives in either foreign or domestic policy and a distinct penchant for "playing it safe," which means generally choosing the more conservative path, trying to exercise maximum control in the economy, cultural life, and in the social life of the citizenry (crackdowns on correspondence and contacts with foreigners, restriction of the flow of information in and out of the country, intolerance of any form of dissidence, virtual halting of emigration). This kind of leadership is not likely to seek out new commercial opportunities with the West and will be suspicious of new ideas coming from that direction. At present, however, because of the apparent disgust-cum-fear with which the Soviet leaders view the American administration, they are somewhat more open to those dealings with other Westerners that might embarrass the U.S. administration and buttress their claim that there could be a good deal of fruitful interaction were it not for the obduracy and irrational hostility of the American administration.

Brezhnev, reacting to Khrushchev's frequent shakeups, had stressed "stability of cadres." Indeed, there was remarkably little personnel turnover at any level during his tenure. Andropov, however, moved toward renovating the Soviet hierarchy and managed to change at least 20 percent of the provincial Party secretaries before his death. There were significant changes in the police and other governmental hierarchies as well. Chernenko, the disciple of Brezhnev and a Party apparatus man all his professional life, put a temporary stop to Andropov's drive for personnel renewal. But Gorbachev, who succeeded Chernenko in March 1985, moved very quickly to infuse the elite with new blood, further promoting some people who had been brought to the Kremlin by Andropov, easing out some of the veteran leaders, and bringing some new faces onto the scene. No doubt, these personnel shifts were the logical complement to policy changes being contemplated by Gorbachev. In his first few months in office, however, Gorbachev seemed to change leadership style more than policy substance. In a manner reminiscent of Edward Gierek in Poland in the early 1970s, Gorbachev sought direct, and much publicized, contact with the working people. While his modest and engaging manner struck a highly responsive chord, he did not try to rally support for a new economic program, but contented himself with exhortations against alcoholism, sloth, and inefficiency, and for conscientious, honest, enthusiastic labor. Though his meeting with American President Reagan in the late fall of 1985 might lead to some change in Soviet-American relations, and consequently in Soviet attitudes toward commercial relations with the West, one should not exaggerate the importance of personnel change for policy change. Gorbachev is unlikely to introduce radical economic or political reforms in the near future.

The reason that radical change is unlikely to occur is that Soviet leaders are intensively socialized and carefully selected. As they move up the hierarchy they attend a series of Party schools and courses which reinforce their political education and serve as filters through which only those with acceptable political outlooks and records can pass. Thus, despite generational differences, the Soviet leadership is able, if not to reincarnate itself, at least to perpetuate the values and mindset that define political orthodoxy. Moreover, Soviet politicians are relatively well insulated from popular desires both by ideological rationales and by the structure of the system. Lenin taught that the possession of "consciousness," that is, a knowledge of the "scientific" laws of history and society, allowed the political elite to claim leadership of the masses, who had only "spontaneity." The claim to knowing more and better continues to legitimize the Soviet leadership and provides a political rationale for setting aside the popular will in favor of the leadership's decision. In addition, the fact that Soviet leaders do not have to win the favor of voters in meaningful elections means that they are free from the pressures of doing what the voters want them to do. Again, this means that once politicians make a decision it will not be countermanded by a groundswell of public opinion or by the findings of the latest public opinion poll.

DEMOGRAPHIC CHANGE AND THE FUTURE SOVIET LABOR FORCE

Long gone are the days when the USSR had seemingly inexhaustible, if untrained, labor reserves in the form of a surplus rural population. A high proportion of the population is in the labor force, and now well over half the population is classified as urban. The most striking development of recent decades is the differential growth of the population. Briefly, the Central Asian and other Muslim populations of the USSR have grown very rapidly, while the European peoples have grown at much slower rates, and in some cases, not at all. Overall, the Soviet population is growing at less than 1 percent a year, down from nearly 2 percent in the 1950s. The growth is mainly in the non-European areas. In 1980, the crude birthrate for the country as a whole was 18.3; it was only 15–16 in the three Slavic republics, but it ranged from 30 to 37 in Central Asia and was 25 in mostly Muslim Azerbaijan. By the year 2000, Russians are likely to be less than half the Soviet population and Muslims will be a bit over 20 percent. This does not mean that Russians will no longer dominate the country—their overrepresentation in the major hierarchies and the fact that the major cities are Russian will ensure their continued preeminence. But, according to Murray Feshbach, the leading Western student of Soviet demography, "virtually all the sharply reduced national labor force growth in 1980–95 will come from the high-fertility, non-Slavic regions, a problem complicated by Central Asian Muslims' reluctance to migrate to labor-short urban areas in their own and other republics." The Soviet armed forces will also have to draw on a larger pool of Central Asian conscripts, now mostly used in construction and other low-skill battalions, and will have fewer relatively better-educated Slavs to draw on. For the civilian economy the challenge will be to attract Asians away from the rural areas and to bring both their Russian language and their technical skills up to the demands of Soviet industry. Moreover, if industry is to remain largely in the European areas, Central Asians will have to be enticed not only out of their rural homes, but out of their republics as well. Large numbers of Central Asians living outside their republics might well pressure the government to break with the Leninist tradition of providing cultural facilities (schools, theaters, publications) only in the native republics. This would have important, and perhaps unintended, consequences for other, extraterritorial nationalities, as well as for non-Russian Europeans (Ukrainians, Moldavians, Belorussians) living in Asia or the Caucasus. The Soviet government is grappling with this dilemma by trying several solutions, including stepped-up Russian language instruction in Asia, diverting Siberian rivers to supply the water needed by potential industries in Central Asia, and trying subtly to encourage the birthrate among Europeans. Whether or not these measures succeed, Central Asians will play an increasing role in the Soviet labor force, and this may have some impact on the nature of Soviet production and the kinds of industries that will be developed. In turn, this may alter the structure of Soviet imports and exports, so that potential Western suppliers as well as purchasers will want to ponder the possible implications of a changing demographic profile of the labor force. A lesser consideration is that the influx of Asians, should it come about, into European and Siberian areas might cause ethnic tensions, and these, in turn, could affect productivity and labor stability in those mixed areas. But there is unlikely to be a sudden and massive movement of peoples out of their national areas, and so the system should have the time and capability to adjust to whatever difficulties may arise from the shifts envisioned here.

CORRUPTION

Much has been written, in the USSR and the West, about widespread corruption in the Soviet economy, which has gone so far that a "second economy" is now the accepted term to describe a phenomenon whose exact dimensions cannot be gauged, but which is certainly of great significance in the overall economic picture. The "second economy" includes, inter alia, the withholding of goods that are then made available only for higher-than-official prices or for return favors, stealing supplies from enterprises for private use or resale, moonlighting to provide private services where the state services are inadequate (medicine, dentistry, automobile repair, plumbing, electrical repairs), using *"protektsiia"* and *"sviazy"* (connections) in order to do things not according to the rules or not in the economic plan, outright bribery, and the use of the "tolkach" (fixer), who arranges deals among enterprises and individuals in order to expedite production, marketing, and delivery. The late Yuri Andropov mounted a serious campaign against such phenomena because they had reached such gargantuan proportions under the flaccid, late-Brezhnev regime that they made a mockery out of official planning for production, distribution, and sales. This campaign was not renounced by Chernenko, and it may be pursued with renewed vigor by Gorbachev.

There is considerable disagreement in the West about how "functional" the extralegal and even illegal activities are to the economy as a whole. Some argue that planning is so centralized, rigid, and unrealistic that the only thing that makes the "first" economy work at all is the "second" one. Others say that while some of this activity is functional, it has reached such proportions as to have distorted the economy and, just as important, it has eroded public morality and morale, exacerbating cynicism and hypocrisy. Whatever one's judgment of the consequences of corruption, it is not at all clear what implications it has for foreigners doing business with the Soviet Union. Although corruption has reached the highest echelons in the Soviet hierarchy, even Politburo members and their families being publicly exposed, the USSR has not made public any scandals involving foreign business transactions. There have been no "Lockheed cases" brought to public attention in either East or West. But even assuming that corruption does not directly enter into calculations about doing business with the Soviets, the foreign businessman must take into account the realities of Soviet production and markets and educate himself or herself about what it takes to have goods produced, supplied, and distributed, so that realistic projections and timetables can be made.

Another social problem that bears at least indirectly on doing business with the USSR is alcoholism. To put it crudely, a combination of the drug abuse and alcoholism in a Western country, such as the United States, gives a rough idea of the dimensions of alcoholism in the USSR (where drug abuse is a much less serious problem). Despite periodic government efforts to wean the populace away from dependence on alcohol—efforts which, some say, are vitiated by the fact that the state's income from alcohol is very substantial—there is every indication that alcohol abuse is growing and that it is having serious social and economic consequences. First, untold workdays are lost because workers are too inebriated to perform their duties, or perform them in such a slipshod fashion that they produce huge quantities of *"brak"* (damaged products). Second, male life expectancy appears to be declining, cutting into the population as a whole and into the labor force. Third, women are increasingly the victims of alcoholism, raising the infant mortality rate, as well as the proportion of defective births. Together with the direct effect of alcoholism on women these factors also impinge on the present and future Soviet labor forces. Thus, the inefficiencies of the economy arise not only from structural defects, but also from social realities. Gorbachev launched a vigorous anti-alcoholism campaign in the spring of 1985. Only one liquor store per residential area was allowed to function, and the stores now open at 2:00 p.m. instead of at 11:00 a.m. The price of liquor has been raised again, and a massive educational campaign, emphasizing the evils of alcoholism, has been launched. Many Soviets and Westerners remain skeptical that this will change long-established habits. Social problems, such as alcoholism, as well as structural ones exist in the agricultural economy, as well as the industrial, and are probably even more pronounced in the former.

Two problems that must concern international business—civil disorder and external threats and terrorism—have not disturbed the USSR in the last 30 years. Authorities are extremely vigilant against civil disorders, which they assume can rapidly turn into politically threatening mass movements. A huge police force, whose exact size is a closely guarded secret, is maintained. A policeman is nearly always within shouting distance. Unrestrained by civil libertarian considerations and operating in an authoritarian environment, the police apply force liberally and have far wider latitude than their American or British counterparts. In addition, large numbers of uniformed personnel—members of the armed forces, border guards—and KGB people are visible, especially in the larger cities. They are supplemented by volunteer militia whose charge is to help maintain public order. These forces are aided in their assigned tasks by the average Soviet citizen's readiness to involve himself or herself in another's affairs and to exercise collective peer pressure on deviants and individualists. Thus, someone who is dressed a bit differently from the norm will draw open commentary from passersby, some of whom will not hesitate to voice their disapprobation directly to the nonconformist. There have been unapproved public demonstrations and even riots in a number of Soviet cities, especially in non-Russian ones, but these are infrequent and are always put down with severity. The swiftness with which demonstrations by political dissidents in Moscow have been dispersed—they have usually lasted no more than a few seconds—is testimony to the difficulty of mounting even a peaceful and quiescent spontaneous public expression. Soviets look with scorn on some of their East European neighbors who have "let matters get out of hand" and have tolerated strikes, marches, and demonstrations, some of which have led to political upheavals. In contrast to the drama of Solidarity in Poland, where millions of people joined a movement that threatened to alter fundamentally the entire system of governance, in the USSR only a few individuals attempted to set up independent, nonpolitical trade unions, and their efforts were quickly and effectively halted.

There have been a few incidents of terrorism, including apparent attempts at assassinating Kremlin leaders, but these have been far fewer than such incidents in the United States. Strict internal curbs on the possession and use of weapons, extremely vigilant guarding of the international borders, and a careful eye on foreign students, visitors, and military and political trainees all minimize the possibilities of terrorism. Obviously, the Soviet Union is not immediately threatened by any of her neighbors, and even China does not constitute a real military problem. Thus, the USSR appears to be a stable, safe system, not seriously challenged in any direct, physical way by internal or external forces.

U.S. GOVERNMENT POLICY AND TRADE WITH THE USSR

There is some irony in the fact that the "capitalist free market" United States has intervened politically in trade with the USSR more than the Soviet government has done; Soviet-American commercial dealings have gone up and down with the swings of the political pendulum. The détente of the early 1970s spurred unprecedented volumes of commercial activity, but the December 1979 Soviet invasion of Afghanistan brought about an American grain embargo. The Republican administration that followed the Democratic one (which had embargoed grain) lifted that embargo, but restricted the flow of technology to the USSR. Most observers agree that neither attempt at influencing Soviet behavior—if that was the real aim of these actions—succeeded. It can be argued plausibly that such actions merely arouse Soviet resentment since they are perceived as attempts by one power to "push around" another, and thereby implicitly deny the parity status the Soviets so desperately want acknowledged. These kinds of actions awaken those nationalistic sentiments and fears of being thought inferior that were discussed earlier in this chapter. Moreover, generally speaking it appears that the Soviets did not suffer economically, except perhaps in the very short run, from the imposition of these measures. The main reason they were able to avoid economic costs is the existence of alternative suppliers, whether of grain or technology, from among the very closest allies of the United States.

If this is true, then one might conclude that future American administrations, having learned the lessons of the 1970s and 1980s, will not attempt to disrupt Soviet-American trade for political and symbolic reasons. This would be a facile assumption. First, because of the change of administrations and political parties, policies and postures are likely to change every four years or so. Second, in many ways there is no incremental learning from one administration to another. Andrei Gromyko was said to have had an advantage over his American counterparts (secretaries of state), so many of them having come and gone during his long tenure, that his was an almost institutional memory of Soviet-American negotiations, while each American secretary relearned the subtleties of this relationship. Similarly, in recent years American administrations have spurned "old Washington hands" (and "old Moscow hands" for that matter), at least in the White House staffs, by now the locus of presidential, and hence foreign policy, decision-making. As new American administrations appear, they may not base their policies toward the USSR on what others might interpret as the lessons of the past. Third, even if a president concludes that intervening in a Soviet-American commercial relationship is unlikely to bring about desired changes in Soviet behavior, he may do so anyway to satisfy domestic pressures for "punishing the Soviets" or "taking a stand and letting them know how we feel." The public's memory is even shorter than an administration's, and there is little doubt that the next Soviet outrage will provoke loud cries for "retaliation" or "a clear message to the Kremlin." Politicians will find it hard to ignore such voices.

One cannot ignore the possibility that the Soviets would also intervene politically in commercial relationships. Yet we can assume that their interest in the relationship would be stronger than the American one, leaving aside a particular firm's visions of penetrating or even capturing a market of 260 million people. The American co-chairman of the U.S.–U.S.S.R. Trade and Economic Council, a private organization of 220 American companies and 125 Soviet foreign trade enterprises, recently claimed that American companies were losing at least $10 billion a year because of government restrictions. But those firms are probably able to find alternative markets, just as the Soviets find French, Japanese, German and other suppliers—and buyers—in place of Americans. Some believe that the Soviets have an inflated view of the influence of American business on politics, owing to their ideology that assumes that political power is based on economic power. Therefore, they might be tempted to pressure businessmen economically so that they will exert political influence to reverse punitive measures or to promote policies favorable to U.S.–Soviet trade. In sum, while the Soviet Union presents few problems of political instability, military vulnerability, labor upheaval, or terrorism, problems often encountered in other parts of the world, trade with the USSR is subject to political interventions from both sides, and these cannot be easily foreseen or controlled.

A NOTE ON EASTERN EUROPE

In many ways Eastern Europe has served as a conduit into the USSR. Western fashions, ideas, culture, and technology have often entered the USSR after having been filtered through Eastern Europe, which is generally much more exposed and receptive to them. The fact that a socialist East European state has adopted a reform or has entered into an agreement with a Western company or government lends them partial legitimacy in the eyes of the Soviets. On the other hand, for reasons mentioned earlier, the USSR does not like to be in the position of "learning" from its junior partners. Therefore, what is done in Eastern Europe does not become automatically acceptable in the Soviet Union.

But Eastern Europe is not just a possible avenue of penetration of the Soviet market. It is also itself a market of more than 100 million people. Although recent experience with Poland, and to a lesser extent with Romania, has had a chastening effect on the willingness of Western banks and firms to do business in Eastern Europe, those East European countries with serious external debt problems have taken seemingly effective measures to reduce their burdens, which cannot be said for other, nonsocialist states. It should be remembered that while the external debt of the Council for Mutual Economic Assistance is about $55 billion at present, Mexico alone owes its external creditors nearly twice as much, France's debt is about $65 billion, and Italy's is about $58 billion. Slowly, some Western banks are resuming dealings with even the more troubled East European economies, even though they have been disabused of the notion that the USSR will come to the rescue of any socialist country in trouble (the "umbrella theory"). Therefore, it behooves us to note very briefly some of the ways in which East European countries, which vary considerably among themselves, differ from the Soviet Union from the perspective of the risks of doing business with the area.

The political cultures of the East European countries are all different from the Soviet one, and they differ from each other. The common political system and economic structures should be seen as superstructural, not basic. Most of the East European countries have strong cultural and historical ties to

Western Europe (especially Poland, Czechoslovakia, the GDR, and Hungary). They do not have the suspicion of foreigners or the burdens of superpower status as do the Soviets. A far greater percentage of their respective GNPs is derived from foreign trade, as none of them is nearly as resource-rich as the USSR. Hungary has loosened its economic system so that, as mentioned earlier, individual firms can do business with foreign enterprises, thus eliminating much of the red tape one encounters in more centralized economies. Before the crisis of the 1980s Poland was encouraging joint enterprises with Western companies and investment in small-scale enterprises, such as motels, by Polish-Americans. The GDR has a unique arrangement ("inter-zonal trade") by which it can use the Federal Republic of Germany as a channel to the Common Market on very favorable terms. Romania, Poland, and Hungary have been quite open to Western trade, while Bulgaria and Czechoslovakia have been much more conservative for both political and economic reasons. Czechoslovakia has more of an economic potential for developing the kind of international commerce that Hungary has engaged in, but its government has carefully avoided incurring debts à la Poland and is fearful that its population would have too much contact with undesirable ideas as a result of increased trade with the West. Thus, one cannot easily generalize about Eastern Europe and the political risks entailed in doing business there.

Nevertheless, it can be said that some problems that are unlikely to arise in the USSR have arisen, and will continue to appear, in Eastern Europe. Except for the Bulgarians, no East European population is as well socialized and stable as the Soviet one. The Poles are the most alienated from the system and will no doubt seize future opportunities to change, although the sheer instinct for self-preservation will curb attempts to uproot it altogether. Moreover, the Polish economy will be in disarray for the foreseeable future since it will require some kind of agreement between regime and population to implement any serious reform. The Czechoslovak population has been rendered quiescent by a combination of force and being bought off with consumer goods. Underneath the surface, however, there is considerable alienation, and while the Czechoslovaks are unlikely to initiate another 1968-type reform soon, they may take advantage of dramatic changes elsewhere in the Bloc to demand some changes at home. The Hungarians seem to have reached an accommodation with the government: as long as the standard of living remains high and individual freedoms are greater than anywhere else in the Bloc, the population goes along. Whether this social compact will survive the departure of Janos Kadar or serious economic dislocations remains to be seen. The recent massive emigration of GDR citizens to the FRG is testimony to the lingering discontent in socialist Germany, some of which has appeared publicly in the form of peace movements and demonstrations. In Romania, the economic situation is critical, and the population suffers real privations. The appeals of nationalism, the cult of the Ceausescu personality, and an autonomous foreign policy have worn off, and only the most repressive regime in the region is able to keep the lid on. Next to Poland, Romania is perhaps the most likely scene of political upheaval in the near future.

Bulgaria, whose economic success has been little publicized in the West, remains the Soviet Union's most dependable ally in the region and is relatively free of economic troubles. The First Secretary of the Party, Todor Zhivkov, has been in power for 30 years, and there is little evidence of political instability or difficulty.

Eastern Europe cannot be lumped together with the Soviet Union for purposes of political and economic analysis, nor can the individual countries of the region. In assessing the political risks attendant upon doing business in the region, the specifics of each country's political culture and current political and social situations will have to be carefully considered.

chapter five
Political Risk in China

Kim Woodard

Between the normalization of U.S.–China diplomatic relations in 1979 and the end of 1984, the international business community has poured some $8 billion into direct investments in China. These investments include about $1 billion in seismic surveys and early drilling programs on China's continental shelf in the search for a new long-range source of petroleum for the world market. Such investments reach maturity and provide a commercial return over a time horizon that is measured in decades. For example, if successful, the offshore oil projects will require a 5–7 year exploration period, followed by a 15 year cost-recovery and production-sharing period. A minimum of 10 years will be required to recover the initial costs of finding and developing each field. Given the size of the required investments and the length of the time horizon for most investment projects in China, correct assessment of long-range political risks will be critical to the commercial viability of those investments.

Yet "correct assessment of long-range political risks" is no simple matter in the Chinese case. What will the political and economic systems prevailing in the China of 1995 look like? In 1985, all the indicators appear to point in the direction of a stable environment for foreign investment. The government is stable, leans toward the West, has adopted an "open-door" policy toward international commerce, is eager to acquire advanced industrial technology and management methods, has plenty of foreign exchange, and is gradually liberalizing certain elements of its communist structure. Yet just ten short years ago in 1975, Mao Zedong was still in power, the country had just emerged from ten years of mass terror under the "Cultural Revolution," a communist regime under Chinese tutelage had seized Indochina, and political and commercial contacts with the West were in the earliest stages of development. The China of 1965 was totally isolated from the international community, while the China of 1955 was considered a Soviet satellite. How much certainty can be attached to a production-sharing contract for offshore oil development that will run until 2005? The correct answer to this question is

The author wishes to acknowledge the contribution of Alice Davenport and John De Pauw to the preparation of this chapter. Any errors of omission or fact are strictly his own.

worth about $1 billion in front-end exploration and development investments for each major offshore oilfield discovered in 1985.

Multinational corporations, and the large oil companies in particular, are familiar with such long-range political risks. They have operated for years in high-risk political environments and accept the risk as routine, much as they have adapted to harsh physical environments like the Empty Quarter in Saudi Arabia or the North Slope of Alaska. Sometimes, as with Angolan oil development, the risk pays off. Other times, as with Iran, it may result in losses. What makes the Chinese case unusual is not the level of risk involved, but the sheer complexity of the risk factors that affect long-range investments in China. China is a large and diverse country, in the throes of rapid modernization and ideological evolution, with a highly complex pattern of regional and global alignments. No single risk factor can be singled out as dominant, but a wide range of political and economic risk factors must be taken into account, including at least the following:

leadership succession and policy continuity,
regime stability and ideological evolution,
success of the modernization program,
commercial, legal, and tax environment, and
regional and global power relations.

LEADERSHIP SUCCESSION IN THE POST-DENG ERA

As a developing country with a communist political infrastructure, China still lacks any effective and stable system for leadership succession, at the local and provincial levels as well as at the central government level. Despite formal provisions for elected congresses at each level which, in turn, are supposed to elect their leadership, the selection system in fact works from the top down through the designation of "approved" candidate lists for each relevant position. The Chinese press has made much in recent years of certain local elections in which the number of approved candidates has in fact exceeded the number of available positions, or in which non-Party members are permitted to run for office, but these instances of local democracy are rare, when they occur, and carefully circumscribed by the existing power structure. The fact is that the Chinese Communist Party (CCP) still designates candidates for most government positions, and that key positions, such as provincial governorships, are simply appointed from above, through channels provided by the Party apparatus.

While this system for leadership succession does function over time as a method for choosing and replacing leaders, it also generates certain rigidities that may cause discontinuities in both leadership and policy. Lacking a fixed term of office or a competitive replacement procedure, the system is heavily loaded in favor of incumbency. Over the past three and a half decades, this has yielded an aging leadership, particularly at the higher levels of government and the Party. Mao Zedong, Zhou Enlai, and Zhu De were key leaders in the revolution in the 1930s and still held office when all three died in 1976. At 80, Deng Xiaoping is very much in control of the Politburo, despite his formal resignations from all but a few Party positions. His "young" protégés are still in their sixties, including Party General Secretary Hu Yaobang at 68 and Premier Zhao Ziyang at 64. The average age of Politburo members is well over 70. Secretary Hu himself has complained publicly about the senility of the aging leadership, a condition that reaches well down into the ranks.[1]

The succession and leadership age structure problem is of more than academic interest in terms of long-range investment risk. As in most political systems, leadership groups become closely associated with political and economic policies they have promoted. In the case of Deng Xiaoping and his group, public policy has encouraged international trade and foreign investment. Deng himself is closely associated with such major shifts in policy as the establishment of Special Economic Zones and open cities, joint offshore oil exploration, promotion of joint ventures and licensing contracts, establishment of separate corporate entities in key industries, promulgation of a legal and tax code that protects foreign investors, and numerous other policies. All of these policies are grounded on the assumption that an "open door" in commercial dealings will accelerate the acquisition of advanced technology and lead to the modernization of the Chinese economy.

Leaving aside for a moment the question of whether Deng's open-door strategy will succeed, it is clear that the strategy itself must survive its creator if investments made in the current commercial climate are to reach maturity over the next five years. Rumors have circulated for some time that Deng would step down in 1985, perhaps at a special gathering of the CCP in September, which has been slated to deal with comprehensive leadership changes.[2] But whether the leadership succession occurs in 1985 or in a subsequent year, Deng will attempt to take with him what remains of the "Long March" generation on the Politburo (Chen Yun, Peng Zhen, Wang Zhen, and Ye Jianying) and to replace them with his own followers. Deng's success in this maneuver will determine the near-term survival of his commercial and economic policies.

How successful will Deng Xiaoping be in placing the imprint of his economic and commercial policies on the next generation of Chinese leadership? The track record for Mao's heirs apparent was an unenviable one. Liu Shaoqi, Mao's first designated heir, was brutally purged and hounded to death in the Cultural Revolution. Lin Biao, who helped to engineer the humiliation of Liu, was shot down and killed in an effort to escape to the Soviet Union after an unsuccessful coup attempt. Hua Guofeng, who succeeded Mao briefly as chairman of the Party, was relegated to political obscurity after only two years in office (1976–1978). Deng himself survived three purges and the Cultural Revolution to succeed Mao. This experience no doubt gives him unique qualifications to deal with his own succession.

Deng has addressed himself seriously to the succession problem ever since his de facto rise to power in 1978. He installed Zhao Ziyang as Premier in 1980 at the head of the government apparatus and Hu Yaobang as Party leader in 1981. Both men are firmly committed to Deng's modernization program. During the 1980–1984 period, Deng initiated a series of steps to push aside both leftist cadres of the Cultural Revolution era and Stalinist cadres from the

1950s. These measures have included adoption of a new Party Constitution, reregistration of Party members, consolidation of the ministries under the State Council, replacement of provincial governors and Party secretaries, direct control of the Military Affairs Commission, decentralization of the Party administrative apparatus, and the application of political litmus tests such as the communiqué of the 3rd Plenum of the 12th CCP Central Committee, which endorsed the modernization program in October 1984. Orderly succession has ranked just behind adoption of the modernization program itself as a key objective of the Deng administration.

As a result of this sustained effort, Deng's appointees hold most of the critical positions at the top of China's three major power centers—the Party, the government, and the People's Liberation Army. Deng has achieved this degree of success by separating the formal and informal lines of power and by using the latter to control the former. He has never himself held the top Party and government positions, although he is chairman of the Central Military Commission, the top military position. Rather, he has chosen to step aside from the formal positions while retaining an iron grip on real decision power through the Politburo. This has permitted advance installation of Deng's protégés in each of the available top slots. Meanwhile, he has become master of the selective resignation, taking the older opponents of his programs with him as he has stepped out of such formal positions as Vice Premier. Deng Xiaoping does not apepar at all on formal organizational charts of the government and retains only his positions on the Standing Committee of the Politburo, chairmanship of the Military Affairs Commission, and the chairmanship of the Central Advisory Committee in the Party. Furthermore, it appears that Deng may break all precedents by dropping his formal and informal power as well, once the next generation has been properly installed.

Although Deng Xiaoping and the modernizers have both established a firm grip on political and economic policy in China and arranged for their own succession, they have not managed to reform the ossified leadership succession process itself. This may favor stability in the short term, as all the advantages of incumbency fall to Deng's preinstalled protégés. There is a high probability that the modernizers, who favor the "open door" toward foreign investment, will remain in the saddle for the short term. Thus the immediate investment risks of leadership succession in China must be judged to be low, compared to other developing country environments. But in the longer term, say over the next 5–15 years, leadership succession will again become an issue, and once again, China may lack an appropriate mechanism for orderly replacement of a generation of top political leaders.

The succession problem itself should also be understood to be just one part of the larger problem of political evolution in China. Leadershp succession is simply the replacement within the existing political system of one set of faces with another, usually younger set. Opposition to Deng's modernization policies still exists: among older cadres who favor the Soviet-style communism of the 1950s, among China's lost generation—former Red Guards and radicals from the Cultural Revolution era, and among military officers who have seen gradual erosion of their political power. The very success of Deng's modernizers in the current power transition could breed frustration among these opposition groups and instability over the longer term.

REGIME STABILITY AND IDEOLOGICAL EVOLUTION

The leadership succession problem is basically the question of which individuals will occupy which positions within the existing political system. A smooth succession for Deng and the modernizers to the next generation of leaders would presumably provide sufficient stability in economic policy to ensure continuation of Deng's "open-door" policies. The resulting policy stability will reduce the level of risk for foreign investors particularly in the near term—i.e., the next five years.

But looking beyond the question of leadership succession, one must also ask about the political system itself. Will it survive as is for a decade or two, evolve slowly to meet changing conditions, or experience further sudden and disruptive upheavals such as the Cultural Revolution? There are serious political risks to foreign investors at either end of the spectrum of systemic change. If the Chinese political system fails to change at all, and simply remains locked into its current nineteenth-century Marxist mold as the economy expands, it will begin to look very much like the Soviet political system within a decade or two—a musclebound giant seriously at odds with the international order and a tough environment for foreign investors. On the other hand, if political change occurs too quickly in China, another serious breakdown of public order, replete with a new wave of xenophobia, could result. Either extreme would jeopardize large-scale, long-term investments such as the offshore oil projects.

There are currently four major elements in China's basic political structure: the Chinese Communist Party (CCP), the People's Liberation Army, the central government under the State Council, and the regional and local governments and organizations. Any change in the Chinese political system, whether evolutionary or cataclysmic, implies either internal restructuring of these basic organizations or changes in their interrelationships. At present the four elements of China's political system are fairly evenly balanced, although government agencies, both central and local, have grown stronger over the past decade, perhaps at the expense of the Party and the military.

The Party

Deng Xiaoping and the modernizers constitute just one faction within the Chinese Communist Party. At present it is the dominant faction, although there are several important opposition factions. The most important opposition groups are the orthodox (Stalinist) communists represented on the Politburo by Chen Yun and Ye Jianying, and the leftists or Maoists who have been pushed out of central Party organs entirely and are now under attack at the provincial and local level as well. Deng and the modernizers have focused their efforts to change the Party from within on restructuring its organization to decentralize authority, on cleansing its ranks of the opposition through reregistration, and on redefining the ideological catechism to reflect their own economic and political priorities.

Decentralization of the Party apparatus accelerated in mid-1984 when the Organization Department of the Central Committee announced that personnel management within the Party would be delegated to the relevant ministries, provinces, regions, and municipalities, rather than concentrated in the hands of the Secretariat in Beijing.[3] The central Party apparatus no longer screens and approves all internal appointments down to the prefectural level. Under the new system, each level screens only those appointments in Party organs one level below and directly under its aegis. Decentralization of the power to appoint was intended to lead to decentralization of decision-making power as well, relieving the heavy load of decisions that are currently sent all the way to the top for resolution. In addition, Party organs are under instructions to get out of day-to-day administrative decisions altogether and to function in the background, setting the rules of the game without playing the game itself.

It is not clear just how fast or how far decentralization of the Party apparatus will go. Indeed, the mandate of the Communist Party is to rule at all levels through government agencies and other organizations. As long as the Party fulfills this mandate, functioning as a permanent inner agency in every organization, it will be tempted to interfere directly in matters of substance. There is, in fact, no clear way to draw the line between setting the rules and playing the game, particularly when Party membership is the most important single criterion for determining personal advancement to leadership positions in each organization. Furthermore, administrative problems will continue to be pushed up toward the center, as each level in the Party seeks to avoid responsibility for difficult or controversial decisions. Many experts believe that decentralization of the Party apparatus is moving very slowly, public rhetoric to the contrary.

There is little question that the existing rigidities in the internal Party structure have a serious negative impact on foreign trade and investment in China. It is frequently difficult or impossible to determine who, in a Chinese organization or delegation, is in fact responsible for making relevant decisions. The Party man often stands back from the center of the action, intervening only behind the scenes. Routine decisions, or operational decisions with time value, are often referred upward in an unseen bureaucracy, while the resulting delays are covered up by requests for further information or by other ploys. The time required to move up and down this unseen decision tree frequently explains the superficial "irrationality" of the Chinese partner. It certainly explains the frustration and irritability of many foreign businessmen in negotiating or implementing deals in China. For some companies, even those with long experience in doing business there, the result may be a unilateral withdrawal from potentially lucrative markets. "Patience" too often becomes a code word for frustration and withdrawal.

Another factor that directly impacts foreign business dealings in China is the lack of technical or commercial sophistication on the part of Party cadres. China's engineers are often given high marks, compared to those from many

Third World countries, by the companies that train them or provide them with technical seminars. Chinese trade officials are often quick to understand the complexities of a proposed deal. But the Party man behind the scenes who is in fact either making the decision or passing it up the ladder unfortunately often lacks the relevant tools for the task. Of China's 40 million Party members, only 17.8 percent have had high school educations, and only 4 percent are college graduates.[4] A large proportion are still totally illiterate. Cadres placed in positions that involve contact with foreigners are toward the upper end of the spectrum of personal capabilities, but they may not have anything like the level of sophistication of Chinese engineers, traders, and other non-Party people in the partner organization. Here again, the most likely result of the separation of expertise and power on the Chinese side is delay, confusion, and a refusal to take responsibility or initiative. A remote or "arrogant" attitude on the part of a Chinese official is almost always a cover for ignorance of the relevant technical and commercial complexities. The result can be more than just a matter of personalities if the investment entails joint management of large capital-intensive projects such as offshore drilling.

Two reform measures have been introduced to deal with the problem of cadre quality within the Party. The first measure, reregistration of Party members, has been underway at the central levels of the Party for some time and will be extended to the local level during 1985. Eventually all 40 million Party members will have to reapply for membership and undergo a screening process. Unfortunately, this process appears to be screening out less than 1 percent of the total membership. Cadres who lose their Party cards have engaged in various egregious errors, such as active participation in violent activities during the Cultural Revolution or in criminal behavior. The process may help consolidate Deng's grip on the Party apparatus, but it will do little to address the cadre quality problem.

The second measure may have a greater effect, but will take many years before a substantial impact is felt in day-to-day operations. In November 1984, the Organization Department of the Central Committee announced a drive to admit more "intellectuals" (high school and college graduates) to Party membership. An education has been treated as an asset, rather than a liability, in selection for Party membership only since 1978. Prior to that time, having a college education bore the stigma of association with class privilege. But even with the shift in attitudes toward educated people, progress in moving them into key Party positions has been slow, more a matter of sheer attrition through aging than of replacement.

Ideology

If structural change in the Party has been glacial, the pace of ideological reform has been impressive by communist standards. Public debate over ideological issues has been a major dimension of China's modernization process not just in the contemporary period, but reaching back to the first intrusions of Western thought several centuries ago. Confucianism, the official ideology and ethical system of pre-modern China, suffered from its close association with the feudal land-holding system. Confucianism also appeared impotent to stem the tide of Western arms and technology that washed up on China's shores in the nineteenth century. The result of these combined failures of the classical intellectual and cultural framework led to deep-seated insecurity in the educated elite and a desperate search for certainty in what seemed a sea of upheaval and change. Marxism, among its other attributes, holds out the promise of "scientific" certainty, which results in a "correct" political line. Once this framework has been accepted, ideological struggle becomes the core of the political process, as each faction seeks to identify its policy formulas as the "correct" line. The "correct" line may vary with historical circumstance over time, but there can only be one "correct" line at a time.

The contemporary Chinese debate over ideological issues therefore has become an important indicator of political stability. Every serious upheaval in the Chinese political system since 1949, and indeed since 1842, has been cast in an intense public ideological struggle. An upsurge of ideological debate can therefore be seen as a harbinger of another period of systemic instability. There is little question that such a debate is currently underway, at least at the highest levels of the Chinese Communist Party. The debate surfaces periodically in the press, as it did on December 7, 1984, when a lead editorial in the People's Daily proclaimed:

> Marx died 101 years ago. Some of his visions may not be appropriate, because great changes have taken place since that time. We can't ask that the works of Marx and Lenin from that time solve our present-day problems. We, the successors of Marx and Lenin, have a responsibility of developing and enriching Marx's works in practice.[5]

This editorial, which was based on the text of a speech by Party Secretary Hu Yaobang, was quickly amended to read "We can't ask that the works of Marx and Lenin from that time solve *all* our present-day problems."[6] But the cat was out of the bag as the international press, both East and West, picked up and amplified the text of the editorial. Neither the editorial nor the speech itself have been publicly criticized or repudiated, but the incident must have created a stir among the orthodox in the ranks of the Party.

The substance of the current ideological debate focuses on economic theory. Deng's modernization program and the "open door" have brought about numerous points of potential conflict between public policy and the central tenets of orthodox Marxism. Private control, if not ownership, of the means of production has sprung up in the rural areas and the Special Economic Zones and will spread to fourteen open coastal cities in the near future. This shift in the control of production into the hands of private individuals and autonomous local organizations is proceeding so fast that Deng has felt constrained to deny that it is happening: "During the last 16 years of this century, no matter how open we are, the economy based on the public ownership system will invariably remain dominant."[7] Deng and the modernizers believe that they can bring to bear the invigorating forces of foreign capitalism and open domestic market to breathe life into a development process that will remain essentially socialist in nature. The entire Marxist ideological framework may be modified as need be, but not sacrificed altogether on the altar of development. Mao's sacrosanct thoughts have received the same treatment, as Party theoreticians turn handstands to "persist in the fundamental tenet of Mao Zedong thought" while rejecting most of its policy implications.[8]

Does the renewed ideological debate that is surfacing in the Party over basic economic policy foreshadow development of another fault line within the Party and perhaps another public upheaval on the order of the Cultural Revolution? Or did the wholesale adoption of Deng's modernization program by the Communiqué of the 3rd Plenum of the 12th Central Committee set a stable framework for economic policy that will persist over the coming decades? The risk to foreign investments of another mass disturbance even a fraction of the intensity of the Cultural Revolution would be substantial. Beijing has been able since 1978 to shield foreign investments, and particularly the offshore oil projects, from the impact of domestic and foreign politics. But if the public order were to dissolve to any degree, foreign projects would immediately become a target for the opposition.

Given the remaining rigidities in the Chinese Communist Party and the presence of substantial opposition elements in the Party, the risk of another public upheaval cannot be dismissed out of hand. There have been scattered reports of violent "sabotage of the reforms" at the local level in both rural and urban areas. These isolated cases have been treated as a reaction by the losers in the reform process—incompetent and lazy factory workers or inefficient farmers who have lost their "iron rice bowls." But it is possible that the remaining "pockets of leftism" in certain areas could provide the tinder for a spark from the center. It should be kept in mind that the risk of a new political firestorm must be contained over a period of decades, not just a few years. Discontent is minimal at present, but could spread rapidly if the pace of growth in personal living standards slackens.

On the other side of the risk equation, it is encouraging that the renewed ideological debate touches on the role of ideology itself. There are more than a few signs that China's intellectual community is moving beyond its craving for fixed points of reference and "correct" political lines. One of the most exciting recent developments on the ideological front was the ardent public call of the Chinese Writers' Association for a renewal of "freedom of creation" in literature and the other arts. This is no dissident movement, but received public support from Hu Qili, a powerful cultural czar in the Party Secretariat who was speaking on behalf of Hu Yaobang.[9] Even Confucius is being culturally rehabilitated, although reinstatement of Confucianism as a guiding ideology is not taken seriously outside of Taiwan. If the public ideological debate has been renewed, it has also been softened. Under Deng, the "correct" line has been to "seek truth from facts"—an ironic absolutist denial of absolutism.

It is clear that "freedom of expression" will continue to have sharply defined official limits, at least for the next few years. Wei Jingsheng, the former editor of *Exploration,* discovered where those limits lay in October

1979 when he was sentenced to fifteen years in prison for "counter-revolutionary crimes." Wei had been a leader in Beijing's Democracy Wall movement and had publicly advocated the "Fifth Modernization"—political democracy.[10] Wei's fate is a reminder that the rigid structure and Marxist ideology of the Chinese Communist Party persist. Any political force that threatens the role of the Party itself is subject to attack. This places a low ceiling on political evolution in China, a form of control that may some day be challenged. Every foreign investment project is eventually affected by the remaining constraints on the political system. Every foreign investor runs the risk that those constraints will be violently challenged.

The Military

Quite apart from the risk that the Party will fracture internally, touching off a wave of public turmoil, a quieter form of structural risk is built into the Chinese political system. As with many developing countries, the military has its own, semiindependent, organizational capabilities. The People's Liberation Army has a long history of political activism, reaching all the way back to Mao's mountain strongholds during the revolution, when for all practical purposes the Party and the army were the same institution. The PLA has continued to function in numerous civilian roles since 1949, moving in whenever production conditions, natural disasters, or social disorder required special attention. The political power and activism of the PLA were demonstrated conclusively during the Cultural Revolution when the army stepped in to replace the Party, which was at war with itself. Control by the PLA in 1971, when I first visited China, reached right down to individual factories and communes where the red star and green uniform of the PLA were present in every leadership group. During his long career, it was never clear whether Mao Zedong identified more closely with the Party or the PLA, although he gave frequent lip-service to the Marxist credo that "the Party controls the gun."

Since Mao's death in 1976, the PLA has been sent back to its barracks, although it still functions in visible economic and political roles. Military modernization was assigned fourth priority among the Four Modernizations, a rank that was directly reflected in budget priorities. The official defense budget (about half of real expenditures on the military) declined from 17 percent of the national budget in the 1977–1979 period to about 13 percent of the budget in 1984.[11] This decline was absolute, from 22 billion yuan ($14 billion) at peak in 1979 to 18 billion yuan ($9 billion) in 1984. The budget squeeze is known to have caused deep resentment at all levels in the PLA. Among other consequences, military pay scales were frozen just at the time when earnings by peasants were doubling and factory wages were rising under the impact of across-the-board loosening in the incentive structure.

The impact of the budget squeeze on weapons modernization has also been substantial. In 1979 the PLA demonstrated both organizational flabbiness and obsolete weaponry when its punitive expedition against Vietnam bogged down a few miles inside the Vietnamese border. Rhetoric calling for weapons modernization has not been matched by budgetary allocations. Commercial discussions with foreign weapons manufacturers have moved slowly or died entirely. Beijing would like to purchase manufacturing technology along with initial equipment packages, but so far has been reluctant to commit to long-range programs that would be measured in billions of dollars.

Modernization of China's indigenous defense industries has also moved slowly. The Ministry of Ordinance controls thousands of factories and machine shops. In some areas, such as nuclear weapons and the missile program, the defense industry has considerable capability, although not for serial production. Conventional munitions plants cover a wide range in technical sophistication, but continue to crank out weapons that were designed by the Soviet Union in the 1950s. Technical advances will be made over the next fifteen years as a by-product of commercial ventures. But technology acquisition by such osmosis is gradual and subject to constraints imposed by Western export controls. At some point, Beijing will be forced to accelerate expenditures on basic research and development in defense. The "guns or butter" debate will probably sharpen considerably during the Seventh Five-Year Plan (1986–1990).

Deng Xiaoping's policy line toward military modernization has centered on the concept of deferred acceleration. Deng argues that a strong domestic economy will yield rising government revenues that can then be plowed back into military modernization, higher pay, etc., a few years down the line. With industrial growth running in the 8–13 percent range and real growth in the GNP of about 5–7 percent per year, this logic has considerable force. Should the pace of economic expansion slow down, however, in the late 1980s and early 1990s as the effects of infrastructure constraints begin to be felt (particularly in the energy, communications, and transportation sectors), expansion in the revenue base for military modernization will disappear. Patience at the top of the military hierarchy will also disappear, if deferred acceleration stretches into a permanent budget plateau.

As with the Party, Deng Xiaoping has also pursued a policy designed to trim down and reform the bloated command structure of the PLA. The largest standing army in the world (4.2 million on active duty and more than 100 million militia) was built on organizational principles appropriate for small guerilla bands operating from isolated base areas. For 30 years it was assumed that China could be protected from attack by "defense in depth"—slow strangulation of the invader by the combined effects of China's huge land area and a vast armed population. But the new mission assigned to the PLA is a combination of nuclear deterrence and conventional defense of the industrial base in northeastern China from a mechanized Soviet attack. In 1982, following the appointment of Zhang Aiping as Minister of Defense, the commanders of the eleven military regions were reshuffled and educational criteria were established for selection and promotion of officers. In 1984, 40 aging generals were forced to retire from the General Staff of the PLA.[12] This shake-up at the top simultaneously removed officers opposed to the reform program and made room for younger, better educated officers to move up.

Meanwhile, an effort has also been made to move aging or ineffective soldiers and officers into what amounts to civilian jobs. Deng has taken the tradition of support for the civilian sectors one step further by transforming hundreds of obsolete defense factories into commercial production of popular consumer goods such as bicycles, watches, and motorcycles. This commercialization policy has the triple advantage of employing thousands of aging or unskilled soldiers, utilization of obsolete machine tool and factory capacity, and the generation of a new, extra-budgetary revenue stream for the PLA. Incentives for the individual soldier include retention of military status, higher pay, and often transfer to an urban area. Public discussion of military budget cuts is now frequently linked to announcement of a new commercialization program.[13]

Given the current level of dissatisfaction in the military, both in the officer corps, which is threatened by constant reshuffling and job insecurity, and in the ranks, which complain of low pay and lower status, the PLA could become a serious source of political instability. Given its historical revolutionary mission, close identification with Maoism and considerable organizational base, the PLA could develop into an institutional center for opposition to the modernization program and the open door. The combination of a large group of disaffected or dismissed Party cadres and renewed political power of the PLA would be extremely dangerous for long-term foreign investment in China. This will not likely occur if constraints on the military budget are eased during the Seventh Five-Year Plan. But it is also true that the easing of military budget constraints over the next five years is contingent on rapid economic expansion and consequent growth in government revenues. Higher defense expenditures are directly conditional on success of the modernization program itself. If economic growth falls to 3–4 percent per year, there will be little room in the budget for new weapons systems or higher military pay.

Deng's program of deferred acceleration for military modernization is, therefore, a strategy that carries risks for foreign investors. If the PLA were to become a center of resistance to the modernization program, the wave of reaction would doubtless be strongly xenophobic and would focus on foreign "exploitation" of China's economy and on the "spiritual pollution" of Western ideology. Deng's power base is centered in the Party and the government, although he has also maintained close tabs on the PLA through his position as chairman of the Military Affairs Commission, one of the few formal posts he has retained. It remains to be seen whether Hu Yaobang and Zhao Ziyang will be able to bridle the military once Deng moves out of the center of real power. On balance, a moderate level of political risk is centered on the possibility of a structural challenge to the evolving Chinese political system by the PLA. This risk will persist over the next decade or more and could intensify if the rate of economic growth falls. Foreign investors should therefore monitor the political role of the military as a key index of long-term stability in the Chinese political system.

The Government

In contrast with the situation in the Chinese Communist Party and the People's Liberation Army, the principal risks associated with China's government institutions is not lack of stability, but the excess stability of bureau-cratic controls. China's central government planning commissions and minis-tries control the entire economy through ponderous layers of bureaucracy that are ill adapted to the decision requirements of a rapidly changing commercial environment. Particularly in industries that are part of the national plan, which includes all of the energy industries, the metallurgical and chemical industries, the transportation and communications industries, the machine-building industries, the textile industry, the ship-building indus-try, and other sectors, decisions that involve more than a small amount of investment capital require central ministry clearance. Almost all decisions that entail expenditure of foreign exchange must be cleared at the ministerial level or must be part of general programs that have been cleared. Special Economic Zones and the new open coastal cities have limited spending authority, but their experimental development programs are subject to close scrutiny at the level of the State Council.

The process of obtaining central clearance can have a devastating effect on local projects. For example, individual land oilfields lack the authority to sign off on equipment or technical services provided by foreign companies. The final decision must always be referred to the Ministry of Petroleum in Beijing. This system invariably causes delays between identification of a requirement at the oilfield level and purchase of the necessary equipment or service. At times, given the lack of accurate information in the deciding agencies in Beijing, it can result in irrational overpurchases or underpurchases. Technical requirements are usually well understood at the oilfield level, but individual oilfield administrations lack even the telex machines necessary to request and accept bids in the short time frames that are critical to smooth operations. The foreign company is forced to communicate with oilfields either by traveling to the field (which can take weeks) or by telex via the Ministry of Petroleum in Beijing, which may or may not see fit to pass along the communication.

There is little question that this system of central control is beginning to break down. For example, importation of foreign equipment and technology has traditionally been handled through Foreign Trade Organizations (FTOs) that are responsible to the Ministry of Foreign Economic Relations and Trade (Machimpex, Techimport, Catic, etc.). This system is a relic of Soviet tutelage from the 1950s and resembles similar organizations in the USSR and Eastern Europe. Adding yet another level of bureaucracy, the FTO takes formal bids and holds negotiations for equipment or technology packages requested and paid for by the industrial ministries. This has usually meant that the foreign company was obliged to sell the equipment three times—once to the local unit, once to the central ministry, and once to the FTO. The role of the FTO is diminishing under pressure from Chinese end-users and has been challenged by commercial trading companies such as Everbright, which is PRC–controlled but operates out of Hong Kong.

The Deng administration has wrestled with overcentralization and govern-ment red tape since its inception, but it is not yet clear whether the driving force of the modernization program will be sufficient to overcome the deep inertia of the government bureaucracy and its iron grip on commerce. Deng has instituted two types of institutional reform designed to break down the government bureaucracy. First, provincial and local governments have been given increasing freedom to design and implement their own commercial development programs. Second, functional units within the ministries, and at times entire ministries, have been reorganized as commercial corporations with semiautonomous authority in specialized fields. For example, the China National Offshore Oil Corporation (CNOOC) under the Ministry of Petroleum now controls all offshore exploration activities that involve foreign partners. All 39 of China's large refineries and petrochemical installations have been detached from local oilfield and city administrations and reorganized into SINOPEC, a cabinet-level corporation that is now the largest company in China with $10 billion in annual revenues.

These efforts to decentralize and rationalize China's commercial infrastructure are a move in the direction of greater fluidity in the Chinese economy and are certainly welcomed by most foreign businessmen. But there remains a degree of skepticism about the effectiveness of decentralization programs that are still tied back into the government planning apparatus and that remain subject to internal control by the Party. Often the short-term result of decentralization has been greater confusion over who holds the power to decide. Negotiations for an electronics factory in Shenzhen may proceed for months before the foreign partner realizes that the Shenzhen administration lacks sufficient capital to pull the project together without approval from the Bank of China.

A very real dilemma is entailed in the decentralization process. If decentralization moves too quickly, it may simply encourage the development of local bureaucracies, rather than creating autonomous companies and ventures. "Regionalism" in the form of entrenched provincial and local bureaucracies has traditionally been viewed in China as a threat to national unity and to the development process itself. China is a vast and diverse country with poor communications and transportation. Local control very rapidly moves beyond commercial motives to the creation of "independent kingdoms." The dilemma of decentralization vs. regionalism is reinforced by the perception that too much local control will destroy the planning process itself, which is the institutional heart of socialism.

From the perspective of risk to foreign investors, however, the principal concern is that the pace of decentralization will be too slow to accommodate the needs of China's rapidly expanding economy. If the government bureaucracy fails to adapt quickly enough to permit healthy and continuing expansion, the result will be slower growth and greater stress throughout the Chinese political system. For example, the current price structure for energy commodities—coal, electric power, and petroleum products—on the domestic market is both internally irrational and incompatible with broader international markets. Coal, natural gas, and fuel oil are underpriced, encouraging wasteful industrial burning of these fuels. Gasoline and the light end of the products barrel are overpriced in relation to the price of crude, concentrating profits at the refining end of the industry and shortchanging the oilfields themselves. Similar examples could be found throughout China's fixed price structure. Yet rationalization of the price structure has been an elusive goal. The element of risk, whether it be in price reform or in another structural element of the Chinese economy, is that the existing government bureaucracy is too deeply entrenched to adapt to the requirements of rapid economic modernization. Given the legitimizing force of the modernization program, failure of key elements of that program could well bring down the government five or ten years down the line. Reforms designed to break down central government bureaucracies have only begun to take hold and may be contingent on vigorous initiatives at the highest levels. It remains to be seen whether Deng's successors will retain the level of initiative in government decentralization that Deng Xiaoping himself has achieved. There is a modest level of long-term risk that decentralization will fail, creating a low ceiling on continued expansion of the economy. If this should occur, the consequent damage to legitimacy of the modernization program and the open-door policy would be substantial.

REGIONAL AND GLOBAL POWER RELATIONS

Western companies intent on opening new markets for their products, services, and technology in China are intensely conscious of each new step Beijing takes in the direction of greater openness to foreign commerce. We focus on the "open door" without always noticing the wall of protectionism that still surrounds most domestic markets in China. Our greatest concern is that the policies of Deng Xiaoping and the modernizers will be reversed, slamming the open door and closing off promising avenues of investment and trade.

If we put on Chinese shoes for a moment, however, a somewhat different perspective on the open-door policy emerges. Zheng Weizi, Director of the Institute of International Studies in Beijing, himself an ardent Dengist, sees the open-door policy in the context of national independence and equality:

> Although China's foreign policy has made corresponding adjustments, the cardinal principle of independence remains unchanged. . . . China has completely ended the humiliation of more than a hundred years of foreign domination and has established really independent diplomacy . . . Independence, self-reliance and initiative is [sic] the core of China's foreign policy, set right from the beginning . . . Also, for some time, and especially during the "cultural revolution," the policy of self-reliance was misinterpreted . . . Open-door policy suits China's present situation.[14]

Seen from a Chinese perspective, the open door is an instrument of policy, designed to facilitate the acquisition of modern technology and to mobilize foreign capital and expertise. The underlying objective of the open door, and indeed of the modernization program itself, is to strengthen China as a totally independent nation in the international system. There is nothing new about this goal, although it has changed names many times to fit new political realities. The underlying drive for national independence and equality has been the most fundamental force driving China's foreign relations since the Opium War of 1842 and the "unequal treaties" that resulted. The drive for independence and equality by this 3,000-year-old political entity resulted in the "Self Strengthening Movement" of the late nineteenth century, the Boxer Rebellion of 1900, the revolution of 1911, the May 4th Movement, the guerilla resistance to Japan, the Sino-Soviet split, and the "self-reliance" slogans of the Cultural Revolution. The underlying drive is not about to disappear in the 1980s, although it may take new political forms as conditions require.

From the perspective of political risk analysis, China's vast array of global and regional relations and the stability of those relations are governed not by policy instruments such as the open door, but by the underlying drive for independence and equality in the international arena. No foreign policy issue that challenges China's sense of independence will be set aside for purely commercial reasons. Territorial issues (Hong Kong, Taiwan, the Sino-Soviet border, etc.) are at the top of the list, but even minor issues of pride, such as the lawsuit over the Huguang Railway Bonds, will also occasionally take precedence over normal commercial considerations.

The discussion below focuses briefly on relations with China's principal trade and investment partners and on regional relations. In each case, policy areas are identified that may involve the risk of conflict between commercial interests and China's drive for recognition as an independent and equal member of the international community.

Sino–U.S. Relations

During the past decade, Sino–U.S. relations have developed from the dramatic Nixon-Kissinger initiative into a stable and growing political and commercial partnership. Trade has grown steadily, with a few short-term setbacks, to its current level of $3 billion per year in each direction and is nearly balanced. Educational and cultural exchanges have also grown to an unprecedented level for a communist country. Common security concerns vis-à-vis the Soviet Union and Vietnam have resulted in regular high-level exchanges of views on regional issues, intelligence-sharing, and arms sales. No event or policy issue has seriously threatened this framework in the past five years, and nothing is likely to disrupt the relationship for the rest of the decade, short of a major internal political upheaval in China. The issues listed below are mere irritants in the context of the overall relationship, but may affect individual trade or investment opportunities.

The most persistent and irritating policy issue affecting Sino–U.S. relations has been continuation of semiofficial contact between the United States and Taiwan, particularly the continuing sale of $500–600 million per year in weapons to Taiwan. The issue was exacerbated at the beginning of the Reagan administration by the Taiwan Relations Act and by Mr. Reagan's public campaign statements on the issue. Beijing strongly objects to any implication that Taiwan is an independent country and treats weapons sales to Taipei as an infringement on Chinese sovereignty. Deng Xiaoping has repeatedly called for peaceful reunification under the "one country, two systems" formula, but has rejected U.S. efforts to obtain a renunciation of the use of force. For its part, Taipei appears to want nothing to do with reunification, although the Taiwan government turns a blind eye to indirect trade with the mainland and has sent sports and cultural delegations to events attended by the PRC.

The Taiwan issue will remain a persistent sore point in U.S.–China relations until such time as Beijing and Taipei are able to come to terms directly. The irritation of arms sales and semiofficial treatment for Taipei will flare up from time to time, but will be subordinated to larger U.S.–China interests. Only a regime change in China, or a similar change in Taiwan, will likely affect the status quo on the issue. A significant risk of serious disruption would be entailed by a declaration of independence by Taiwan and U.S. recognition of the island as a separate country. Certain commercial ventures may be subject to risk because of the issue. For example, arms manufacturers who sell to one side risk the wrath of the other, although some defense companies are trying to play both sides of the Taiwan Straits. Exploration of the potentially petrolific East China Sea will probably have to wait for at least tacit agreement between Beijing and Taipei. But on the whole, the Taiwan issue does not pose serious levels of risk on companies investing on either side or both.

Trade protectionism is another outstanding issue between the two countries. Given the vast availability of low-cost labor in the Chinese manufacturing industries, this form of tension is likely to persist. Nevertheless, it is more likely to affect trade opportunities than direct investments. Indeed, one of the powerful motivations drawing foreign capital into joint ventures and other direct investments in China is precisely the desire to take advantage of Chinese wage rates that are deliberately set just below average rates for the Asia-Pacific region. Even if certain projects do run into overt protectionism on either side, the general posture of both governments on trade issues has been that everything is negotiable if only the other side would be reasonable. Indirect protectionism, such as the "preference clause" in the offshore oil exploration projects, will be a far more serious impediment to foreign commercial activity in China than trade quotas.

Aside from protectionism, the legal environment in each country causes problems for the other in a number of areas. For example, U.S. export controls and the need to license sensitive technology for export to China still cause serious delays in many projects, despite liberalization of export controls in the last few years. On the Chinese side, protection of proprietary information and intellectual property is a serious problem. Statutory impediments are likely to affect U.S.–China commerce for some time, but cannot be considered serious risks from a political perspective. It is very unlikely that Beijing would deliberately abrogate the basic framework of legal and tax codes that are slowly being put in place to protect and regulate foreign investment and trade. In cases where new laws have been introduced, China has bent over backward to allow existing contracts or previous statutes to retain force if the foreign partner insists on application of the original agreement.

Only one area in the U.S.–China relationship will consistently block pursuit of commercial opportunities, and that is in technologies that have strategic defense applications—particularly to China's nuclear weapons and missile programs. China has had nuclear weapons for 20 years and continues to insist on development of its own independent nuclear deterrent. The PRC has finally joined the International Atomic Energy Agency, but has never acceded to any nuclear weapons control agreement except the Treaty of Tlatelolco, which established a Latin American nuclear weapons free zone. President Reagan negotiated and initiated a commercial nuclear cooperation agreement with Beijing in April 1984, but because of intelligence indicating Chinese assistance to Pakistan's nuclear weapons development program, the cooperation agreement has not yet been submitted to Congress for approval. In the absence of the agreement, U.S. nuclear vendors are unable to compete with European and Japanese companies for contracts in China's fledgling nuclear power construction program. U.S. concerns regarding the agreement center on possible reexport of sensitive technologies and on the precedents that would be set for other Third World countries that seek similar technology.

In all three of these issue areas—the Taiwan issue, trade relations, and strategic weapons technology—the United States is attempting to preserve what it sees as its basic interests, while Beijing is attempting to achieve what it perceives as parity. All three issues touch sensitive nerves in China's drive for independence and equality. All these issues will persist as irritants in the relationship, but none of them poses serious political risk to foreign investors, barring a regime change in China.

With the exception of Britain, which must perforce deal with the Hong Kong issue, the countries of Western Europe and Australasia have tended to follow the U.S. position on political and defense relations with China. European countries are inclined to be more liberal on export control issues than the United States, and are somewhat more aggressive in offering subsidized export credits to China.

The Asia–Pacific Region

Over the past decade, China's diplomatic and trade relations with its Asian neighbors have gradually moderated, eliminating most of the tensions that were characteristic of the 1960s. Japan has been at the heart of the process, leading the way with formal recognition in 1972, and building bilateral trade that reached $13.2 billion in 1984. The Japanese government has gone out of its way to be accommodating to the Chinese, deliberately softening the edges of public disagreements and providing about $250–300 million per year of low-interest, long-term loans for Chinese development projects. Beijing has reciprocated by toning down the rhetoric over such issues as the jurisdictional dispute in the East China Sea, and by opening up opportunities, particularly in northeast China, for direct Japanese investment. Despite the improvement of political and commercial ties, the relationship retains an edge of Chinese bitterness and Japanese guilt over the brutal occupation of Manchuria before and during World War II.

Korea remains the most important flash-point in East Asia. Chinese efforts to reduce the level of tension are significant, but are constrained by Pyongyang's many ties to the Soviet Union. Moscow is very wary of direct North-South talks and has continued to take a hard line on reunification and other issues. The North is deeply dependent on Soviet military aid and trade to sustain its ossified economy. The Soviets would like to have access to naval facilities on the northwestern coast of the peninsula to circumvent any potential blockade of the Tsushima and La Perouse Straits and to put pressure on China's coastal defenses. Another constraint that may affect Chinese initiatives on the Korean issue is the instability caused by the dynastic succession in the North to Kim Il Sung's son. Kim Jong Il will visit the Soviet Union in 1985 for the first time since his childhood. Uncertainty regarding his ties to Moscow and his reported emotional instability could present obstacles to long-term peace on the Korean peninsula.

The other area of direct confrontation between Chinese and Soviet objectives in Asia is Indochina. Since the end of the Vietnam war, Moscow has backed Vietnamese domination of Laos and Cambodia, while China has backed anti-Vietnamese insurgents and strongly objects to the unification of Indochina under Hanoi's control. The Soviet Union has also extended considerable military and economic aid to Vietnam and has based aircraft, surface vessels, and submarines at the former U.S. bases at Danang and Cam Ranh Bay. China terminated its aid program in 1975 and is engaged in a festering border conflict with Vietnam that has spread into a vitriolic jurisdictional dispute over control of the Tonkin Gulf and the Paracel and Spratley islands. China occupied the Paracels by force in 1972 and faces occasional harassment of its offshore exploration programs in disputed areas by Vietnamese gunboats.

Despite the intensity of the Sino-Vietnamese border conflict, which tends to escalate whenever Vietnam steps up attacks on the Cambodian resistance, it is difficult to identify any firm linkage between the conflict and levels of risk for foreign investors. Certainly foreign offshore drilling rigs and production platforms in the Gulf of Tonkin are vulnerable to Vietnamese attack and therefore subject to high levels of risk in the event of escalation in the border conflict. In 1979, however, no foreign trade activities in southern China were affected by the open border war. Foreign offshore rigs, which were not present in 1979, have occasionally been harassed since they moved during 1980, but have never been directly attacked. Vietnam actively cooperated with search and rescue attempts after the "Glomar Java Sea" sank in a typhoon in October 1983. A direct attack on offshore rigs would probably result in confrontation with the United States, since several of the rigs and crews are of U.S. origin. At present, Hanoi is engaged in gradual easing of tensions with Washington, a process that it would not likely reverse by attacking U.S. nationals.

Aside from the offshore oil projects, it is difficult to project precisely how foreign investment in China would be affected by serious conflict between China and Vietnam. Heavy industrial projects, such as coastal refineries, might be subject to attack, as would projects located on Hainan Island. But the prospect of direct Vietnamese attacks on industrial targets in the Hong Kong/Guangzhou corridor is remote. The most important effects for foreign investment in southern China would be indirect—disruption of the transportation and communications infrastructure and a tightening of Chinese security measures.

As for the fate of Hong Kong itself, the die is cast. Britain and China initialed the Joint Declaration on the Question of Hong Kong in September 1984, after two years of difficult negotiations. The Joint Declaration provides for the reversion of Hong Kong to Chinese sovereignty and governmental control on July 1, 1997. It also contains a long list of specific provisions designed to protect the rights of Hong Kong citizens and the continuity of commerce over a 50-year period. The reversion treaty was a major international victory for Beijing, symbolizing precisely the independent and equal status that China has sought since the 1842 Treaty of Nanking. This last chapter in the history of colonialism in China will also provide a dramatic experiment with Deng's concept of "one country, two systems," a test that may have implications for Taiwan's future.

From the perspective of political risk, of course, the reversion of Hong Kong to China represents a clear and present danger of expropriation for all foreign investments in Hong Kong itself. Despite the explicit provisions of the Joint Declaration protecting such investments, foreign capital (and Hong Kong capital) will probably flow slowly but steadily out of the colony for the next thirteen years. Some major trading companies (e.g., Jardine Matheson) have already reincorporated elsewhere in the world. Land values and the stock market have fallen. But given the amount of time left for removal of foreign assets, the Chinese run a greater risk from a commercial collapse in Hong Kong than do foreign investors.

Hong Kong will probably be treated as part of China in support activities for offshore oil exploration, even before it reverts to Chinese control. Many other areas of direct investment and trade into the indigenous market may also open up through Hong Kong–based channels. Whereas Hong Kong has for the last 35 years been China's commercial window on the world, it may in the next 15 years become the world's window to China's vast domestic markets. Investments placed through the Hong Kong window may prove to be *less* risky than investments negotiated with the central ministries in Beijing.

China's diplomatic and trade relations with South and Southeast Asia are both stable and gradually improving. The main concern in Southeast Asia had been that Beijing would use indigenous communist movements and overseas Chinese populations to its own political ends. The Association of Southeast Asian Nations (ASEAN) and China are drawn closer together by common opposition to Vietnamese domination of Indochina. In South Asia, the border dispute with India is once again under discussion, but will probably prove intractable for some time to come. But the areas involved are too remote to pose significant political risk to investment on either side.

The Soviet Union and Eastern Europe

After two decades of hostility and border incidents, Sino-Soviet relations are finally on the mend, if only incrementally. Contact began with two rounds of "funeral diplomacy" when Foreign Minister Huang Hua attended Brezhnev's funeral, followed after a short interlude by Deputy Prime Minister Wan Li at Andropov's funeral. Both Chinese officials were well received, and quiet discussions took place that resulted in four rounds of negotiations from 1982 through 1984 directed toward stabilization and improvement of relations. The most obvious initial benefit of these talks was the resumption of trade. Two-way trade has grown from $300 million in 1982 to $1.2 billion in 1984. Further expansion in trade is anticipated—to $1.6 billion in 1985 and possibly to as much as $6 billion by 1990, a level equivalent to 1984 Sino–U.S. trade. The Russians have agreed to resume cross-border trade in Manchuria, Mongolia, and Xinjiang. They will concentrate generally on selling China low-cost standardized heavy industry equipment, not high-technology gear, which primarily will continue to come from the West. Rising trade with the Soviet Union will undoubtedly present new competition in the China market for the West in certain product and commodity lines.

Political and security issues between China and the Soviet Union are likely to prove far less tractable than commercial relations. Major differences include the presence of half a million heavily armed Soviet troops on the Chinese border, deployment of the SS-20 Intermediate-Range Ballistic Missiles in East Siberia targeted on Chinese cities and industrial centers, the Soviet-supported Vietnamese invasion of Cambodia, the Soviet invasion of Afghanistan, and a wide range of less important issues. None of the major issues is likely to be resolved quickly through negotiations. But as with U.S.–Soviet relations, the very fact of face-to-face talks will stabilize relations and lead to a reduction in tension. Over time, these continuing contacts will substantially reduce the risk of conflict along the Sino-Soviet border.

China has also renewed its relations with East European countries since 1983, increasing trade and cultural contacts. Most political contacts focus on inter-party relations, and some nostalgia is expressed for the halcyon days of the world communist movement. But if any movement takes place at the party-to-party level, it will be in the direction of greater independence of East European communist parties from Moscow, not toward greater integration.

No foreign relationship more clearly reflects China's drive for independence and equality than that with the Soviet Union. The Sino-Soviet split was born of Russian arrogance and interference in domestic Chinese affairs. Each remaining area of friction involves more than a little Chinese pride. The confrontation will soften over the next fifteen years, but underlying differences will remain. The only real risk to foreign investors of the new climate in Sino-Soviet relations is the relatively remote possibility that the remnant Stalinist faction in the Chinese Communist Party would somehow regain the upper hand and return the country to a more rigidly Marxist model of economic development. There are those in the Party who would return to the Soviet-style communism of the 1950s, but they are few indeed.

LONG-RANGE POLITICAL RISK IN CHINA

This concludes our review of various risk factors that may affect large-scale foreign investments in China. The basic conclusion, whether one considers the domestic political system or foreign policy, is that China not only appears stable, but in fact is relatively stable and likely to remain so for at least the next five years. After three decades of intense political turmoil, economic development has replaced revolution as the most important legitimizing force in the Chinese polity. Deng Xiaoping has placed an entirely new generation of leaders at the top of the party, the government, and the military. This new generation is even more firmly committed to the modernization of China's economy than the Deng administration itself. China has come to view economic modernization, rather than doctrinaire Marxism, as the most likely avenue to independence and true equality in the global community.

None of this is to suggest that there are *no* political risks entailed in doing business in China. Certain parts of the institutional structure, such as the military, could become deep reservoirs for renewed radicalism and xenophobia. Failure of the modernization program to yield sustained improvement in average standards of living could turn into rejection of the open-door policy and a return to orthodoxy. Most important, the lack of a regularized means of replacing the political leadership through elections or other institutional mechanisms puts a low ceiling on the adaptability of the system to new economic and political conditions. Thus China's long-term political evolution is likely to be a halting and uneven process.

On the foreign policy side, one must conclude that the political and commercial partnership with the United States that emerged in the early 1970s reflects commonalities of interest on both sides and will therefore persist over time, despite remaining areas of friction. China's relations with its Asian neighbors have also matured and are likely to remain stable, although some of the countries around the perimeter of Asia's giant will remain guarded in their enthusiasm for China's newfound international status and power. Only the relationship with the Soviet Union remains largely negative in tone. The Sino-Soviet stand-off will also remain a fact of life in East Asia through the end of the century, barring major regime changes on one or both sides. But the threat of open conflict with the Soviet Union has declined significantly since 1982, and it is unlikely that either side would see much advantage in renewed hostility.

Perhaps the greatest threat to foreign investments in China is that change will proceed too slowly—particularly the changes that are required in the bureaucratic decision process that affects every development project. The modernization program is already placing great stress on China's planning system, price structure, communications and transportation infrastructure, and other key organizational elements required of a truly modern society. Inertia, not momentum, will be the biggest risk in the long term.

NOTES

1. "Chinese Leader Asserts Some Officials are Senile," *Wall Street Journal,* November 2, 1984, p. 36.

2. Parris H. Chang, "China's Deng Plans Purge of Critics in 1985," *Wall Street Journal,* December 24, 1984, p. 7.

3. "Major Steps to Change Personnel Management," *China Daily,* July 21, 1984, p. 1.

4. "Party Branches Urged to Admit More Intellectuals," *China Daily,* November 21, 1984.

5. "Theory and Practice," *Renmin Ribao,* December 7, 1984, p. 1; in *FBIS,* December 7, 1984, p. K1.

6. *Renmin Ribao,* December 8, 1984, p. 1; in *FBIS,* December 10, 1984, p. K21.

7. "A Talk by Deng Xiaoping at the Third Plenary Session of the Central Advisory Commission on 22 October 1982," *Xinhua,* December 31, 1984; in *FBIS,* January 2, 1985, pp. K1–K6.

8. Christopher S. Wren, "Peking Reshaping Ideology to Fit New Economic Policy," *New York Times,* December 17, 1984, pp. A1, A10.

9. John F. Burns, "Writer's Congress in China Demands Artistic Freedom," *New York Times,* January 1, 1985, pp. 1, 4.

10. "China's Forgotten 'Counterrevolutionaries'," *Asian Wall Street Journal,* December 11, 1984, p. 2.

11. John F. Burns, "40 High Officers Retire in China in Army Shake-Up," *New York Times,* December 31, 1984, pp. 1, 4.

12. *Ibid.*

13. "Aide Calls for PLA to Cut Costs," *China Daily,* December 22, 1984, p. 1.

14. Zheng Weiji, "Independence is the Basic Canon," *Beijing Review,* January 7, 1985, pp. 16–19, 38.

chapter six

Venezuela: Oil, Democracy, and the Quest for Sound Political Leadership

Gustavo Coronel

A BRIEF HISTORICAL BACKGROUND

Throughout the last century and the first five decades of this century, Venezuela was the scene of war, revolutions, regional strife, and dictatorships. The first popularly elected president, Rómulo Gallegos, came to power in 1948 and lasted just ten months in office before being overthrown by the armed forces.

After its independence, Venezuela became the stage for a succession of violent events at the regional level between leaders usually more vulturous than talented. In contrast to exceptional Venezuelans such as Bolivar, Miranda, Bello, and Simon Rodriguez, these regional chieftains usually had a myopic sense of history and pooled their efforts to convert the country into one of the most backward South American nations. By the end of the last century, Venezuela was bankrupt, torn apart by the greed of these regional leaders and that of the major European powers, all intent on obtaining some of the spoils.

Oil created a new Venezuela social fabric. The countryside was abandoned mixed blessing. At the time of its discovery it definitely helped to shift the attitude of the external world from contempt to interest. By the early 1920s dozens of international oil companies had arrived in the country and were actively pursuing exploration activities. The luckier ones found and started to produce some excellent-quality oil.

Oil created a new Venezuela social fabric. The Countryside was abandoned in favor of oil production centers where money ran freely and life was more exciting. The demographic shift also brought about a change in personal values and attitudes. Many a farmer turned into an oilworker and became a different man. After all, the exploration for oil was a gamble that promised immense and almost instant wealth. The instant wealth syndrome became one of the most pronounced characteristics of Venezuelan society from the early 1920s to the present.

International oil companies established a relationship with the Venezuelan dictator J. V. Gómez (1908–1935), which, in the eyes of the Venezuelan people, ranged from deference to coziness. In retrospective, it seems that the price paid by the companies was quite high, that of being perceived as supporters of the dictator against the will of the people. Oil companies decided to buy the present at the expense of some of the future. There is little doubt that the nationalistic flashes and the anti-foreign sentiments that have surfaced sporadically in Venezuela during the last decades have had much to do with the perception of foreign enterprises as historical allies of authoritarian, unpopular political regimes.

It took a group of hot-headed university students and a few understanding elders to nurse Venezuelan democracy along after the years of despotism. Among the former were Rómulo Betancourt, Jovito Villalba, and Rafael Caldera; among the latter, Eleazar Lopez Contreras, Gomez's minister of war, and Isaias Medina, Lopez's minister of war. These two mature men, although political products of the years of dictatorship, came successively into the presidency of the country to plant and nurture the seeds of democracy. During the period 1935–1945, democracy in Venezuela grew at an accelerated rate, although never too fast for the impatient, younger political generations.

From 1945 to 1948, Venezuela entered what could be defined as the political rapids. During these three years there were two coup d'etats, the second one of which plunged Venezuela into a new, ten-year-long military dictatorship. During those sad years for Venezuelan democracy the main political leaders of the country, in exile when not in prison, finally came to realize that if they wanted to assure the consolidation of democracy they had to agree on some fundamental issues and establish political floors and ceilings to eliminate unnecessary dissent and friction. This led, after the fall of the dictatorship in 1958, to the formulation of a broad political pact to support Venezuelan democracy regardless of the party that came into power. This ability to enter into multipartisan agreements concerning basic national issues has remained as one of the most successful ingredients of Venezuelan democracy.

The period 1958–1978 was one of democratic consolidation, a process lubricated by oil. Oil income during those years compensated for the many imperfections of the system and, up to 1970, was used in a reasonably efficient way to build a basic national infrastructure of roads, hospitals, dams, and schools and to stimulate a process of industrialization based on the substitution of imports. This emphasis on basic needs was abandoned in the 1970s with the abrupt increase in oil income produced by the first oil shock of 1974–1975. In those years, fiscal income suddenly quadrupled, converting Venezuela in a classical example of economic indigestion. Without enough absorptive capacity to utilize wisely this enormous income, the country created the Venezuela Investment Fund to store the surplus of foreign exchange that could not be utilized immediately. Unfortunately, this very sensible move was replaed by the desire of the incumbent Acción Democrática (AD) administration to turn Venezuela into an industrial giant within a very limited time span. This led to a massive investment program in capital-intensive projects, such as steel mills, hydroelectric complexes, petrochemical and aluminum plants. Imports grew at 25 percent per year, but employment levels did not increase, and delays in the construction of the gigantic projects forced the progressive utilization of the investment fund reserves and, worse, led to massive external borrowing that was mostly contracted on a short-term basis, although all the projects were of a long-term nature.

It was not surprising that, by 1979, Venezuela was suffering from significant economic disturbances.

ESSENTIAL POLITICAL AND SOCIAL BEARINGS

The dominant theme in the Venezuelan political and social scene of the last 30 years has been that of a rich oil country with a deeply rooted democratic instinct looking, so far in vain, for the high-quality political leadership that could make it fulfill what appears to be a stupendous potential.

The 1979–1983 administration of Luis Herrera Campins was such a profound disappointment for Venezuelans that some analysts and observers felt conditions were ripe for abrupt social or political change. Instead, the results of the December 1983 presidential and congressional elections were convincing proof of the preference of Venezuelans for an orderly democratic evolution. There was very low absenteeism and, as it had been widely forecast, the party in power received a dramatic rebuke as a result of its colorless performance. The main opposition party, Acción Democrática, came once more into power, obtaining 57 percent of the total vote.

The combined vote of AD and COPEI, the outgoing government party, rose to 92 percent of the total. The political left, represented by socialist-Marxist parties MAS and MPE, and the small Venezuelan Communist Party obtained 7 percent of the vote, while the candidates of the moderate right shared the remaining 1 percent. As in the preceding four national elections held since 1959, voting took place normally.

No other administration in the last 25 years had given Venezuelans so many reasons to become totally disenchanted with the system. Yet the voters had already become mature enough to distinguish between permanent institutions and a transient administration. Their clear endorsement of a democratic solution left no doubt as to the degree to which Venezuelan democracy had become consolidated.

The elections also indicated that Venezuela was closer than ever to a two-party system, both of the parties located around the center of the political spectrum. Extreme political positions were not perceived as valid options by the Venezuelan voter. The behavior of voters suggests that Venezuelan common political sense has developed faster than wisdom at the political top.

The preference of Venezuelans for the center of the political spectrum can be traced to their traditionally liberal philosophy of life, commonly expressed as a strong tendency toward social equality, as an easy acceptance of change, and through a very informal behavior. This liberal attitude has been successfully exploited by the political left to liquidate all hopes the political right might have had to become a significant force in 20th-century Venezuela. The intellectuals of the left have utilized ridicule to describe Venezuelan conservatives as throwbacks to a distant past, as Stone Age troglodytes. As a result of this persistent campaign, several younger generations of Venezuelans have grown conditioned to being ashamed of being conservative.

The liquidation of the political right at the hands of the left did not give this group victory, however. The political left in Venezuela has been totally unable to capture the imagination and the hearts of the people. More and more, leftist advocates have been reduced to the intellectual realm and to academia, which has become the home of transitory leftists who rapidly abandon their beliefs as they enter the "real world." The Venezuelan "real world" is inhabited by political moderates, who largely conform to no social boundaries, age, or occupation.

In voting to preserve the system while soundly rebuking the incumbent administration, Venezuelans also demonstrated their determination that the democratic model could and should be improved from within, that it could generate enough momentum to become efficient. The Venezuelan love for democracy has come to be, as Shaw once said of second marriages, "a triumph of hope over experience." In the Venezuelan case, this has already been a marriage of 30 years, one that has seen many crises come and go and is no longer a fluke but a very robust institution.

THE POLITICAL AND ECONOMIC PROCESS

The Ingredients of the Crisis

The mounting external debt, weakening oil markets, and lackluster political leadership contributed to a rapid deterioration of the economic and social climate in Venezuela during the period 1979–1983. Loss of confidence in Herrera's administration led to severe capital flight, which reduced the foreign currency reserves to some $10 billion by the end of 1983, barely half of what they had been in 1981. By this time the country faced a real economic crisis, and several steps had to be taken by government to resist further deterioration: exchange controls, import restrictions, interruption of payments on the principal of the external debt, and intense negotiations to reschedule payment of the very large short-term component of the debt.

Why the crisis? In addition to the reasons already mentioned (weak oil markets, higher interest rates, and the large short-term component of the external debt), other economic factors contributed to the present situation. Among them:

- The accelerated growth of total public expenditures, which in 1972 represented 40 percent of the GDP and in 1982 reached 72 percent of the GDP.
- Current government expenditures, which increased at some 18 percent per year during the period 1979–1982.
- Decreasing capital expenditures, from 60 percent of total expenditures in 1974 to only 30 percent in 1980. The reduction in capital expenditures and the delay in the completion of pending projects clearly increased the gap between government income and total expenditures.
- The transformation of the Venezuelan Investment Fund into the shareholder for many of the largely inefficient public enterprises. About $8

billion from this fund was sunk into public companies in the period 1975–1981.

- Increasing short-term borrowing on the part of public enterprises, not always with the knowledge and approval of the central government.
- The absence of adequate and managerial resources to handle large projects and the long lead times involved in those projects.
- The stagnation of internal production and of private investment which had been evident since 1976, as shown by the following statistics (million bolivares):

	1976	1977	1978	1979	1980	1981	1982
Private investment	14,346	19,132	18,927	15,783	10,050	8,478	6,982
Index	100	133	132	110	70	60	48

Source: Venezuelan Central Bank.

- The erratic behavior of the internal interest rates, which helped to stimulate capital flight.
- The increasing level of nonessential imports, which grew at some 20 percent per year in the period 1975–1980, cutting deeply into the financial surplus and the investment fund and finally obliging the country to borrow abroad.

The dimensions of the crisis are illustrated by the size of the external public and private debt, estimated by the Finance Ministry of Venezuela in mid-1983 as US$32 billion and by external observers in mid-1984 as US$36 billion. Of this total debt, more than 50 percent matured in 1983, while an additional 12 percent matured in 1984. An agreement was reached in late 1984 to refinance 94 percent of the total external public debt, and negotiations were under way during 1985 to settle the financing of the external private debt.

About 86 percent of the debt is in the hands of foreign commercial banks, only 4 percent is with Venezuelan banks which are members of lending groups led by international banks, and the remaining 10 percent is with international financial agencies.

The Lack of Leadership

There is no doubt that a negotiated solution to this significant external debt is an item of the highest priority for Venezuela and the incumbent AD administration. Still, it might not be the most important of the Venezuelan problems. In the longer term, the main problem of the country seems to be the low quality of its political leadership. The country still is under the trauma of the 1979–1983 Herrera Campins administration, when the sense of national direction seemed to disappear under the thick fog of folksy rhetoric.

The deterioration of the Venezuelan political leadership has not been an abrupt development. After Rómulo Betancourt (1958–1963), Venezuela has not had a truly charismatic political leader, although his successors have kept alive a tradition of presidentialism which, in their hands, has rapidly turned into a political liability. Probably fundamental in the decay of Venezuelan political institutions has been the lack of determination shown by political leaders to convert them into more modern, popularly accepted organizations that would reinforce the legitimacy of the system. Not only does the president still pretend to be all-powerful and to be able to pontificate on every conceivable subject, but he also feels obliged to dedicate much of his time to attend all kinds of minor social and political events. Congress members are elected in block, on a party basis and without much concern for individual quality. The judicial bodies have become deeply politicized and, in a general sense, can no longer be considered fully autonomous institutions. State legislatures look oddly misplaced in a highly centralized political system, and its vacancies essentially serve as rewards for outstanding regional political activists.

It seems clear that Venezuela has been much more successful in building a democratic infrastructure than in making it evolve into a more workable tool for real social and political progress. The reasons for this are largely attitudinal. Once democracy was reasonably established at the cost of much work and sacrifice on the part of the political elites of the 1950s, oil-derived income started to flood into the country, creating a taste for the easy life, which seems to be a main characteristic of most countries which acquire a sudden overabundance of financial resources. This addiction to opulence contaminated all segments of the Venezuelan social fabric, including the political elites. As a result political corruption replaced political idealism.

The Main Actors

The main political and economic actors in Venezuela are the following:

- The political party now in power, Acción Democrática, a social-democratic organization. Acción Democrática is essentially a party of the middle and working classes. It has had, more than a well-defined political doctrine, a line of distinguished leaders with whom the popular sentiment has been able to identify. This group has included politicians such as Rómulo Betancourt, Gonzalo Barrios, Alberto Carnevali, and Juan Pablo Pérez Alfonzo, and intellectuals such as Rómulo Gallegos and Andrés Eloy Blanco, all of whom played an invaluable role in the democratization of Venezuela. During the last 30 years Acción Democrática has consistently migrated from the left to the center of the political spectrum. For the present, the main strength of the party still lies in its control of the labor unions through the powerful "Confederación de Trabajadores de Venezuela" (CTV), in its continued appeal to much of the Venezuelan middle class and peasants, and in its generally superb regional organization, an objective which the party actively pursued since its creation. Acción Democrática has rarely been a monolithic organization, however. Nowadays there exist at least three tendencies within the party: *the orthodox wing*, followers of Betancourt, led by the elder president of the party Gonzalo Barrios; *the Carlos Andrés Pérez group*, led by former president Pérez, who clearly desires to run for the presidency once again in 1988 and who commands an important segment of the party machinery and has preserved a high level of acceptance among the rank and file; and *the Jaime Lusinchi group*, now in power, enjoying the benefits of being at the top and whose future political fortune will essentially depend on how successful the administration turns out to be. For all practical purposes, it should be assumed that the Lusinchi group and the orthodox wing of the party will remain very much in agreement with the way government should be run during the present administration. The strong Carlos Andrés Pérez group will be less clearly identifiable with the austerity measures that will be attempted by Lusinchi, since the Pérez group still believes in industrialization policies based on capital-intensive projects rather than on a slower, more cautious process of national development.

- The opposition party, COPEI, a Christian Democratic organization. COPEI started out in the early 1940s as a conservative party, closely identified with the Catholic church. From the moment of its creation the party has been led by Rafael Caldera, a brilliant lawyer and university professor who became president of the country in 1969–1974. The party has moved in time toward a position slightly right of the political center and has lost some cohesiveness during its two presidential terms. Today there are two distinct groups disputing the party leadership. One, still the strongest, is *the Rafael Caldera group*, led by the founder of the party and comprising the original group of leaders, together with a very talented younger group led by Eduardo Fernández, Caldera's heir apparent. The other is *the Luis Herrera group*, under the wing of the former president, where absolute leadership is less clear and somehow shared by Pedro Pablo Aguilar, Pepi Montes de Oca, and Luis Herrera himself.

  The Herrera group, still smarting after the sound electoral defeat of December 1983, could be further weakened in the medium term by charges against some of its members of mismanagement and corruption during its administration. There is no question, however, that Acción Democrática and COPEI together represent the overwhelming majority of voters in the country, and there is little possibility that this situation will change in the medium term (8 to 10 years).

- The political left, essentially represented by MAS, is a Marxist-socialist party that saw its rather accelerated growth come to an abrupt halt during the December 1983 elections. MAS is led by Teodoro Petkoff, a former guerrilla activist who in recent years has shifted to the center in an effort to convert MAS into an acceptable party of the establishment. This has produced a reaction from the orthodox Marxists of the organization to the extent that the party is now undergoing a severe crisis of identity and has already lost many members. The other organizations of the left are mostly clustered around the figure of José Vicente Rangel, a respected socialist congressman who has played a distinguished role in the defense of human rights in Venezuela.

- An emerging movement, centered around the figure of Jorge Olavarría, a magazine editor and liberal politician of considerable appeal among the uncommitted Venezuelan middle class and moderate university student groups. This grassroots movement obtained three seats in congress during the December 1983 elections, enough to place it as the fourth political organization in the country.

- The labor movement organized under the very powerful Confederación de Trabajadores de Venezuela (CTV). CTV is under the political influence of Acción Democrática (AD). Its president, J. J. Delpino, is an AD party member and a close friend of Manuel Peñalver, also a labor leader and secretary general of Acción Democrática. CTV has entered into a broad political pact of uncertain duration with the government and the business sector to accept smaller and farther apart salary increases for its membership as part of a package of economic measures designed to improve the overall economic situation of the country. CTV is actively promoting the concept of comanagement or labor representation at the managerial levels in both state and private companies and has found powerful allies in some members of the Lusinchi cabinet. The Venezuelan version of labor representation at managerial levels is likely to be highly symbolic, quite different from the more aggressive Bolivian version, and it might take between three and five years to make noticeable progress. In general, organized labor is a very strong ingredient of Venezuelan political stability and, although it has suffered some mishaps in recent years, such as the scandal of the Worker's Bank in which prominent leaders of CTV were involved, it will remain in the foreseeable future as an essentially positive force in Venezuelan politics.

- FEDECAMARAS, the powerful Federation of Chambers of Commerce, which brings together the leaders of the Venezuelan business sector. The nature of its membership has changed during the last decade to include more of the smaller regional chambers of commerce. This change has brought about a new type of leadership, closer to the interests of the small business groups than to the traditional, family-run economic groups that have controlled the federation for many years. Although the traditional groups have recovered much of their lost power, FEDECAMARAS is now perceived as a much more open and, in a way, less powerful organization than a decade ago. FEDECAMARAS exerts its power through the highly imbricated network of commercial, family, and friendship relationships that exist between their members and the political elites. In this fashion, many government regulations undesirable to business are diluted and generally transformed into more palatable products. This is possible because Venezuela is a relatively small country where there is a strong sense of togetherness, a remnant of the long years of the Gomez dictatorship in which entire families would be persecuted by the security forces of the dictator and befriended and protected by neighbors and acquaintances.

- PRO-VENEZUELA, a nationalistic association created some 30 years ago by industrialist Alejandro Hernández to promote Venezuelan industrial and cultural development. During the years, this association has become a valuable forum for the discussion of many national problems, but its influence has steadily declined due to its increasing leftist, occasionally xenophobic posture.

- The military which, during the 1940s and the 1950s, played a dominant role in deciding who the Venezuelan political leaders would be, has undergone a significant change in attitudes and philosophies. Through a process started in the early 1960s by Rómulo Betancourt and followed by all other democratic presidents, the political sector has actively interacted with the military elites, duly recognizing their role as the safeguards of national security and substantially contributing to improve the quality of life of officers and soldiers. As a result, the military elites have been progressively absorbed into the Venezuelan social and political mainstream, with many top officers becoming engaged in professional careers in such fields as law and engineering, essentially abandoning their once-strong sense of identity as a power-seeking group. At the same time, the military institution has become politicized, many of its members now leaning toward one or the other of the main parties of the system. As a result, promotions are often accelerated or delayed in direct relation to political loyalties. Politicization has also contributed to weaken the perception that the military had of themselves as an exclusive and monolithic group. In addition to these factors there has been a strong, self-generated drive within the military to make the institution more professional, which is very much to the credit of the younger generation of military officers. For all of these reasons, the military can be considered as an institution actively working for the stability, rather than subversion, of the Venezuelan democratic system, and this trend is unlikely to change.
- The oil industry technocracy, an elite that arrived rather late to the Venezuelan political stage but which had a decisive role to play in the rational approach Venezuela took in nationalizing its oil industry in 1975. The group of high-level managers who control the Venezuelan oil industry is no larger than 120, assisted by a group of some 300 middle managers and a technical core of perhaps 2000 engineers and other specialists. This relatively small group has been instrumental in making it possible for the Venezuelan oil industry to generate income in the order of $14–17 billion per year for the last nine years. Perhaps more important than the purely financial and technical aspects has been the example of administrative responsibility this group has given the country. Although managing billions of dollars per year, the group has been involved in very few scandals. The most spectacular of these concerned an isolated group of five to ten middle managers and outsiders and was brought to the attention of the country by the industry leaders themselves. There is little doubt that the example set by the oil industry technocracy during the last ten years has been a major source of hope in the ability of Venezuelans to keep their institutions free from corruption and in their will to clean whatever contamination might have appeared. The oil industry technocracy has strong leaders and a group, AGROPET, formed during the national debate on nationalization, which acts as a vigilant organization to ascertain that the nationalized oil industry does not become politicized or

corrupt. Oil industry technocracy represents one of the strongest assets of Venezuelan democracy.

• The Catholic church remains as a very strong political and social force in Venezuela, although significantly less so than 30 years ago. It is well organized but lacks strong leadership and financial resources. The church has traditionally been a supporter of Venezuelan democracy, and there are no signals that such a role would change in the future. There are two groups within the Venezuelan church: the orthodox followers of Roman Catholicism and a group of younger priests who advocate a blend of Catholicism and Marxism for the solution of the problems of the poor. The orthodox group is, by far, the dominant one. Hence, the Catholic church in Venezuela tends to serve more as a lever of control than as an agent of active social change.

THE RESULTS

The actors described have interacted in the last decades to produce an economic and political environment characterized by:

1. A hyperthrophic public sector that started out as one more example of a mixed economy and became, in time, an acute case of state capitalism. The original idea was that of reserving to the state only strategic, basic industries. Yet, public bureaucracy and a shy private sector made it possible for more and more industries to become state-owned. At present, there are some 350 state-owned enterprises, most of which are poorly managed and chronic money losers. Employment in the public sector accounts for almost 25 percent of the total workforce in the country.

2. A sustained and deliberate national effort toward industrialization, which started in the early 1960s. This has been another of the issues in which all sectors have agreed in order to make the country less dependent on oil. The industrialization drive has centered around the concept of import substitution rather than being export-oriented. During the period 1950–1970, industrial growth was rapid as illustrated by the increasing participation of manufacturing in the Gross Domestic Product, which went from 10 percent in 1950 to about 16 percent in 1970. Moreover, whereas in 1950, nontraditional manufacturing represented only 23 percent of the total, in 1980 it had reached 47 percent, excluding oil refining. By 1977, the number of industries having more than 100 employees already accounted for 75 percent of all production. Although a latecomer compared to other countries in the region, Venezuelan manufacturing grew so rapidly that it went from last place in 1950 to a tie with Colombia for first place in 1978, growing at the rate of 8 percent per year.

3. A significant growth in foreign investment in the field of manufacturing, from $400 million in 1965 to over a billion dollars in 1978, accounting for 35 percent of total investment. The role played by foreign investment has been very important. Most of the industries that were installed in Venezuela during the period 1950–1970 were either subsidiaries of foreign industries or majority joint ventures with Venezuelan capital. In 1974, 90 percent of total foreign investment in Venezuela was represented in physical assets, and most of this

was of U.S. origin. On the other hand, however, the overall industrialization effort has become progressively stagnant. The rates of growth started to decrease from 11 percent in 1950–1958 to eight percent in 1958–1964 and to five percent in 1974–1980. This was the result of the inability of Venezuelan industry to export due to its high production costs, generally low productivity, and insufficient qualified personnel.

4. A rigid, almost religious adherence to a progressively overvalued currency that minimized incentives to produce internally what could be bought cheaper abroad. The overvalued currency stimulated an important outflow of capital. Venezuelans became avid travelers and bought much property in the United States, Europe, and the Caribbean. Internal tourism practically disappeared, and the average middle-class Venezuelan became more conversant with Miami, Puerto Rico, or Madrid than with the Venezuelan mountain or beach resorts.

5. A distrust of foreign investment on the part of the political elites. This distrust has historical roots that go back to the Gomez dictatorship, when multinational oil companies were perceived to be aligned with the dictator. The military coup that deposed democratic president Gallegos in 1948 was seen as partially encouraged by the international oil companies, in retaliation against the higher taxes levied upon them by the AD government. Many of the Venezuelan political leaders who were imprisoned, tortured, or exiled by dictatorships came back to power with the strong feeling that foreign executives and foreign corporations were not their friends. To distrust we should add resentment, the product of a deeply rooted inferiority complex possessed by these political leaders vis-à-vis the representatives of foreign capital, essentially the oil industry executives. Years later, this resentment was transferred on to the Venezuelan oil executives who inherited the management of the oil industry after nationalization. It has not yet disappeared. Although the success of the nationalized oil industry has greatly helped to ameliorate this negative attitude, its complete disappearance will probably take a long time.

6. A historical tendency toward the centralization of political and economic power. Regional Venezuelan authorities are not elected, but are appointed by the central government. Similarly, state finances are controlled by central executive levels. This philosophy of overcentralized government has effectively inhibited regional development by limiting the capacity of the regions to establish their own priorities or do their own planning.

7. A strong state paternalism on the basis of which not only economic and political guidance are left in the hands of the state, but also most of the social and community initiatives. Probably as a reaction against this paternalism, there exists a moderate but persistent tendency toward civil disobedience, commonly expressed in the chronic vandalizing of public assets such as telephones, buses, and school or hospital facilities. A remarkable exception to this tendency has been the total respect shown by the population toward the new Caracas Metro, which everyone helps to keep impeccably clean.

8. Intense political rivalries and politicization of all economic and social activities. Politics is the national Venezuelan sport. It is the most obvious way

to fame and power for many poor and ambitious young Venezuelans. University deans, presidents of professional societies, even beauty queens are elected on the basis of their political affiliation. As a result, political activity in the country is devoid of the violence that is its frequent companion in many other Latin American countries, and frequently resembles a sports event. On the negative side, political activity seems to prevail over other equally vital activities in the fields of science, education, sports, and industry, absorbing a disproportionate percentage of the national energy.

9. The hypersensitivity of public opinion toward the oil industry. Oil is the largest source of income for the country and will probably remain so in the forseeable future. Moreover, the oil industry is very poorly understood by most Venezuelans, even the most cultured. As a result, the never-ending discussions about the industry in newspapers, magazines, and public fora are usually misinformed and mediocre. Decision-making at the highest political levels is afflicted by a lack of factual knowledge about the oil industry and by an overemotional approach to many important issues such as the development of the Orinoco heavy oil deposits, the remodeling of the refineries, or offshore exploration.

STRENGTHS AND WEAKNESSESS AND IMPLICATIONS FOR INTERNATIONAL BUSINESS

Venezuela has several strong points that help to explain both the success of its democratic experience and the underlying stability of its business environment. It also has weak points that account for some of its present political, economic, and commercial problems. Among the strengths:

1. The example set by some exceptional men who have become a source of pride for Venezuelans. Miranda, Bolívar, and Bello were universal Venezuelans who set extremely high standards for their countrymen and have provided many of them with a constant source of inspiration.

2. The liberal attitude of Venezuelans in politics and social life. Venezuelan society is highly equalitarian with little or no racial conflict, is open and participatory, and of extremely high mobility. Successful figures in politics, art, or sports usually remain accessible to the common people and try not to behave fatuously. An exception to this trait can be found in many state bureaucrats, specially those immediately below minister levels, who often tend to have an exaggerated opinion of their importance.

3. The ability shown by the political and economic establishment to enter into broad pacts regarding political issues. We have already seen how this ability allowed for a strong consolidation of the democratic system and is again at work, trying to take the country out of its economic crisis.

4. A growing and dynamic middle class with many habits of work patterned after the example of their counterparts in the industrial economies.

5. An absence of labor unrest or excessive salary demands, a situation due to the maturity of labor leaders and to their close imbrication with the political parties of the establishment. Although it could be argued that this situation

does not always work to benefit the rank-and-file members of the sector, it certainly seems thus far to have worked to the benefit of political and economic stability. It is probable that labor unrest will increase in the short term under the Lusinchi administration as economic conditions take a turn for the worse due to the high payments that will be required to amortize the external debt and as Lusinchi pays less attention to labor.

6. A well-established habit of democracy, which has now become a cultural ingredient of Venezuelan society. The average Venezuelan is conditioned to think of orderly and peaceful political change as his only valid option.

7. Sustained oil income, which in the last five years has been in the vicinity of $15 billion per year and which, barring some unexpected events, should not decrease significantly in the next five years.

8. No demographic pressure. With a million square kilometers of territory, Venezuela has only some 15 million people. Yet the population is not evenly distributed, and the major urban centers, notably Caracas, already show a decidedly unhealthy density of population that has led to a significant lowering of the quality of life for large segments of the Venezuelan people.

9. A lack of propensity to nationalize. With the exception of the basic extractive industries, iron and petroleum, Venezuela has shown no serious desire to take over private firms. Even when the nationalization of those two industries took place, due consideration was given to the need for a negotiated settlement and payment of compensation. There are no ideological ingredients in the Venezuelan system that call for systematic nationalization of private enterprises.

Impressive as this list of strong points is, there is also a list of weak characteristics which, specially in the last few years, has made of Venezuela a country in need of a major overhaul of its economic and political environment. Some of these weak points:

1. The increasing mediocrity of political leadership, as illustrated by the poor performance of the main political actors of the last decade. The country has given enough signals of distress and danger in the last ten years for any competent group of political leaders to have taken charge and changed courses. This did not happen because of the incompetence of the country's political leadership. There are indications that this weakness is now being recognized and addressed, but no sudden, dramatic improvement can reasonably be expected.

2. The obsolescence of some democratic institutions, such as the state legislatures, the lack of truly popular representativeness in the national Congress, and the deep politicization of the judiciary all have contributed to the delegitimization of the democratic system and to much disenchantment of the Venezuelan people regarding these institutions.

3. The low quality of education at all levels, which continues to be a major weakness of the system. This low quality is most apparent in the universities where the student body is largely politicized and rather indifferent to academic life. The political ingredient in Venezuelan universities dates back to the years of the Gomez dictatorship, when students became the only orga-

nized and overt source of resistance and protest. With the advent of democracy, students did not go back to their books but have remained engaged in politicking, giving rise to a new breed—the professional student who tends to remain indefinitely at the university doing political proselitization.

4. Chronic border disputes with Colombia and Guyana that have diverted considerable time, talent, and energy from more fruitful endeavors. Again, resolution of these disputes essentially requires political courage, since no alternative selected could ever be to everybody's liking.

5. The failure of one of the main sustained goals of democratic governments, agrarian reform. This failure has been due to insufficient government monitoring of projects and the acute lack of opportune financial and technical assistance. The emphasis is now placed on commercial agriculture, a reasonable alternative given the high level of urban population in the country and the urgent need to increase agricultural output.

6. Widespread corruption, the consequence of the financial indigestion experienced by the country during the last ten years. Since 1974 some $200 billion has been pumped into Venezuela as a result of increased oil prices. This enormous amount of money could not be absorbed into the economy. Much of it filtered down into all the crevasses of the Venezuelan social structure, where many of the people were unable properly to earn it but not unwilling to keep it. The abuse of authority as a means of personal gain became more and more frequent, a moral breakdown compounded by the impotence or indifference of the government. By the 1980s most of the Venezuelan public administration experienced significant corruption. This practice covered a wide range of levels, from petty corruption or "the bending of official rules in favor of friends" to aggravated corruption, the need for payment to authorities to perform their administrative duties. Corruption in Venezuela has reached the level of an almost global conspiracy and has become a major enemy of efficient political democracy.

The country is now fully aware of how seriously corruption has eroded its social and political fabric. The 1983 report of the Venezuelan General Comptroller indicates that the Herrera administration had their hands on some 600 billion bolívares during its term (about $120 billion). When the external debt is added to this amount, total expenditures of the Venezuelan government for the 1979–1983 period can be estimated in the order of $150 billion, an expenditure incurred without much visible sign of improvement in the quality of life for Venezuelans. The Comptroller lists corruption as the leading cause for this gigantic waste. The new administration has started an open war against this formidable enemy and, although no miracles can be expected, it is refreshing to see the emergence of a critical attitude toward the extremely permissive environment that has existed for the last ten years.

OUTLOOK

As we have seen, petroleum and democracy are the basic ingredients of the Venezuelan social fabric. Petroleum took millions of years to form and required much foreign initiative to find and develop. Democracy has been a wholly Venezuelan creation, and its consolidation has taken significant effort on the part of several generations of Venezuelans. The blend has not been all positive. With oil income came corruption, and rapid growth led to significant economic distortion. Nevertheless, great strides have been made, and Venezuela has become one of the leading economic and political powers in the region.

Today the country faces serious but essentially manageable economic problems. These problems will tend to persist in the medium term but should diminish in intensity as Venezuelans adjust to a new economic environment and have an opportunity to revamp some of the country's weaker political and administrative institutions.

Venezuelan economy in the future will follow one of two possible scenarios. Under a first scenario there would be the adoption of internal austerity measures that would help to restore economic balance as well as a successful handling of external debt negotiations, events that would significantly increase the level of confidence in the government and the country. These essentially short-term measures would be followed, in the medium term, by the modernization of political institutions, a high-priority issue in the agenda of the current administration. Beyond the mid-term, the country would follow a model of development in line with its size and resources.

Under a second scenario the political leadership would fail to abandon the pattern of waste and mismanagement that has prevailed in the country for the last fifteen years. Necessary social and economic measures would be delayed or canceled because of their perceived high political cost. Continued weakness of the international oil markets would bring Venezuelan income down to levels of some $10 billion per year. The combination of these unfavorable events could conceivably lead to civilian unrest, labor agitation and, even, to an interruption of democratic rule and the emergence of an authoritarian government.

Some important economic and social indices would tend to behave somewhat differently under each of the two scenarios briefly described above. Among them:

Levels of Activity in the Oil Industry. Regardless of the prevailing scenario, the oil industry will maintain its role as the main generator for Venezuelan economic development. In the medium term, emphasis will focus on the maintenance of present levels of production potential and in the progressive substitution, in the domestic market, of natural gas for liquid hydrocarbons, to liberate increasingly larger volumes of liquid hydrocarbons for export. In the longer term, five to ten years, the industry will accelerate development of the Orinoco heavy oil area, since these deposits will be required to maintain the country as a leading oil exporter. Also in the longer term and under any scenario, private capital might be allowed to participate in the oil sector, probably in the form of risk ventures in the offshore, unexplored areas.

Areas of Public Investment. Under the first scenario, public investment will probably shift emphasis from large capital-intensive industrial projects to medium-sized or small labor-intensive projects in the fields of agriculture, light industry, petroleum and mining, and food processing. Under the second scenario there would be a continuation of interest in the large basic industries, which would probably lead to another round of external borrowing.

Bureaucratic Red Tape would be likely to continue at undesirable levels under any scenario, although modest improvements can be expected in the mid-term.

Civil Disorder and Labor Agitation are very unlikely, except as a short-lived event under the second scenario. Economic adjustments in Venezuela will not need to be as painful as in some other Latin American countries in which there has been much social unrest.

Succession of Leadership would be very predictable and orderly in the case of the first sceanrio; much less predictable under the second one. The Venezuelan democratic system has generated a long line of hopefuls for the highest political levels, and this guarantees an orderly transition which could only be broken in the event of a coup d'etat.

To conclude, the main advantages and disadvantages of doing business in Venezuela can be summarized as follows:

Advantages	Disadvantages
A stable political system	Slow and inefficient administrative institutions
A relatively large domestic market	Scarcity of skilled labor
High national income	Corruption in the public sector.
A growing middle class.	

chapter seven
Saudi Arabia

Hermann Frederick Eilts

Saudi Arabia encompasses the greater part of the Arabian Penninsula and it is bordered by Jordan, Iraq, Kuwait, Qatar, Bahrain, the United Arab Emirates, Oman, the Yemen Arab Republic, and the Peoples' Democratic Republic of Yemen (Aden). Much of its territorial area is gravel and sand desert, interspersed with occasional, usually small agricultural and pastural settlements. No formal census has ever been taken, but its population is estimated at about 5 million native Saudis and another 2.5 million expatriates. Of the latter, well over four-fifths are from various Arab communities: Egyptians, Palestinians, Sudanese, Iraqis, Yemenis, and Hadhramis. Annual population growth rate is estimated at about 2.4 percent. Literacy is about 25 percent, but it is growing with the constant improvement in primary and secondary education. Some 60 percent of the Saudi population is estimated to be 30 years old or less.

It is a conservative monarchy, rooted in the orthodox Hanbali school of Sunni Islam, and regards the Koran *(Qur'an)* as its constitution. King Fahd ibn 'Abd al-'Aziz Al Saud, 62 years old and a son of the founder of the third Saudi empire, has been monarch since 1982. The kingdom of Saudi Arabia regards itself as part of the Third World group of states, and is also the largest and most prominent member of the (Arabian) Gulf Cooperation Council. In the latter context, it is seeking to harmonize its economic and security policies with those of five fellow members in that organization—Kuwait, Qatar, Bahrain, the United Arab Emirates, and Oman.

Saudi Arabia enjoys a special distinction in the Muslim world. In its Western Province, customarily known as al-Hijaz, are located the *Haraymain*, the two most sacred cities of Islam, Mecca and Medina. Because it is one of the five "pillars" or religious obligations of Islam, some two million Muslims from all over the world make the *haj* (pilgrimage) to Mecca and its environs each year. Since most Muslim pilgrims now come and leave by air, the annual *haj* is today compressed into roughly a two-month time frame. From a logistical point of view, it is an extraordinarily well-conducted example of religiously inspired mass tourism.

Apart from being the spiritual focus of Muslims everywhere, the kingdom is blessed with the largest petroleum reserves in the Middle East, i.e., an estimated 168 billion barrels, including those in the Neutral Zone. As such, it is second only to the USSR and the United States in estimated recoverable petroleum reserves. It currently produces about 5 million barrels of oil per day and, in its role as a member of the Organization of Petroleum Exporting Countries (OPEC), sees itself as the "swing" producer in that organization. Until three years ago, it was producing at the rate of between 8.5 and 10.3 million barrels of oil a day and retains the capacity to do so. It also belongs to the Organization of Arab Petroleum Exporting Countries (OAPEC).

Petroleum was first discovered in Saudi Arabia in the mid-1930s, with commercial production commencing after World War II. Largely through the ever-growing national income derived from expanding petroleum exports, the kingdom has since 1970 been engaged in a massive economic development effort. Its third Five Year Development Plan, covering the period 1980–1985, is about to be completed with a final-year expenditure of an estimated $74 billion. A fourth such Five Year Development Plan will begin in 1985–86. According to the minister of development, it will aim at encouraging the private sector to assume many responsibilities formally shouldered by government. Other goals are to encourage private and social integration into the Gulf Cooperative Council (GCC), to raise the standard of living and welfare for the Saudi populace, to complete basic economic infrastructure, to provide and maintain services for already-completed projects, to diversify the nation's productive base from oil and petrochemicals to industry and agriculture, and to develop indigenous manpower.

In past development plans, the kingdom focused on building up a petrochemical industry, utilizing low-cost natural gas associated with oil production. Huge industrial complexes have been constructed at the port of Jubail, on the Arabian Gulf, and in Yanbu al-Bahr, on the Red Sea.

The kingdom's estimated gross domestic production (GDP) for 1984/85 is approximately $120 billion. This would mean a per capita income of $17,000 per native Saudi, exclusive of foreigners. Of its GDP, industry accounts for about 57 percent of the total (of which crude oil amounts to 46.5 percent); services, 45 percent; and agriculture, 2.3 percent. In recent years, its annual growth rate has fluctuated considerably. From a high of slightly more than 10 percent in 1979/80, it dropped to almost minus 11 percent in 1982/83, and will probably be about 5 percent in 1984/85. Government expenditures under the third Five Year Development Plan amount to some 40 percent of the GDP, exclusive of defense expenditures and foreign aid.

The physical facade of the kingdom has altered materially in the past two decades. What were, 20 years ago, at best small towns, Jidda, Mecca, Riyadh, and Dammam-Khobar are now megalopoli of a half a million or more people. Similarly, what were formerly small villages scattered throughout Saudi Arabia have now in many instances become towns. Huge electrification programs, based upon cheap energy, have proliferated throughout the country. Schools, hospitals, and clinics, in many cases employing expatriate professionals, have been opened everywhere. A network of first-class highways crisscrosses the kingdom. Saudi Arabian Airlines, one of the largest carriers in the Middle East, flies to every part of the kingdom, as well as to foreign destinations, including New York. In truth, a minor miracle has been wrought in physically uplifting the face of Saudi Arabia. It has literally cost billions of dollars to do so, but the result is impressive. And Saudi Arabia's economic development continues to grow under the direction of King Fahd and the minister of development, even if at a somewhat slower pace because of reduced oil income.

It should be emphasized that in a country such as Saudi Arabia, whose legal system is based on traditional Islamic law *(shari'a)*, no distinction is drawn between the political, economic, and religious aspects of individual or corporate conduct. The dichotomy between church and state, so common in the West, does not exist. However discretely politics and economics may be pursued in the kindgom, both are in the final analysis governed by Islamic law. Not surprisingly, therefore, the influence of the Muslim *'ulama*, or religious savants, is strong in all phases of government and society.

DOMESTIC SAUDI ARABIAN POLITICS

In recent years, and especially after the Iranian Islamic Revolution of 1979 and the almost concurrent attack by Saudi tribal and expatriate Muslim fundamentalists against the Great Mosque in Mecca, there has been considerable speculation in the United States about the kingdom's internal political stability. Some sought to draw an analogy between Iran and Saudi Arabia, with dire predictions that the kingdom would soon face domestic internal political upheaval, perhaps violently achieved. Such predictions of doom seem to be poorly informed. While not without problems, Saudi Arabia has demonstrated remarkable political stability and is likely to continue to do so in the foreseeable future.

Leadership Succession

King Fahd, who assumed the throne of Saudi Arabia in 1982, while cautious in implementing promised political liberalization, has a reputation for progressivism. The prime minister and heir apparent is his half-brother, Prince Abdullah ibn 'Abd al-'Aziz Al Saud. Although the two siblings have differences of view, they are able to cooperate in the affairs of government, and considerable royal family cohesion exists. The succession is at least nominally assured, although its implementation, when necessary, will still require reaffirmation by members of the Saudi family, the formal endorsement of the religious leaders, and the oath of allegiance by major political and tribal figures. At that time, too, the royal family will have to designate a new crown prince and heir apparent from among the senior princes and seek endorsement from the religious leaders. The established Arab principle of seniority within the family is usually followed, although older members of the royal family may waive rights in favor of younger members.

The Saud family has had a past history of fractiousness, but it is noteworthy that the last four successions were implemented peacefully and smoothly, despite the fact that one required the disposition of a monarch for imcompetence and another followed the assassination of a king. There is a recognition on the part of the senior princes of the Saud family that, whatever their personal differences, they must unite in the interests of preserving the family's status and for the sake of stability in the country.

The monarch and the heir apparent are also prime minister and deputy prime minister, respectively. In these capacities, they preside over a royal cabinet, composed of members of the royal family and commoners. Royal family members largely hold defense and security portfolios; commoners tend to hold technical and/or developmental portfolios, e.g., the minister of petroleum, minister of development, minister of finance, etc. The business of the kingdom is conducted through the cabinet and the bureaucracy, always subject to the king's approval, and is generally carried on in praiseworthy fashion. Sensitive security issues are handled within the confines of the royal family and by subordinate security officials trusted by them. The already-mentioned massive and impressive development programs of the kingdom, while executed in large part by expatriate labor, are nonetheless a tribute to the purposefulness and efficacy of cabinet government.

Based as it is upon Islamic precepts, the economic philosophy of the kingdom is one of private enterprise. The Saudi Arabian government, as the direct recipient of the nation's substantial petroleum income, has been the contracting element for virtually all private enterprise activities, especially those connected with Five Year Development Program projects. Nevertheless, the nation is awash with private entrepreneurs of all types, and an effort is now being inaugurated to persuade the private sector to assume some project activities formerly handled by government. There is keen competition among private Saudi businessmen to maximize individual firms' profits.

With one exception—the petroleum industry—there is no history of nationalization in Saudi Arabia. Indeed, any such concept is contrary to Saudi Arabian and Islamic practice, which recognizes private property and the sanctity of contracts. In the case of the petroleum industry, because of the kingdom's total dependence upon it, the Saudi Arabian government has in effect bought out—through the medium of increasing equity participation—the Arabian American Oil Company (Aramco), which had first discovered and thereafter developed the oilfields until the mid-seventies. Saudi Arabia continues to utilize Aramco for the exploitation of petroleum and related matters. Now, however, instead of being under the direction of its "stateside" parent companies, it is subject to the orders of the minister of petroleum and his colleagues.

The Middle Class

A substantial middle class, made up largely of businessmen, teachers, and bureaucrats, has developed in Saudi Arabia during the past 30 years. Much of the bureaucratic, commercial, and educational activities of the country is in its hands. To date, however, the middle class has been largely politically passive. It exercises influence in the administrative areas, but it has not thus far played a major role in national decision-making in the kingdom. Social mobility exists for members of the middle class, in terms of improving their well-being and that of their families, although many would like a greater opening of the political process and a larger voice in national decision-making. Some believe that their high-sounding titles in the ministries are incommensurate with their limited decision-making authority. There is a desire for greater public participation in the political system, coupled with a view held by some that the country is too much of a single family preserve, but there is no evidence to date that this feeling has created any serious wave of disaffection toward the monarchy. The fact of the matter is that Saudis of all classes and ranks share a vested interest in maintaining the political independence and territorial integrity of their nation from perceived covetous regional neighbors, even as they aspire to a greater opening of the political process.

The Fringes of Islam: An Apparent but Unproven Threat

All native Saudis are Muslims. While many have been trained in Western universities, most readily accept the strictures of Islam, even when they return after extended absences. As already indicated, the conservative Hanbali school of Islam predominates in the government of the nation, but there are also adherents of the Hanafi and the Shafi'a schools of Sunni Islam, especially in the Western Province. In the Eastern Province and in the Medina area, there are about 300,000 and 50,000, respectively, Twelver Shi'i Muslims. Adherents of the same brand of Shi'i Islam as one finds in Iran, they have on two occasions in the past four years demonstrated against the Saudi Arabian government, largely at the instigation of the Iranian Islamic government, for alleged discrimination against them. While Shi'is have long been regarded as heretical in Saudi Arabia, the Saudi Arabian government is nevertheless seeking to work out an accommodation with them. The importance of the Shi'i community in Saudi Arabia does not lie in its numbers, which are less than 8 percent of the total population, but rather in its strategic location in the area of the petroleum facilities. Many Shi'is are employed in the oilfields and refineries of the Eastern Province. Hence, to the extent they are disaffected, they pose a potential threat to those facilities. It is worth noting, however, that on the two occasions when the Shi'is of the Eastern Province did demonstrate, they did not direct their ire at their places of employment, i.e., petroleum facilities.

No Organized Labor, but Militant Expatriate Workers

Organized labor does not exist in Saudi Arabia. Unions are banned. The Saudi theory is that labor, like other elements of Saudi society, benefits from the welfare state concept that characterizes the kingdom's socio-political approach. There have been one or two strikes at the petroleum facilities in the past, but these were largely instigated by expatriate labor. Heavily reliant as Saudi Arabia is upon expatriate labor, this element of the labor force—and it is by far the greatest—has the potential for labor agitation. The Saudi authorities watch carefully and utilize preemptive techniques, *including arrests and deportations*, when dealing with expatriate labor agitators.

The Question of Civil Disorder

Apart from the 1979 attack on the Great Mosque in Mecca by a group of some 200 Saudi and expatriate Muslim fundamentalists, which was a traumatic shock for the Saudi authorities, and the two aforementioned Shi'i demonstrations in the Eastern Province in 1979–1980, there has been no serious civil disorder in the kingdom in recent years. To be sure, there were demonstrations against Aramco, the American Consulate General in Dhahran, and the offices of the U.S. Military Training Mission in Dhahran during the June 1967 Arab-Israeli war, but these were prompted by spontaneous outrage over perceived U.S. support for Israel and American responsibility for the defeat of the Arabs. They were quickly put down by the Saudi Arabian National Guard, but not without damage to property (but not to life) at the hands of the mob. This could recur in the event of a new, major Arab-Israeli war.

The Political Process

The Saudi Arabian government is authoritarian. Unlike so many of its neighbors, however, it is generally benevolent. While it maintains police and intelligence organizations, it has not oppressed its public. On the contrary, any Saudi may present any petition that he likes to the king, the crown prince, or to the provincial governors of the country in the daily *majliss* (public audiences,) that these officials hold. Despite protests from Saudi exiles about alleged abuses in the kingdom, there are very few political prisoners. In its punitive procedures, Saudi Arabia adheres to Islamic law prescriptions, including flogging or jailing for drinking, stoning for adultery, amputation of limbs for stealing, decapitation for murder, etc. But these, it should be emphasized, are not capriciously utilized and only after the most careful review by an Islamic court.

The Military

The Saudi Arabian military, under the direction of a full brother of the king as minister of defense and civil aviation, has been loyal to the regime. It has benefited from modern weapons acquisitions, training programs, excellent cantonments, and other perquisites. Apart from the Saudi Arabian air force, which has of late been engaged in security overflights in the Arabian Gulf area, the military has not been exposed to battle and has sustained few casualties. Members of the royal family are strategically placed in various military command positions and are thus enabled to monitor the loyalty of the army.

External Threat

The kingdom has long considered itself "encircled." The nature of the encirclers has changed over the years, but an external threat remains in existence. Today the principal external threat to Saudi Arabia is perceived to be the Iranian Islamic Republic, with its "revolution for export," not only directly but also through the possible spillover effects of the Iran-Iraq war. Saudi-owned tankers have in recent months been attacked by Iranian aircraft, which required the Saudi Arabian Air Force to fly protective missions. The danger of the Iran-Iraq war escalating, and of resultant Iranian attacks on Saudi Arabian petroleum installations and Saudi- or Kuwaiti-owned tankers, has prompted a closer security cooperation among the GCC members and also closer Saudi cooperation with the United States in defense matters. Saudi Arabia remains unwilling, however, to provide the United States with military facilities on its territory.

A second perceived military threat is Israel. The latter, rather short-sightedly it would seem, views Saudi Arabia as a major enemy, and the Saudis are concerned that Israel may at some point unexpectedly lash out and strike at the kingdom's military or petroleum facilities. Should this happen, it fears it cannot count on the United States for meaningful support.

A third perceived external threat comes from the Peoples' Democratic Republic of Yemen, although the Saudi Arabian authorities have sought to alleviate this threat through the medium of economic assistance for that country. Still another is leftist-dominated Ethiopia across the Red Sea.

Terrorism Limited

Terrorism has not generally been a problem in Saudi Arabia. To be sure, during the June 1967 Arab-Israeli war, the American Embassy and the U.S. Military Training Mission headquarters in Jidda and the offices of a private American defense contractor in Jidda were bombed, and anti-American demonstrations took place in the Western Province. The bombings, it transpired, were the work of Palestinian expatriates. Given the large number of frustrated Palestinians still working in Saudi Arabia, a potential terrorist threat from this source exists. The Saudi security authorities are alert to this phenomenon and monitor potential dissidents or terrorist elements as closely as they can. The Saudi security authorities are generally quite good.

Traditional Religion and the Fear of Modernity from the West: A Deterrent to Foreigners Living in Saudi Arabia

As a result of the massive economic development that has taken place in the kingdom during the past two decades, some concern has been expressed by the conservative *'ulama* (religious savants) that those traditional socio-religious values upon which the state was built may be threatened. An element of xenophobia exists in the country, especially in its Central Province. This has caused foreign expatriates to be viewed in orthodox Muslim circles as potential social pollutors. Western expatriates, especially Christians, tend to be segregated either in compounds or in largely foreign quarters of urban centers with relatively little social contact between them and Saudi nationals, except in the workplace. Strict dress codes are enjoined, which include foreign women resident in Saudi Arabia, who are also not allowed to drive. Muslim expatriates in Saudi Arabia, men and women alike, are expected to adhere to rigid Islamic behavorial codes. The importation and drinking of alcoholic beverages is forbidden, with violators subject to jailing and flogging. Life in Saudi Arabia for the Western expatriate, while bearable and profitable, is closely circumscribed. Christian worship services are prohibited.

Regional Relations with the Capital

The kingdom is administratively divided into five provinces: Eastern (Hijaz), Central (Najd), Western (Hasa), Northern (Jabal Shammar), and Southern ('Asir). In the early phases of the Five Year Development Plans, the focus was on improving national infrastructure in the first three of the aforementioned provinces. In the most recent development plan, the Northern and Southern Provinces have also been covered. Since a member of the royal family now governs each of the five provinces (in the Eastern Province it is a member of a collateral branch of the family), each has been able to solicit and obtain from the central government financial and personal support for accelerated economic development in his province. While a considerable element of administrative decentralization exists, national ministries, such as education and health, operate in all provinces in coordination with provincial governors. One does not find significant local or regional power plays, although obviously Riyadh and the Micca-Jidda region tend to be favored, but each provincial governor does his utmost to obtain a greater share of the development budget pie.

Political Participation and the Challenge for Social Change

Saudi Arabia has to a considerable extent become a social welfare state. The benefits of massive oil income are shared, even if not equally, with the public at large. Low-cost land and interest-free loans are available to any Saudi wishing to build his own home. Indeed, construction of all types is one of the most prominent features of the Saudi landscape. In contrast to the public's participation in Saudi Arabia's economic development "boom," its participation in the political process remains limited. No political parties are allowed, press coverage tends to be self-censored, and radio and TV programs are carefully controlled by the ministry of information and monitored by the *'ulama* to ensure that socially unacceptable programs are not aired. For years there has been talk of modest political reform, including the promulgation of a Basic Law, the strengthening of the existing but largely dormant consultative assembly, and the establishment of provincial assemblies. Thus far, however, these promised reform measures are still being studied in committees, and there is no saying when any such political reform measures may be introduced. When and if they are, one can assume that they will be gradualistic in implementation.

At the same time, the Saudi political elite is narrow. The elite consists of members of the Saud family (estimated to be about 5,000 strong); the religious hierarchy, headed by the Shaikh family (descended from the religious founder of Islamic unitarianism); and, to a lesser extent, Western-trained, non-royal family members who head major ministries. The royal family, headed by the king, and especially its score or so of senior members, holds most of the political power. They are expected to rule in accordance with the concepts of the *Qu'ran* and Islamic law. The latter is administered by the *'ulama*, who watch closely for any potential signs of innovation or deviation from Islamic precepts.

It has come to be realized, however, that Islamic law does not adequately cover all aspects of 20th-century life, especially those relating to high finance and massive economic development. Hence, a series of extra-legal royal ordinances has been issued to cover areas such as mining, some elements of commerce, contracting, etc. Such ordinances are invariably drafted with *'ulama* participation to ensure that they do not trespass upon the all-encompassing authority of Islamic law. Non-royal members of the elite wield such authority as they have through their ministerial posts, which usually means in limited technical areas. Where socio-political matters are involved, it is the royal family and the *'ulama* who determine acceptability or unacceptability. Chambers of Commerce in the major provinces play important arbitrational roles in contract disputes between Saudi and foreign firms on issues not adequately covered by traditional Islamic law.

Social reform in Saudi Arabia is developing in slow fashion. In the past four years, and especially since the fundamentalist attack on the Great Mosque of Mecca, there are signs of some social regression. The pace of modernization, many Saudi leaders have concluded, has been too rapid to be readily absorbed by an essentially orthodox Muslim society. This, coupled with concern over public criticism of the Saudi leadership by the Iranian Islamic Republic and the latter's avowed "revolution for export," has brought about a rigidification of the Saudi social structure. Pressures for social change exist, and sooner or later there will again be some relaxation of social standards, but these will be slow in coming.

Many Saudis, both men and women, now travel abroad and are exposed to foreign cultural influences through such travel, through foreign radio or telecasts, and through occasional contact with the expatriate community working in the country. While some Saudis are repulsed at their experience with foreign cultures, others would like to see some opening of their rigid social structure, even if this is cast in Islamic terms. This pressure for change presents a challenge to the Saudi leadership.

THE POLITICAL CULTURAL DIMENSION

Saudi society has traditionally been regulated by twin pillars: belief in a single God and the family. As is the case in other Middle Eastern countries, the family in Saudi Arabia is extended rather than nuclear, with the eldest member being titular head. Peer pressure within the family, whose members are expected to act in accordance with Islamic mores, has in the past been an effective device to assure individual member conformity. Some may travel abroad or attend foreign universities, but when they return they revert surprisingly readily to family-approved norms. The family regulates each member's behavior, offers help and encouragement to its members, and is in general a source of strength to its members.

In recent years, however, the infusion of hugh amounts of money into Saudi society has tended to weaken somewhat the influence of the aforementioned twin regulators of social conduct. To the distress of many older Saudis, an element of materialism has inevitably entered the cultural scene. As a result, tensions exist within Saudi society as the quest for materialism challenges traditional individual and group behavior. Materialism is often equated by Saudi traditionalists with westernized modernization, causing the latter and its perceived agents to be suspect in the eyes of more orthodox Muslims. It is the *'ulama* who lead the social battle against westernization and materialism. It is not surprising, therefore, how exceedingly difficult it is for a Western expatriate in Saudi Arabia, however culturally attuned he may be to Islamic mores, to engage in meaningful dialogue with orthodox religious leaders.

At the behest of the Saudi *'ulama*, and with the acquiescence of the royal family, committees of Public morality, a kind of religious police, monitor individual and public behavior. They seek to ensure that Muslims pray five times a day, that shops are closed during prayer times, and that alcoholic libations are not drunk. As such, they represent a religious/communal control mechanism, although many Saudis privately express concern over what they often regard as illiterate and narrow executors of this function. At the moment, and especially since the attack on the Grand Mosque in Mecca, the committees of public morality are again having a heyday. In pursuit of their responsibilities, as they see them, they often harass not only Saudis, but also expatriates.

The Saudi Arabian government, in addition to national and local police forces, utilizes several intelligence organizations to monitor possible dissidence. These intelligence organizations tend to be in competition with one another. Investigatory methods still tend to be somewhat rudimentary, with rumors often given excessive evidentiary weight. The saving grace in the system is that the Saudi *shari'a* court system, including an appellate and supreme religious court, insists upon strict procedures conforming with Islamic law. Guilty verdicts require adequate evidence.

Potential Sources of Instability

Some destabilizing elements exist in the Saudi polity. Thus, for example, the kingdom's Shi'i (Shiite) minority remains an uncertain factor despite efforts by the Saudi leadership to integrate it into the state. The fact of the matter is that the orthodox Saudi *'ulama* have historically looked askance upon Shi'is and find it difficult to accept such Muslim sectarians as full-fledged citizens. Concern on the part of the Saudi security authorities that Shi'is may be influenced by Iran aggravates the situation.

A second potentially destabilizing element consists of divisions within the royal family. Such internecine divisions were prominent in the eighteenth century and led to the collapse of the second Saudi empire. The present senior members of the Saud family are all strong, self-confident individuals, and it is hardly surprising that they differ on some policy matters. All evidence to date suggests, however, that whatever divergencies exist, they are argued out within the closed confines of the Saud family until some kind of a concensus is reached. This, unfortunately, can be a time-consuming process, sometimes leaving critical decisions dangling for long periods of time.

U.S. GOVERNMENT IMPEDIMENTS TO DOING BUSINESS WITH SAUDI ARABIA

Generally speaking, U.S.–Saudi Arabian relations have been and continue to be close. There is a long history, going back to the initial American involvement in petroleum exploration and exploitation in Saudi Arabia in 1934, of economic association between the two countries. American economic planners from the private sector (Harvard, Stanford Research Institute, and others) were prominent in the formulation of the early Saudi Five Year Development Programs. Since 1974, a joint Saudi Arabian–U.S. Commission has been in existence, designed to enable the kingdom to draw upon American public and private resources in promoting national development. On the American side, the U.S. Treasury has been the executive agent for such economic collaboration.

To be sure, political differences exist between the two countries, brought about by a Saudi perception of excessive U.S. partiality toward Israel in the Arab-Israeli dispute. The Saudis were bitter about the American-inspired Camp David agreements and the subsequent Egyptian-Israeli peace treaty. Nor has the U.S. failure in Lebanon, which was seen by many Saudis as a test of American reliability, commended itself to the leadership and people of the kingdom. The Saudis consider the United States to be unsympathetic to legitimate Palestinian national aspirations. Nevertheless, despite the nagging doubts that these political developments have created in the Saudi mind about U.S. capability, both countries have in effect agreed to disagree on their respective approaches to the Arab-Israeli problem.

Two balancing factors in the U.S.–Saudi Arabian political equation are the kingdom's dependence upon this country for security assistance (not only in the provision of armaments to the Saudi military, but also possible tangible American help in the event of an Iranian or other external attack upon Saudi Arabia) and the substantial Saudi Arabian financial investment in the United States. Three American military missions are permanently stationed in Saudi Arabia to help train the Saudi military and National Guard and for the construction of military cantonments. For the past three years, too, four U.S. Awacs have been stationed in Riyadh and fly surveillance cover over the Arabian Gulf areas. Thus, a "special relationship," however frayed it may sometimes be, exists between the United States and Saudi Arabia in the security and economic spheres.

That "special relationship" has sometimes been marred by recurrent

Congressional efforts to require disclosure of Saudi Arabian investments in this country. The Saudis have insisted upon confidentiality about their investments in the United States. Thus far, at least, the executive branch of government, supported by the American banking community, has successfully opposed such bills. Concern exists, however, that they may be reintroduced, and there is some evidence that the Saudi Arabian authorities are diversifying their investment portfolio in order to place more funds outside this country.

As a member of the Arab League, and as a bitter opponent of Israel, Saudi Arabia adheres strictly to the Arab secondary boycott of Israel. Moreover, while it insists that it does not discriminate against persons of Jewish faith and is only opposed to Zionism, it has traditionally been reluctant to grant visas to Americans of Jewish faith and has thereby incurred the ire of the Jewish community in this country. As a result, frequent efforts have been made in the Congress to enact anti-boycott legislation.

In 1965, amendments were passed to the Export Control Act of 1949 and again included in the Export Administration Act of 1969, indicating U.S. opposition to boycotts of friendly countries and requiring American firms to report to the Department of Commerce if requested to participate in such boycotts. Since all foreign firms, including American, who bid on Saudi contracts are sent boycott questionnaires by the Saudi Arabian Arab Boycott Office, this legislation was viewed by the Saudis as a direct challenge to their right to determine their own boycott policies.

In 1976, the Justice Department initiated suit against the Bechtel Corporation for allegedly violating the Sherman Act by complying with Saudi requirements, banning contracting firms from dealing with blacklisted subcontractors in fulfillment of their contracts. While the case was negotiated out of court in January 1977, its net effect prohibited any U.S. company under contract in Saudi Arabia (or any Arab country) from refusing to deal with firms blacklisted by the Saudis or discriminating against them. American firms were legally prohibited, under penalty of fines, from replying to Saudi Arabian anti-Israeli boycott questionnaires. The result of this legislation and subsequent litigation was a standoff. Saudi Arabia refused to budge significantly in easing its Arab secondary boycott procedure; American firms were prohibited from executing boycott questionnaires. In consequence, Saudi Arabia has also diversified its foreign contracting activities, and there are complaints that many American firms have lost out to foreign competitors.

A second congressionally enacted obstacle to the provision of American contractual services to Saudi Arabia was the Tax Reform Act of 1976, which requires the Treasury to deny offenders of anti-boycott legislation their right to foreign tax credits, to tax benefits, and to deferral of taxation on foreign income earned from business in countries participating in a boycott. The Export Administration Act Amendments of 1977, subsequently incorporated in the Export Administration Act of 1979, established rigid procedures for American firms engaged in business in boycotting countries, including Saudi Arabia. Occasional efforts have also been attempted by the Congress to enact legislation that would prohibit American firms from refusing to send persons of Jewish faith to Saudi Arabia, but whether or not such persons can actually travel to the kingdom is, in the final analysis, a function of its visa policies. Only Saudi Arabia can decide to whom it will grant visas.

Still another disincentive to U.S. exports to Saudi Arabia was a 1976 U.S. tax cut ruling that required the computation of income tax exemptions for Americans working abroad to price housing at full overseas value rather than equivalent value in this country. This, in effect, discouraged foreign contractors working in Saudi Arabia from hiring Americans because of higher income tax liabilities and brought about a 30 percent decrease in American employees of U.S. firms working in Saudi Arabia between 1976 and 1980. To alleviate the situation, Congress in 1978 enacted the Foreign Earned Income Act, but IRS regulations construed this so narrowly that it did little to help the situation. Finally, Congress enacted the Economic Recovery Act of 1982, which increased exempted income and excluded from the income tax computation for Americans working abroad to a phased maximum of $90,000.

A fourth disincentive to American commercial activities in Saudi Arabia has been the Foreign Corrupt Practices Act of 1977, establishing new accounting procedures intended to prevent the concealment in other business expenses of illegal payments to foreign agents or officials who might be involved in foreign government contracting decisions. American firms were concerned about the act, not because they wished to perpetuate corrupt practices in Saudi Arabia, but because of the inadequate drafting of the law, making it difficult to determine what was and what was not permissable. Moreover, non-American competitors, who could operate without any such restrictions, were advantaged by this legislation. While practices perceived as corrupt in the West, including excessive commissions, have existed in Saudi Arabia, the Saudi authorities do not condone them and perceive U.S. restrictive legislation as a slur on their reputation.

As a result of these enactments, although U.S. firms still garner just over one-fifth of the Saudi Arabian import market, they have not been able to increase their share of that market. The Saudis have resented the kind of pillorying that they have received in the Congress and from many parts of the American public media as greedy "oil shaikhs" and have demonstrated their resentment by turning to non-American firms for imports wherever possible. There is cause to be concerned that these pieces of legislation, unless amended or more clearly written, will continue to be obstacles to Saudi selection of American firms for the procurement of goods and services.

COMMERCIAL CONDITIONS: ENVIRONMENT FOR INVESTMENT

Although Saudi Arabia is not in need of foreign capital investment, it has generally welcomed such investments where they facilitate achievement of Saudi development objectives. Any foreign investment must be approved by the Foreign Investment Committee of the Ministry of Industry. A Saudi agent is required in all such instances, except in armaments, government-to-government, or foreign military sales contracts. In the case of the latter three-type contracts, dealings must be directly with the ministry of defense without a Saudi agent. In the case of non-defense contracts, two types of agents exist in Saudi Arabia: the commercial agent and the service agent. The commercial agent operates solely in the private sector. The service agent operates in the governmental contract sphere. There is a legal maximum of 5 percent as an agency fee, although smaller fees are often arranged. The agent has no voice in the management of the company.

The Saudi Arabian government requires registration of all foreign companies operating in Saudi Arabia as a condition of their being permitted to function in Saudi Arabia. Registration, i.e., licensing, is a separate matter from contract conclusion. The signing of a contract by a foreign company with a Saudi Arabian governmental agency does not automatically confer registration. Indeed, it is to the advantage of the foreign company if registration can be accomplished prior to conclusion of contracts. Should this not be possible, registration must be accomplished after contract conclusion if the foreign firm is to benefit from the customary five-year tax holidays generally permitted to such firms.

Foreign firms seeking to do business in Saudi Arabia may enter into joint venture arrangements with Saudi business firms. Any such arrangement, in effect, makes the Saudi participant a partner in the venture rather than a simple agent. Two types of joint ventures exist in Saudi Arabia. The first is a contractual joint venture under which the foreign firm and the Saudi partner agree to bid for and, if awarded the contract, execute a project. In this case, Saudi law does not confer juridical personality on the joint venture; hence, an agent is still required unless the joint venture's activities are in the defense procurement area. The foreign firm still requires temporary or commercial registration.

The second form of contractual joint venture is the "mixed company." Under Saudi registration, most foreign firms choosing to go this route establish a Limited Liability Company (LLC). Such an organization consists of two or more participants, partners in the enterprise, each of whom has liability limited to its respective shares in the capital of the company. Formation of such LLCs is subject to approval by the Foreign Investment Committee of the ministry of industry. The Saudi Foreign Investment Committee usually insists upon initial capitalization of one million Saudi riyals (about $300,000), although higher amounts are sometimes demanded depending upon the magnitude of the proposed project. LLCs, provided they have a minimum of 25 percent Saudi participation, can apply for five-year tax holidays and also receive bid preference in seeking project contracts. All such joint ventures must be registered and licensed in Saudi Arabia.

There are no legal restrictions on the repatriation of capital and profits, although sometimes bureaucratic procedures may create delays. There are no limits on foreign investment in Saudi Arabia, but a minimum of 25 percent Saudi ownership is required by law. In fact, given the interest on the part of Saudi Arabian firms in engaging in joint ventures, they frequently demand 50 percent Saudi participation. These matters must be negotiated between the foreign firm and its putative Saudi associate(s).

Labor availability is a serious problem in Saudi Arabia, especially skilled and/or semiskilled labor. Given the smallness of the Saudi population, coupled with the huge magnitude of the kingdom's development efforts, it is difficult to find indigenous labor. Nevertheless, the Saudi Arabian government nominally expects foreign firms working in the kingdom to engage at least 75 percent of its labor requirement from Saudi nationals. Since this is frequently difficult, even impossible, it remains more of a goal than a reality; many foreign firms must perforce utilize less than the prescribed percentage of Saudi labor. Many have had to bring in expatriate labor.

Expatriate labor constitutes at least four-fifths of the overall Saudi labor force working in Saudi Arabia. The extent of expatriate personnel to be brought into the country in connection with any particular project undertaken by a foreign firm/joint venture is a negotiable matter. The Saudi Arabian government carefully monitors expatriate labor brought in by foreign contractors. Any foreign worker must have the sponsorship of a Saudi Arabian national, and entry visas are often extraordinarily difficult to obtain. Saudi Arabian embassies abroad must submit, with few exceptions, names of proposed expatriate workers to the ministry of foreign affairs and the ministry of interior, which must approve any such visas. Since 1967, this has become a somewhat cumbersome procedure. Expatriate workers in the kingdom often find it a difficult and protracted process to arrange entry visas for wives and children. Exit visas are also required for expatriate labor, which can also involve time-consuming procedures. In recent years, the Saudi Arabian government has sought to diversify its expatriate labor and has brought in more technical personnel from Far Eastern countries, such as the Philippines, Korea, and Japan.

Foreign firms operating in joint venture capacities are subject to corporate taxation after the conclusion of the tax holiday. Corporate taxation is levied at the rate of between 25 and 45 percent of corporate earnings, with the burden falling on the foreign firm.

Saudi Arabia has no record of contract repudiation. There is a history, however, of both Saudi government organizations and private firms frequently interpreting contracts differently from the foreign firms and demanding additional goods and services. Where contract disputes develop, mediation and arbitration by local Chambers of Commerce is the most accepted practice, although foreign firms would be well advised to stipulate in contractual agreements how differences of contract interpretation will be resolved.

ECONOMIC CONDITIONS: RISKS AND INDICATORS

Saudi Arabia is one of the wealthiest Third World nations in the world. Its substantial petroleum revenues have over the years enabled the kingdom to pursue, simultaneously, massive development programs, equally large defense programs, and a substantial foreign assistance program and to maintain sizable investments abroad as well as reserves at home: Nevertheless, in recent years, largely because of the oil glut and attendant loss of income, Saudi Arabia has found itself in somewhat more difficult financial circumstances. In 1982/83, for example, revenues amounted to $71.8 billion and budgetary expenditures to $71.1 billion. While still substantial, this represented a 33 percent drop from record revenues and expenditures from the previous year.

Saudi Arabian investments and reserves, while not formally divulged, are estimated to be in the neighborhood of between $65 billion. In formulating the Saudi budget for 1984/85, there are indications that the Saudi authorities may have to withdraw from their investments and reserves about $30 billion if planned projects and services are executed on time. The actual drawdown may be less, however, since Saudi Arabia has regularly underspent on its budget projections because of delayed completion of projects.

In 1983/84, Saudi Arabia had a budgetary deficit of $10 billion. This is expected to climb to $13 billion if the approximately 16.9 percent increase in expenditure has to be disbursed during the fiscal year. Revenue is expected to increase by slightly more than 15 percent because of a new consumer's tax on locally used petroleum products, designed to harmonize Saudi oil prices with those in existence in other GCC countries.

Thirty percent of the Saudi budgeted expenditures for 1984/85 (estimated at $74 billion) are devoted to defense projects. The defense budget is roughly 30.7 percent of the total budget and represents a slightly more than 5 percent increase over the previous year's defense expenditures. Foreign companies engaged in defense-related contracts are now required to invest up to 30 percent of the total value of contracts in joint ventures with 100 percent Saudi partners in order to manufacture strategic goods currently being imported. Thus, in the defense sphere at least, Saudi Arabia is adopting an import substitution strategy largely focused on obtaining technology transfers of strategic items.

Since so many of Saudi Arabia's goods and services must be imported from abroad, the kingdom has been subjected to global inflation rises. Within the country itself, however, inflation appears to have been only about 5 percent a year. The Saudi Arabian riyal represents hard currency, readily convertible. It is tied to the dollar and, because of fluctuations in the dollar, has recently been devalued from 4 to 3.51 riyals to the dollar. Some further slight devaluation is expected, depending in large part upon the strength of the dollar.

Despite Saudi Arabia's relatively good liquidity ratio, at least compared to other Third World states, there are frequent delays in payments to foreign contractors. The ministry of finance has adopted a practice of doling out riyal allocations to the various contracting ministries and limiting these allocations, allegedly to control internal inflation. This has often meant that ministries have not received in a given month the riyals required to pay foreign contractors, who have increasingly had to wait a month or more beyond payment due dates before receiving their funds. Awkward though this is to foreign contractors, most Saudi Arabian ministries have good records of discharging debts to foreign contractors with reasonable promptness.

No requirement would seem to exist for any radical debt restructuring for Saudi Arabia. Nor have the Saudis been in default on major debt payments, although they have sometimes sought deferred payment arrangements.

Although Saudi businessmen and the Saudi Arabian government have invested large sums in the United States, Europe, and elsewhere, this is more the result of surplus capital availability than of capital flight. There is some suggestion that the threat to Saudi security posed by the protracted Iraq-Iranian war may have caused some wealthy Saudis to place greater funds abroad, but no accurate figures are available as to the magnitude of such transfers.

Saudi Arabia's already mentioned massive social welfare program is, of course, a type of subsidization. As far as basic commodities are concerned, the market has generally regulated prices with no direct Saudi Arabian government subsidy program. As the fourth Five Year Development Plan goes into effect in 1985/86, with its emphasis on the private sector, the present indirect form of subsidization implicit in the social welfare program is likely to decrease.

CONCLUSION

In short, while problems exist in dealing with Saudi Arabia, and time and patience are often required to resolve them, the kingdom remains a promising investment area. Both the unity between Islamic institutions and the monarchy and the well-developed levers of social and political control militate against the potential threat to stability in Saudi Arabia from fringe Muslim groups, expatriates, the inroads of materialism, and the effect of bickering within the royal family. Another "Iran" is not likely soon in Saudi Arabia.

chapter eight
Australia

Henry S. Albinski

Myths and cliches about Australia abound, more so than about most familiar societies. Australia has been referred to as "the Saudi Arabia of the Pacific" and as "the nation" of the 21st century, as well as an intractably strike-afflicted society, addicted to leisure and contented with values of ordinariness. Reputable political risk analysis must of course probe well beneath the surface of such generalizations, both because of and despite their carrying a grain of truth.

This effort to place Australian conditions in useful perspective highlights four major categories of analysis. The first category is a nontechnical review of Australian economic circumstances, which in themselves are incentives or disincentives for overseas ventures. The second category moves to the Australian climate of opinion and political culture pertinent to the reception of an overseas economic presence. The next category, divided into several subparts, addresses relevant Australian political actors, formations, and constituencies. The last category spotlights the decision-making dynamics that might be construed as facilitating or impeding the well-being of overseas economic interests.

THE ECONOMIC ENVIRONMENT

For those wishing to trade with or to establish extractive, product, or service enterprises in Australia, it is well to remember the country's status in the global and regional context. Australia is by any reasonable measure an advanced society, composed of a diversified economic base, a high standard of living and of material expectations, and of an educated and skilled population that takes its consuming and spending cues from the West rather than from its Asian/Pacific neighbors. Although in the relatively prosperous period of the second half of the 1970s Australia's real private consumption expenditure was below the OECD average, the country nevertheless has enjoyed one of the world's higher per capita income levels. The proportion of umemployed within the workforce has been more difficult to decrease than in most Western countries emerging from recession, and the percentage of persons nominally under the poverty line has been rising for some years. Nevertheless, few households are without a wage earner, and the socioeconomic safety net has been set at a reasonably high level. In other words, the vast majority of Australians continue to live comfortably, and those who are not prosperous for the most part avoid privation.

Australians overwhelmingly reside in large, coastal cities. On balance, these circumstances contribute to a greater rather than lesser outgoing style of life and of public economic values and enterprise. In a society with historically narrow differentials between upper and lower income earnings, conspicuous consumption is increasingly apparent. This reflects not only a widening of income gaps, but more significantly of overall increases in affluence. While rank-and-file Australians tend to save, saving often becomes the basis for purchasing private homes and motor cars, the ownership of which places Australia inordinately high on a per capita world scale.

Australia's modest population size of 15.5 million should be taken in context. Australia is larger than some European countries and, while smaller than many Asian countries, nevertheless has far greater capacity to absorb consumer goods and services than many poorer countries several times its size. Its population growth rate has in recent years been modest, running at 1.5 percent or less per annum. But this is more than the basically static population levels of Britain, West Germany, and other Western nations. Australia, moreover, has long been a net importer of people, with intake numbers generally rising with improved economic cycles. Some of its migrants, such as older persons who arrive under family reunion schemes or Indochinese refugees, do not make quick and major economic contributions, nor do they readily become heavy consumers. Many new arrivals—for example, British, New Zealanders and regular Asian migrants—do rapidly augment wealth creation and indulge in national habits of extensive discretionary consumption.

In part because of its relatively narrow, indigenous capital and technological base, Australia has traditionally been a major recipient of overseas investment. The postwar discovery of vast new natural resource deposits, of rapid population growth, and of more diversified and sophisticated economic and living styles has generated an especially prominent flow of overseas investment, with U.S. sources predominant. About 50 percent of resource investments are currently from overseas sources. Next to Canada, Australia has become the second most transnational corporation–penetrated nation within the OECD group. For immediate purposes, the point to be made is that there is a long and firmly established habit of Australian reliance on foreign investment and money markets.

Moreover, whatever related social or political inferences may obtain, the overseas economic presence directly or indirectly has become responsible for a large share of Australia's present prosperity. To illustrate, about 55 percent of the equity in Australian mining and petroleum activities is in foreign hands. The mining industry itself accounts for about 5 percent of GDP and 40 percent of the value of Australia's exports. Resource exports have by now nearly caught up with overseas earnings from primary products, long the staple of Australia's export trade. About 12 percent of the Australian federal (Commonwealth) government's income accrues from the mineral industry, and various state imposts probably yield a comparable proportion of their revenue. While the resource industry is capital-intensive, there also is a high overseas concentration in some key, labor-intensive industries, such as automotive production, with consequent implications for employment. In other words, especially in a period of national prosperity, of rising public material expectations, and of mounting government absorption of its share of national spending, the overseas economic factor makes a critical difference.

The overseas economic presence in Australia should not, however, be construed as having overshadowed domestic capital and industry. To put the matter squarely, Australia does not have cause to consider itself under the thumb of, or otherwise abjectly beholden to, outsiders. A significant proportion of multinationals' investments reflects local borrowing and undistributed profits. Most new, direct foreign investment is in the form of joint ventures or partnership arrangements with local companies. Australian companies are not only expanding their investment activities in foreign resource undertakings in particular, but—as with the purchase of Utah by BHP, Australia's largest company—have begun takeovers in "reverse."

For a variety of reasons the Australian manufacturing industry has been slumping in scale and competitiveness. This has prompted serious discussion about the need to reindustrialize, probably along lines that would emphasize high-technology, service industry investments. While such steps would largely be aimed at encouraging indigenous activity, the overseas contribution should not be discounted. Australia is well down the line among OECD nations in the proportion of GDP it devotes to R & D. The private sector contribution to this modest effort is especially low, but within the private sector the overseas company branches render a disproportionately high contribution. Any concerted national effort to reindustrialize would therefore plausibly encourage rather than discourage or disregard existing areas of R & D strength.

CLIMATE OF OPINION AND POLITICAL CULTURE

The considerations mentioned above suggest that the foreign presence has, in economic terms, become habitual, substantial, and significant for growth and prosperity. It has not become so pervasive as to suggest that it overwhelms, and it is increasingly comingled with Australian firms and markets, and their objectives and profitability. The Australian public itself, viewed as a society or as a political force, must of course be factored into the equation. In effect, the question is whether Australian cultural dispositions and popular outlooks would seem to confirm the acceptability of overseas economic interests. The analysis can conveniently be divided according to socioeconomic values, the impact of nationalism, and the degree to which disruptive conditions are or may be in store for outsiders contemplating economic activity in Australia.

Australia's experience has produced a political culture characterized by a preference for the convergence of wealth, status, and opportunity. The survey data reflect substantial public self-perception/assignment of middle-class membership. It in fact has been argued that Australia is a one-class rather than a classless or class-polarized society. Middle-class values actually do dominate, and available data suggest wide areas of consensus on basic socioeconomic questions among persons who, on objective criteria, can be regarded as spread over upper-middle, middle, and lower-middle/working strata.

In context of present discussion, several key attitudinal features should be noted. First, the absence of a severe radical and especially radical left temper, and of estrangement over basics, contributes to a consensus that converges near a moderate, center-to-center left point, even though, on surface, political rhetoric at times would seem to belie this conclusion. Second, while the Australian public is not renowned for upper aspirational levels, it cherishes a good, secure, and enjoyable life, including in its material emanations such aspects as private ownership and the right of choice generally. At bottom, bourgeois values are an integral part of the Australian makeup. Moreover, while Australians expect that government authority will organize a proper system of social protections, they are suspicious of overbearing and especially of concentrated authority. The result is that while Australia has incrementally acquired a mixture of federal and state social schemes, of public ownership in various utility, communication, transport, and other spheres, and of complex regulations and subsidies, it nevertheless lacks public support for new nationalization ventures and other forms of private sector reduction or emasculation. This has been revealed not only in survey data, but for instance in the electorate's consistent reluctance via constitutional amendment referenda to approve enlargements of federal power.

Pragmatic, politically centrist, and bourgeois values are at large not inimical to an overseas economic presence. Even so, nationalist impulses must in their own right be examined and accounted for.

Australia had a sense of community feeling before it became a nation. But nationalism in the sense of overt patriotic celebration of the nation-state has been soft-pedaled. Attempts by political leaders to mobilize politically nationalist opinion did not take serious shape until the late 1960s. Since then, such appeals have been sporadic, not consistent. Some such appeals, as the "New Nationalism" presentation of the Whitlam government in the early and mid-1970s, were a combination of asking the public to rouse itself on behalf of protecting Australia's legacy, self-respect, and control over its own economic and cultural destiny, and raising the consciousness of an otherwise apathetic public. Subsequent Labor and non-Labor governments have variously stood behind programs of Australian self-expression or avoidance of indiscriminate foreign swamping, but have not held up nationalism as anything like a fetish. The supposedly nationalist message of Robert Hawke, who led Labor back to federal office in 1983, was more anodyne than bold: "Bringing Australia Together Again."

What is being stressed in this context is that Australian society has not suffered from a cultural identity crisis, and that its leadership has not tried to whip up strong nationalist emotions. While the country's experience has left traces of cultural parochialism, this has not been equatable with xenophobia. The country's entire experience has been dependence on outsiders for its security and for its market outlets. Political nationalism has been weak, and the nationalism that dominates mostly refers to a community of social and personal values.

Flourishing and distinctive cultural and artistic contributions, as expressed recently in the film industry, have added to a sense of Australian self-confidence without accompanying tantrums against established overseas influences. Agitated voices have been raised in various quarters against the combined weight of American cultural, economic, and defense-related penetration, but this has not approached a majority view. The United States and Americans continue to enjoy a broadly based acceptance. Australia's intimate defense and security connections with the United States, however, have become increasingly contentious. It bears watching whether a widening and exacerbation of this debate could contaminate economic ties with the U.S. It conversely is of interest that one of the Hawke Labor government's motives in maintaining close security ties with the U.S. has been to reassure the American commercial community that Australia continues to be a highly desirable and respectable country in which and with which to carry out business.

Australia's prevailing nationalist environment extends to public perceptions of overseas economic interests. So far as survey data can usefully be brought to bear, it is helpful to recall the circumstances of the early 1970s, when suspicious sentiment seemed to run strongest. This was in the final stages of the Vietnam conflict, when America's intentions and reputation were being brought into question. It was a period of conscious nationalist treatment by the government in office, shortly after a hastily introduced, foreign-sparked resources boom had deflated. It also was a time when overseas firms had not yet absorbed lessons of sound public relations and civic responsibility. Circumstances have changed since then. Not only has image-building among TNCs considerably improved, but the public has had more time in which to acquire a better appreciation of major overseas interests' role in national economic growth, of cyclical declines as well as improvements in their profitability, of the frequent cooperation between domestic and foreign firms, and of movement toward the domestication of Australian-based management. "Big Business" as such is regarded with some apprehension by Australians, be it domestic or foreign. But, as seen, there is no impulse to nationalize, expropriate, or otherwise break up big business. Australians are in fact more apprehensive about the power of organized labor than of big business. By mid-1984, after the mildly nationalistic Hawke Labor government had been in office for more than a year, corporate and overseas corporate images, in particular, were registering noticeably improved public reception in opinion polls.

Last, it is useful to glance at the environment in which a miscellania of social circumstances operate. For example, in part because traditional political cultural dispositions did not find them appealing, life quality and related social justice issues have been somewhat slow to enter the Australian public agenda. Now that environmental, conservationist, freedom of information, civil protection, women's and minority improvement, and other programs have been given impetus, there may be a temptation to conclude that the imperatives governing domestic and foreign private sector operations are being disregarded. It may be somewhat unsettling for overseas economic interests to discover that this kind of social change process is taking hold. But the changes are simply coming later and in more condensed form than they appeared in many other industrial democracies, not more dramatically or radical in content. It is arguable that overseas firms and commercial interests have already found and will continue to find it easier to make necessary adaptations than holds true of Australian businesses, insofar as the foreign concerns have the benefit of American and/or other non-Australian experience with such changes behind them. On balance, perhaps the most troublesome social change issue for overseas operators will be Australia's effort to reconcile Aboriginal land rights with mining company interests.

Demonstrations and other forms of mass protest are not uncommon in Australia; such manifestations became popular during the Vietnam conflict. More recently they have been staged on behalf of causes such as nuclear disarmament, Aboriginal rights, cessation of uranium mining, and the removal of U.S. defense facilities from Australia. As expected, these causes attract considerable, overlapping membership. And, as expected, the marches and other demonstrations attract a distinct minority of the population. Some protests, such as against uranium mining, are by definition directed against what are commercial operations. All the same, it is useful to notice that when commercial operations have been protested against, the target has not been overseas economic interests or even corporate/private sector interests as such. When such protests have occurred, commercial operations have been impeded only marginally. Violence in the context of such demonstrations is rare, and when it surfaces it is condemned by governments of all political persuasions as well as by the mass public.

In the broad law-and-order sense, Australia is not in fact a particularly violent society. By advanced nation standards, it does not rank high in violent crimes and criminal resort to firearms. Personal safety is greater in Australian than in American cities. While organized crime has established a foothold in Australia, it has not become a threat to the social order. Politically inspired attacks with intent to kill, kidnap, extort, or disrupt are extremely rare. Neither terrorist nor vigilante groups have intruded in ways prejudicial to public safety. Australia lacks anything resembling a secessionist or other systemically threatening movement. Political and business leaders have remained immune from assaults aimed at them as symbols or representatives of an objectionable political or socioeconomic system. In this sense, overseas business interests and facilities and their representatives do not function in a harassing and dangerous environment.

ACTORS, FORMATIONS, AND CONSTITUENCIES

The Workforce

The Australian workforce, especially in its organized, trade union form, has long been an object of keen attention and even of controversy. The foreign investor/employer potentially interested in Australia must first take into account the pure and simple scope and entrenchment of organized labor. Unionization had its major impetus as far back as the 1890s, at the time with strongly radical overtones. The early ideological radicalism faded, but the parallel growth of the unions and the Australian Labor Party and of their substantially mutual aims and similar constituencies brought them into close, working relations. The union-party nexus is not as tight as it is in Britain, and the relationship has never been carefree. All the same it is a relationship in which each side has needed the other. Although they do not vote as a bloc, trade union delegates are substantially represented in Australian Labor Party decision-making councils, such as federal and state conferences and executive committees. Union-party ties in Australia should, moreover, be construed as a sign of the intrinsic and established position of the working class, as a basic ingredient of the nation's economic and political competition. The union movement has approached becoming a de facto embodiment of goals of comfort, security and well-being for Australian society, not just for the union members for which it nominally speaks. Federal and state governments have over time tampered with the details of trade union–related legislation, but the essential position of organized labor must be regarded as a given, even if a number of unionists themselves, as well as the general public, feel that unions are too powerful.

The argument about union pervasiveness is underscored by the sheer numbers of the Australian workforce enrolled in unions. The proportion has for decades been among the highest in the world, and its present figure of 56 percent places it in first position worldwide. The phenomenon is not a coincidence. The creation of federal and state organs of arbitration and conciliation before World War I placed a premium on union representation at and judgments from these bodies. The social temper of the country has itself contributed to unionization as a natural outlet. Professionals and public servants, not just blue-collar workers, have shown an impulse to unionize, and teachers and nurses are among the white-collar unions that have militantly presented their claims.

It is arguable that investors and employers would in some respects welcome a large, powerful, and disciplined trade union movement—one with which they could deal authoritatively and reliably. Australian conditions do not however satisfy such expectations. The organized trade union movement is extremely fragmented. There are in the neighborhood of 300 separate unions. There is a long-established umbrella organization, the Australian Council of Trade Unions, but it does not come close to encompassing the range of separate unions and of unionists. It does enjoy a measure of suasion over its constituent unions, but is not in a position to dictate. Hence, despite the ACTU's presence, demarcation disputes between unions are frequent, leading to work stoppages to which employers did not contribute and which they cannot resolve. It has not been uncommon for high-leverage unions in key industries, such as resources and on the docks, to wage industrial disputes and have the example of their settlements serve to embolden other unions to lay their own claims.

Australian strikes generally have drawn much publicity. Applying such indices as man-days lost, by industrial nation standards Australia is not disproportionately strike-prone. Australian strikes are in fact often brief, but they tend to be distinguished by some troubling features. One is that they frequently develop over very minor issues, or involve jurisdictional quarrels between unions. In such instances, management is hard-pressed to devise reasonable and responsible wage and condition-of-work policies with high assurance that such measures would promote tranquil industrial relations. Another factor is that Australian industrial action often occurs in pivotal industries such as transport and communications. Australian ports are probably the world's most strike-prone. If stoppages do not last long, it is in part because their impact very rapidly becomes serious, and management, whether private or public sector, is likely to settle. The communist leadership of some unions contributes to their militancy, but the communist/noncommunist leadership distinction is not a reliable guide to union behavior generally. Moreover, in recent years, strike action has become more prevalent in the manufacturing industry, which has been undergoing decline and worker displacement.

It is in this setting that Australian workers and their unions have historically resisted production method changes that appeared to threaten familiar and job-preserving ways. In recent times their apprehension has particularly focused on automation and technological change. This has and foreseeably will continue to make industrial changeover, and therefore competitiveness and productivity, a nagging Australian problem. Employers were especially downcast by a recent Arbitration and Conciliation Commission judgment. In effect, employers will henceforth need to arrange for far greater consultation with unions/workers before introducing major changes in production methods or the structure of their companies. Should redundancies eventuate, longer notice and heavier severance pay must apply.

The Australian worker is already widely regarded as combining low productivity, strong protection for his job and job conditions, and a generous pay scale. As previously mentioned, there is a deeply embedded tradition of the worker as a deserving citizen, and one who should have ample leisure and security as well as be free from exploitation. Among the consequences have been labor costs driven up by sub-40 hour workweeks (but 40 hour wage scales) in an increasing number of industries, multiple wages for overtime and weekend work, extensive paid vacations, long service leaves with pay, and the frequent practice during strikes that employers continue to pay nonstriking workers whose services are not required.

Wage scales and awards have over time been dealt with in various ways in and outside the ambit of conciliation and arbitration machinery. In general, the machinery—which is essentially autonomous—has set basic and over-award wages for a host of industries and occupations, but unions have been able to negotiate with employers for further concessions. Periodic wage indexation, to reflect consumer price index movement, was introduced in 1975 and abolished in 1981. Even when it was in effect, there was considerable labor-management bargaining for scales above indexed levels. Indexation was reinstituted in 1983. The Arbitration and Conciliation Commission awards semiannual adjustments in keeping with inflationary movements, and in a few instances allows greater settlements due to pay anomalies. The maintenance of this system is largely dependent on a bargain struck between the ACTU and the ALP, which is also the party of government federally. The government promised to push inflation down, to extend certain social benefits, to bring taxation relief to lower- and middle-income workers and their families. The ACTU in turn pledged to exert itself to dissuade unions from pressing employers for settlements above the indexed levels.

The ALP–ACTU "accord," as it is known, is an improvement over open-season bargaining. But firms and management are not sanguine. First, there is no warranty that the accord can stick over an extended period. The ACTU's ability to hold individual unions in line is problematic, and many workers could grow impatient with no real-term wage improvements. Second, even if the accord holds, there is a considerable private sector complaint that the present system does not ameliorate problems of wage-push inflation, since inflation-reflected indexation is noticeably higher than productivity improvement.

Hence, from the vantage point of overseas economic interests, the Australian working and trade union scene has worrisome features, and features that foreseeably will not disappear or be seriously attenuated. The results of a 1984 survey of Japanese company offices operating in Australia, though by no means alarmist, were nevertheless critical of conditions such as poor industrial relations, substantial worker privileges, low productivity, and high tariff protection for inefficient industries (for which organized labor is only one major protagonist). These have been among the considerations leading Japan to undertake a diversification of its sources of Australian iron ore, coal, and other commodities.

The Australian Labor Party

Like its close but often uneasy ally, the trade union movement, the Australian Labor Party has been a long-standing Australian fixture. It arguably is the centerpiece of the party system, toward which the other, "nonlabor" parties react. Its electoral fortunes have been historically uneven, and it was out of federal office continuously from 1949 to 1972. As of 1984 it was governing federally and in four of the six states, and its short- to middle-range electoral prospects seemed bright.

The ALP is an amalgam of trade unionists and of professionals, of socialists and of pragmatic social democrats. The present breed of federal and state ALP parliamentary elites is skewed toward nonideological, practical-minded reformism. This is reflected both in their programmatic leaning and in their style, and it coincides with Australian public preferences. The ALP government under Robert Hawke, elected in March 1983, has exhibited particular capacity to preempt the center/center-left Australian mainstream, and has gone out of its way to demonstrate commonsense practicality in its handling of economic policy. One of its intentions has been to distance itself in the public mind and among overseas observers from Gough Whitlam's ALP government of 1972–1975, which was widely viewed as economically incompetent and flawed in various stylistic ways. It should, however, be remembered that the Whitlam government entered office after 23 years of party absence from power, that there was an understandable zeal for change, and that the ministry was woefully inexperienced.

The Hawke government has worked with the unions, especially in promoting the accord on wage restraint, in an effort to keep wages within limits and to reduce both the actual as well as the reputational damage of industrial stoppages around the country. It has been quite successful in this. The government proceeded to lift some legislative encumbrances that the union movement had resented, and has planned noncompulsory, "industrial democracy" guidelines for greater worker representation access to company records and labor-management consultation.

However, the government's animating economic principle, held by Hawke and his Treasurer Paul Keating, has been that the ALP could achieve many of its traditional social objectives through fostering the efficiency of the market. Some of this has meant the drawing up of plans for nationwide industrial reform to retrack the economy over a long haul, higher growth path. This would entail not only rather more industrial democracy practices, but restructuring toward high technology, dismantling excessive tariff protection, undertaking various industrial incentives, and financial deregulation. The Hawke government early in its tenure took the business community into its confidence, and then continued to maintain close and constructive contacts with it. For the most part, the Australian private sector and overseas interests as well have given the government good marks for its efficiency and economic sense. By the second half of 1984, government policies included selected tax breaks for industry to encourage investment and thereby employment and economic growth. There also were some specific incentives for the resources industry; for example, money spent on general mining exploration could become deductible against income from any company source. Deregulation was undertaken of the traditionally stodgy banking system, and overseas banks were now able to enter areas of activity previously barred to them. The decision to allow the Australian dollar to float proved popular throughout most of the business community.

The ALP government has taken or promised to take some measures that have left a mixed reception among overseas economic interests. Even its pragmatic leadership shares a measure of the party's sentiments about nationalism, Australian self-determination, and suspicion of wide open and especially foreign-derived development at the expense of other goals. Moreover, despite his command over the government and his popularity with the public, Hawke must realistically extend concessions to various sectors of his party. Hence a record of both advance and withdrawal, of compromises with both party and outside interests. The government's long-promised creation of a controversial national hydrocarbon corporation faced stiff opposition from the private oil industry and other quarters. The government continued to delay appropriate legislation, but did not withdraw its intention. The government passed a Resources Rental Tax, but readjusted its targeted petroleum sites and also taxation rates after heavy representations from the resources industry. The 1984 ALP federal conference did not give carte blanche to uranium mining, but two operating mines in the Northern Territory were to continue, and the exploitation of rich deposits at Roxby Downs in South Australia was allowed to go forward.

The Hawke government has generally preserved its predecessor's attitude toward foreign investment at large. Apart from some long-standing, technical exceptions of form rather than substance, Australian and foreign companies continue to be taxed at the same rates. There are no restrictions on the repatriation of nonresident-owned funds, and exchange control approval is not required. Exporting companies remain the sole negotiators for export contracts. The number of minerals and materials theoretically subject to export controls has been falling, and succeeding governments have regarded intervention only as a last resort.

Under the ALP, foreign investment guidelines and practices have been tightened slightly, but not enough to cause concern among most overseas investors. Economic benefit, equity, and other previously followed national interest tests have essentially been kept, although the Foreign Investment Review Board has proved somewhat more stringent than under Liberal-National Party governments. The ALP government entered office with a party policy requiring that the prevailing rate of 50 percent Australian equity for new natural resource, business, and other projects be raised to 51 percent. At the 1984 party conference, the government leadership was able to win a rewording that now refers to 51 percent "where feasible," which de facto could continue to mean less than majority Australian participation. The government has moreover retained special provisions under which overseas companies holding more than 50 percent participation can by steps "naturalize" themselves.

The upshot of this review is that an ALP government of the temper and outlook characteristic of the one now led by Hawke and Keating is essentially congenial to overseas interests. It functions along pragmatic lines and indeed finds much virtue in the contributions (to national economic prosperity) of both the domestic and overseas private sectors. A number of its plans for industrial regeneration, if adopted and successful, could prove more beneficial to private sector vitality than the more laissez-faire approach of predecessors. The ability of the government to sustain good relations with and to decompress the claims of, and industrial disturbances attributable to, organized labor can be much more productive than when a more confrontational posture was assumed by nonlabor governments.

The key, however, is who will occupy the leadership roles in a Labor ministry. Hawke and Keating are publicly popular but lack a broad personal base within the party itself. Both are regarded in many party circles as simply too committed to pragmatism and political convenience, while Hawke is resented for his personal grip over colleagues and for his lavish public following. Should leaders of this type fall by the wayside for whatever reason, the party would very likely pass into the hands of persons from the center-left faction. These are moderates rather than radicals, but more committed to combining principled and progressive policies with political and economic realism. While Hawke's position should not be endangered while he is able to win elections handily and the economy is in reasonable shape, the Labor Party does have a lengthy history of commotion and fragmentation.

Private Sector Groups

The discussion of labor unions as a major constituency in the Australian system pointed to a considerable amount of organizational fragmentation, to varying degrees of militancy among unions, and to the only modest capacity of the umbrella ACTU to ensure common approaches within the industrial movement. The private sector in Australia has an equally high stake in policy outcomes, and its own capacity to represent and to influence can be treated along similar, organizational and behavior criteria. As preface, it should be kept in mind that Liberal-National Party governments have been the rule rather than the exception at the federal level, and private sector groups have therefore done most of their dealing with them, not with Labor. While relations between business and nonlabor governments have had their ups and downs, business has for the most part preferred nonlabor governments and has been their principal financial sponsor.

In the past few years and especially since the advent of the Hawke government, the corporate community's position as a coherent, interest-articulating group has been less predictable both as to its preference and as to impact. There has been sparring between manufacturing and resource industry spokesmen. The former, whether representing domestic or overseas firms, have generally been much more committed to preserving protective tariff barriers. But some companies, BHP being a prime example, have diversified their connections in ways that have made them both manufacturers and partners in resource development, thus preventing them from becoming fully tied to a particular constituency and its specialized interests. Some umbrage has been taken by domestic Australian businesses at the heavy flow of overseas capital into resource projects because of the purported strains on the domestic price of money. But other manufacturers, apart from teaming up with resource industry partners, have themselves been served fresh investments, and the recently opened opportunities for overseas banks are widely seen as invigorating the financial scene to the benefit of the private sector generally. In fact, since 1980–1981, the share of overseas funds directed to the extractive industry has been proportionately modest and, as previously mentioned, resource-based TNCs have been increasingly involved with Australian partners. Overall, both the manufacturing vis-à-vis resources industry and the domestic vis-à-vis foreign business distinctions and strategies for influence expression have become less clear, on balance probably to the advantage of potential overseas entrants.

Another factor has at least temporarily confused the picture of private sector interest activity. Groups representing sectors of the business community have themselves been changing. In the late 1970s, in a move toward unity among business groups, the Confederation of Australian Industry was formed. It now faces competition for employer and free enterprise spokesmanship from a newly created Business Council of Australia and from a resuscitated Australian Chamber of Commerce. The Business Council, composed of major company (domestic and foreign) chief executives, is opposed to business organization around sectoral interests and strives for wider, free enterprise perspectives. As the ALP government undertakes industrial renewal programs, the impact of umbrella groups generally will probably be weakened by the reassertion of special sectoral claims.

A third component is the private sector's place in the context of a Hawke Labor government and the prospect of long-term Labor rule. A number of the leading Australian business figures are highly visible in the national community. They have often had close establishmentarian connections with the Liberal Party. Since this community of "leaders" or of "influentials" is relatively small, their spokesmanship has traditionally provided business with additional access and leverage. Yet the Hawke government made it an early and important priority to draw leading business interests into dialogue. This began with a much-publicized labor/industry/government "summit" shortly after the government's election, and has been continued through both conventional and newly fashioned channels of consultation. As seen, moreover, the government has on occasion not just listened to but accepted advice from private sector sources, and has been eager to devise both programs and to cast an image that would build business confidence. A number of business leaders have been impressed—by Hawke and Keating particularly, but also by what they have regarded as a surprisingly constructive approach by an ALP government as such, and very much in contrast to their recollection of the Whitlam government. Many also feel that, despite what are felt to be its occasionally wrongheaded policies, Labor has at least followed a more systematic economic path than that toward the close of the Fraser government. Moreover, they cannot quite be sure what to expect from a restored Liberal-National Party government. Such views obtain among overseas as well as domestic sides of the private sector. It is an unusual position in which business interests have found themselves and whose implications have yet to be fully discerned.

The Coalition Parties

Coalitions between the Liberal and National (formerly Country) parties have been the mainstay of Australian federal politics. Business interests have ordinarily preferred these parties, since both have been rather more oriented toward free enterprise, the business sector, and overseas investment than has Labor.

The National Party, the smaller of the two in the coalition alignment, began and has continued as a party of large- and middle-size rural industry sectors and of country and small-town voters. Its generally conservative disposition would in principle appear to recommend it to business interests, but its rural/primary industry base would on surface appear unsuitable. In recent years, however, the National Party has thrown its support behind natural resource development, viewing that industry as an economic ally on such counts as resistance to high tariffs and vigorous overseas marketing. Also, as a party with a shrinking natural electoral clientele, it has worked to broaden its base—to become "national"—and to avoid clashes with manufacturing interests, as for instance over tariff policy. In effect, it has been able to acquiesce to the manufacturing interests fostered by the Liberals in exchange for various subventions and favorable regulations for the rural sector. It has shown itself astute in the politics of quid pro quo. Overall, therefore, neither the political disposition nor the broad programmatic approach of the National Party is uncongenial to overseas economic interests.

The Liberals, the senior coalition partner, have supplied prime ministers and most other ministers when nonlabor has governed. While carrying a fairly wide spread of tendencies within its ranks, the party is centrist rather than genuinely conservative, and has understood that its appeal must extend into working and lower middle-class sectors if it is to remain electorally viable. It nevertheless prides itself on being more conscious of economic realities than it finds Labor to be, and whom it often accuses of overregulating, overspending, and overindulging the trade union movement. A comparison of recent L-NP government performance with that of the Hawke ALP government does not, however, substantiate such claims. In 1983, the outgoing Fraser government left behind a very considerable public deficit, in part because promised, stringent economies had not been fulfilled. The L-NP had not actually implemented some earlier promises of major scale privatization. Its relations with organized labor were poor, and strike incidence was noticeably higher than after Hawke settled into office. There was an atmosphere of economic policy drift when the coalition was unseated in March 1983.

Andrew Peacock, who replaced Malcolm Fraser as Liberal leader, brought with him a reputation as a "small-l" liberal. The rebound of the economy and Hawke's popularity nevertheless imposed very difficult policy prescription choices on a Liberal Party striving to rediscover its bearings and to redeem itself electorally. Liberal deputy leader John Howard, a former coalition government treasurer, has his eye on the party leadership and in the meantime has contributed to an essentially "dry" Liberal economic policy platform. The policy calls for a shaving back of the Arbitration and Conciliation Commission's ability to set wage structures, although the system at large is probably too much a sacred cow to be eviscerated by any prospective Australian government. Liberal policy also stands for sharp reductions in deficits associated with tighter monetary policy generally, a transfer of some tax burdens from direct to indirect levies, and movement toward further deregulation.

Even with an early L-NP electoral rehabilitation, it cannot be assumed that the coalition's announced policies would bring a swifter and more durable Australian economic revival than under a Hawke-Keating style of Labor government, and the industrial scene in particular would likely become more agitated. As suggested earlier, traditionally pro-Liberal business and commercial interests have not been alienated by Labor's performance. Despite their anti-Labor instincts these interests are not persuaded that the coalition parties have settled into a programmatic mode that is either fully marketable electorally or that in all prime respects is economically feasible.

The Fraser government's attitude toward foreign investment as such was generous but not uncritical. The Hawke government's general absorption of earlier tenets and guidelines is partially testimony of moderate rather than one-sided continuity in this area. Naturalization of foreign companies, more stringent rules governing land acquisition by outsiders, and the progressive closing of tax avoidance loopholes utilized by foreign investors were among L-NP government measures. The L-NP federal opposition has promised deregulation of the resource industry, and would not pursue the national hydrocarbon authority promised, but not implemented, by Labor itself. While it has pledged itself to lower taxes on the resources sector, it has hinted of the retention of the Resources Rental Tax. Again, for the overseas investor there is little to choose between the two principal Australian party groups, assuming as before that leadership and factional balance changes do not impose a different cast of mind on Labor.

THE DECISION-MAKING FRAMEWORK

Political risk assessment in developed countries in particular must not only concern itself with cultural temper, elites and groups, and public policy alternatives. There must also be some appreciation of the framework in which decisions are made, and of its dominant customs and styles. It helps to illuminate the sources of authoritative decisions and in what de facto ways such decisions are shared, reinforced, or attenuated within the system. It is necessary to understand whether decision-making and policy implementation are usually consistent and reliable, and at what points in the system interested constituencies can hope to establish their claims. The Australian scene can usefully be summarized according to how political decisions are made at the center, how politically nonresponsible sources of advice or pressure impinge on the center, and according to the influence of federalism.

At the federal level, where most significant decisions are taken, the political process is reasonably clear. As in other Westminster-style systems, the government of the day is predicated on a majority in the lower house (House of Representatives). Primarily because of the electoral system (single member constituencies with preferential voting), minor party and independent candidates capacity to gain a representational foothold is extremely difficult. Hence the House is not a melange of parties, but basically divides between Labor and the L-NP coalition group. Party discipline is firm, meaning that the leadership of the governing majority can expect House support for its legislative program. While the parliamentary caucus role of backbenchers is not absent, especially on the Labor side, the Prime Minister and his senior colleagues overshadow the agenda-setting process. While interested groups cannot ordinarily count on eliciting influential spokesmanship from individual Members, the government party and its leadership provide considerable focus and predictability in the shaping and timing of decisions.

Australia is, however, bicameral. The upper house, the Senate, cannot be dismissed as an inconsequential actor. The Senate is a party house in that party positions there are congruent with counterpart parties in the House, and discipline is strong in the Senate as well as the House. The principal complication is that the state-based, proportional voting system employed for the Senate elections makes it exceedingly difficult for any single party/coalition group to muster an absolute majority there, even at times when there is a strong national electoral swing toward one party or another. Minor parties and independents are able to establish representation and for most of the last two decades have held the balance of Senate power. Since the Senate's formal legislative authority is considerable, this factor can affect the speed and content of legislative policy determined by the government of the day. Since the late 1970s, this has been reflected in the behavior of a small group of Australian Democrat Senators. The Democrats frustrated aspects of the Fraser government's program and, although they lean more toward Labor than the Liberal–National Party coalition, under the Hawke government they have not hesitated to hold out for their own objectives. They are in fact rather more openly nationalistic and suspicious of major overseas economic interests than is the current Labor leadership. Apart from amendments to government bills and other concessions that can be wrung in such circumstances, the presence of an obstreperous Senate can produce a House-Senate impasse on legislative measures that in turn can precipitate a double dissolution and an early election. Relatedly, such an impasse can be used as a tactic by a ruling government to call an early election in order to maximize presumed electoral advantage for itself. In either case, Australian parliaments are less likely to run their full course, thereby introducing a feature of uncertainty as to who will be governing and for how long.

At federal as indeed at other tiers, the decision-making process includes various informal, nonauthoritative sources of influence. As in other political systems, the bureaucracy plays a prominent role in policy-setting as well as implementation. In the Australian context, the Commonwealth bureaucracy is characterized by size and pervasiveness, by generally strong expertise and freedom from corruption, and by an ethos of self-confidence and importance. Taking national experience as a whole, the received wisdom is that Australia has a genius for bureaucracy.

The federal bureaucracy's strength is in part reflected in conventional methods of organizational influence, including the authority of the senior ("permanent") secretary) figures vis-à-vis their own departments and their political ministers. Especially in key economic departments such as Treasury, there has been a tendency for senior officials to be cautious rather than adventurous in policy outlook. Departments can and do disagree with one another. Interdepartmental committee activity and the measure of oversight and continuity imposed by the practice of chairmanship from the Department of the Prime Minister and Cabinet over such committees does mitigate advisory fragmentation, but can result in lowest common denominator advice from the bureaucracy at large when a complex issue is being addressed. Recent steps to recruit top public servants laterally, as from business and academic life, have not been adequately tested by experience, but at least in theory such nonconventional appointments are designed to introduce fresher and less organizationally hidebound leadership into line departments.

Apart from an abundance of traditional bureaucratic forms, Australia has evolved a pervasive network of advisory and rule-setting agencies. One of the most prominent is the Arbitration and Conciliation Commission, whose work deeply affects wage award guidelines and thereby much of the country's economic direction. Another agency, the Prices and Surveillance Authority created under the Hawke government, monitors prices in selected, key industries. The Authority operates by suasion, and compliance with its findings is voluntary, but the nominated companies are subject to fines if they fail to comply with price rise notification requirements. As its name implies, the Foreign Investment Review Board receives, screens, and then recommends to the government whether foreign investment/ownership proposals should be accepted. It is guided by prevailing government policy, and more contentious cases can be brought up for determination at Cabinet level. Its own handling of proposals does matter, however, insofar as prospective investors may find themselves encouraged to proceed, discouraged from proceeding, or encouraged to resubmit proposals along amended lines. The three examples listed illustrate the subject range of regulatory and advisory bodies operating in the domain of economic policy, and the range of actual influence that can be exercised. Some such bodies by definition attract representations from interested private sector sources, while others are less subject to such intervention. The central point is that overseas economic interests wishing to deal with Australia must be aware of the character and responsibilities of various institutional layers, of the dispositions of individual agencies and their members, and of their susceptibility to receiving advisory inputs from interested economic constituencies.

Moreover, there has been a growing tendency for Australian governments to surround themselves with nonstatutory or otherwise nonregulative advisory bodies for both short- and long-range advice. Such bodies have increasingly been built on multiconstituent rather than single-sector membership. A prime example is the Economic Planning and Advisory Council, which is the roof organization in the economic area. It comprises unionists, businesspersons, farmers, consumer representatives, and the federal and state governments. Much of its founding rationale was to offset the advice of the traditional bureaucracy, and predictably the Council's work is not especially congenial to those involved in conventional channels of advice.

It is a matter of perspective as to how interested outsiders should view developments toward the diversification of advisory and oversight bodies. To repeat, the overall intent inherent in these developments is not simply to widen the range of advice to political decision-makers or to decentralize some features of rule-making. The intention is also to draw various private and public sector constituencies to deliberate together on common economic issues. The content and quality of such bodies' advice apart, it is assumed that such a diffused yet reasonably representative consultative system carries value for overall economic management. It definitionally incorporates, rather than excludes, interested constituencies and hears their concerns and advice.

In so doing it in degree simplifies the political task of policy announcement and implementation. This is particularly useful for a Labor government which, in wishing to keep business as well as other constituencies on side, assiduously fosters what it describes as consensus politics.

The Australian decision-making process is especially influenced by the country's federal environment. Through a combination of constitutional judgments by the High Court and of political exigencies, the national government has become dominant over revenues, and thereby has been in a position to dominate economic priorities and decisions. Moreover, while judicial review has not supported monopolistic federal ownership of various enterprises, it has in recent decades favored an expanded definition of federal jurisdiction at state expense. Recent court decisions, in considerable part relying on the Commonwealth's exclusive access to external affairs powers, have upheld Canberra's preeminence in such spheres as offshore resource rights, Aboriginal land purchase entitlements, and the protection of designated areas for conservation purposes. These broad trends arguably redound to the benefit of prospective overseas economic interests seeking more than less focus and predictability in the way that policy is set and administered.

The six states, however, are not without incentive nor without political and legal resources with which to promote their separately defined interests. Their borrowing capacity on capital markets is subordinated to federal priorities. But through such devices as land tax concessions, start-up subsidies, loan guarantees, and reduced power rates they vie for new business or for the retention or expansion of established businesses. Private sector interests can in this sense be seen as capitalizing on interstate competition for their presence. Political constraints at times require that federal government policies, whatever their merit, be fine-tuned to accommodate state governments and their publics. This, for instance, has happened regarding national policy governing Aboriginal land rights. Such land rights can run counter to and even directly interfere with state-based development goals. As a case in point, the ALP government in Western Australia has not been unsympathetic to mining industry concerns about the effects of national Aboriginal legislation regulating resource development projects in the state, and has worked to dissuade the federal ALP government from being overzealous.

Another side of the coin is less attractive to overseas interests, as states play out their political inclinations or seek to direct rather than allow laissez-faire investment and development, or as they simply search for lucrative sources of revenue. Regarding the extractive industry, for instance, the states can let or cancel leases, set royalties and transport imposts, establish environmental standards, and regulate energy rates. Not only can investors be caught in a crossfire between federal and state priorities, but they can face quite real, state-originated disincentives. One of the objectives of the Hawke government's Resources Rental Tax is to consolidate and simplify levies on the resource industry. But this assumes that the states can be persuaded to drop a number of their own levies, which yield considerable revenue and which in some respects are viewed by the states as symbolically important in the wider framework of federal-state relations.

SUMMARY AND CONCLUSION

Political risk assessment applied to Australia suggests a picture of considerable nuance. The assessment does not validate either a halcyon or a depressing conclusion. The balance that emerges, however, is well on the favorable side. Australia is economically receptive to further overseas interventions, while established operations continue and even expand. The Australian public is not hostile to an overseas economic presence. Despite strikes and other interferences, the country's social setting is orderly, and groups expressing discontent with private sector activities, with an overseas economic presence or with prevailing socioeconomic assumptions, generally do not foreseeably threaten to interdict the entry and operation of outside interests. The leadership of the main party groups, while not committed to permissive overseas investment policies, is moderately disposed and welcomes most new ventures. Nor are the principal political constituencies of the parties antagonistic toward broadly prevailing policy outlines. The framework within which Australian decisions are taken, while in respects diffused and at times frustrating, is probably no more injurious to overseas private sector interests than obtains in most industrialized nation political environments. To reemphasize, the underlying Australian prognosis is positive.

part three

APPROACHES TO DEVISING METHODOLOGIES AND MODELS

chapter nine

The Bootstrapping Approach:
An Alternative to Old Methods Restyled

Robert O. Slater

In the field of international politics, we have often witnessed debates between so-called "empiricists" and "traditionalists" concerning the relative merits of the two approaches. It has become more and more evident over the years that the two approaches are neither distinct nor mutually exclusive. In many cases, each approach may address the same problem from unique yet complementary perspectives. The field of political risk analysis is a recent example of the debate between approaches. Born from a rather strange combination of experts on political instability, regional areas and economics/ business, proponents of risk analysis share a common perception that the private business community is desperately in need of more systematic and informed assessments of factors that may affect the risk associated with a particular investment decision. Events during the past several years, such as those in Iran and Lebanon, have done a great deal to stimulate interest in political risk analysis and have pointed to the weaknesses that exist in the way political risk is sometimes currently assessed.

While the number of individuals and organizations offering approaches to assessing political risk has increased dramatically, serious questions remain as to whether these approaches actually add valuable information and whether they will impact on foreign investment decisions. At times it seems that the substance of these approaches is somewhat obscured by the zeal to convince potential clients that the approach provides insightful and invaluable assessments of the political risk in foreign countries. While the "Madison Avenue" approach may produce short-term successes in marketing political risk approaches, any long-term success will more likely be determined by the track records of political risk analyses and whether they have any impact on investment decision-making. It is difficult to define the depths of corporate interest in political risk analysis beyond the simple willingness to subscribe to a particular risk assessment service. If the sources of political risk analysis are not innovative in providing meaningful assessments, it is likely that the field will be denigrated as a fad.

To this end, the work on political risk thus far has been somewhat self-defeating by presenting arguments for empirical or traditional approaches that are sometimes inaccurate or simply irresponsible. Those individuals within the private sector who are candidates for such approaches may not be highly trained in social science and are sure to view such debates as indicative of insecurity or possibly insincerity. The lack of constructive debate continues to haunt the field. Claims are frequently made that one approach is clearly superior to another—almost as if the product being marketed were a box of cereal.

Numerous inaccuracies or misleading statements do little to help the cause of political risk analysis, although they might help "sell" the political risk analysis service. Several points are contradictory or simply incorrect, and are not supported by findings in the extant research on either quantitative approaches or expert judgments. While this is an extreme case, it is typical of the type of debate that haunts political risk analysis. Continuing this level of debate may guarantee political risk analysis an early death!

The objective here, however, is not to debate the accuracy of such statements, but to attempt to take an *objective* look at approaches to political risk analysis and to concentrate on the following types of issues:

- What are the dominant research approaches and methodologies in political risk analysis?
- Are these approaches most suitable, or are there more appropriate methodologies?
- Do quantitative approaches have a place in political risk analysis?
- Is a "track-record" required before a risk analysis approach is likely to be convincing?
- What are the long-term prospects for political risk analysis?

The objective of our discussion is to focus on the *research* aspects of political risk analysis. This is not a review of the literature; there are an ample number of reviews, although far too few critiques. Instead, this essay attempts to stimulate further discussion in order to promote a more critical approach to assessing the foreign political risks involved in investment and trade.

APPROACHES TO POLITICAL RISK ANALYSIS

The effort to assess the foreign political environment has taken two rather distinct approaches. The first, which we will label "traditional", entails the evaluation made by a single country expert—a competent historical analysis by a highly qualified country specialist. This specialist is likely to have considerable knowledge of the politics, culture, etc., of the given country. A small group of experts is sometimes used since it tends to contribute a more well-rounded analysis that is not quite as subject to the biases of one individual.

The second, and more "empirically" oriented approach, utilizes subjective evaluations. Country experts, not unlike the ones used in the more traditional approach, are called upon to evaluate (or rate) a country along a variety of substantive factors. These factors are predefined for the expert and are chosen to reflect factors of instability and stability. The rating system is often applied to a number of countries at once so the degree of assessed risk can be compared. Investment recommendations are, then, based on a restricted, organized set of data rather than on an overall history. There are countless examples of such an approach, and we will return to these shortly.

Before we discuss specific approaches, it is important to consider the relative strengths and weaknesses of these two general types of approaches. The use of the traditional country analysis often provides a strong, in-depth analysis of the political situation. The analysis gives an overall view to an investor who has had little experience with the country, and is also valuable to the more knowledgeable investor in that it provides an overview of the investment climate, from a political cultural perspective. Yet, a number of severe limitations and problems restrict the contribution of this approach to the overall assessment of political risk. First, the analysis is entirely dependent on the ability of one expert. If this individual changes and another of similar ability and background is not available, the new individual's framework may be considerably different, resulting in lack of comparability. It is also difficult to estimate the capability of the individual country expert without a track record. Traditional types of analyses do not tend to lend themselves to determining success and failure rates. It is also difficult to assess what impact the traditional analysis has made on the investment decision itself.

Second, the expert is not likely to be capable of evaluating, in depth, more than one country. Thus, an investor is faced with the problem of either hiring the number of experts needed to cover the countries of current or potential investment interest, or of using the services of a number of outside experts. The building of a mini-bureaucracy of country experts—a system resembling a group of State Department desk officers—appears to be an attractive alternative, particularly for the larger companies and banks. Yet the track records of larger bureaucracies, made up of country analysts, causes one to speculate as to the efficacy of such an approach. The alternative, to use outside consultants, is often costly in absolute terms, and the interaction between the firm and the individual is minimal.

Third, the country expert is not always capable of assessing a foreign political situation in precise enough terms for decision-makers. This is particularly true when political scientists with purely academic backgrounds are brought into the thick of the practical, spot-decision–filled world of the business professional. Yet a seemingly paradoxical situation also may arise when "old business hands" are brought in to consult on country risk. Their contribution to the assessment of risk may be no more attuned to present decision-makers' needs than that of the academic. In the past, it has generally been the case that the evaluator of the political environment has been a chief executive officer in the country. Although his practical background in day-to-day operations of overseas plants may have been impressive, his training in the field of political analysis is probably negligible. His understanding of political risk may therefore be confounded by an overemphasis on economic factors without a comprehensive understanding of the supports and demands of the sociopolitical system.

The use of panels of country experts has been seen as at least a partial answer to the problems of traditional analyses. Yet it is no surprise that the use of more empirical methods for the analysis of political risk have not been particularly encouraged by much of the investment community, although various quantitative means for assessing financial risk have been employed for some time. Critics have also questioned the basic validity of applying such methods to the dynamic and subjective political scene. For those considering the possibilities of employing empirical techniques, the problem of operationalization must be surmounted. What sorts of data can be collected that will facilitate indication of political risk? How can this data be organized? More precise predictions, whether expressed in probabilistic or other empirical terms, are impressive only when they improve on "traditional" methods with which many businesses feel more comfortable.

Panels of experts were seen by some as a way to "measure" political risk while at the same time avoiding "overquantification." Groups of country experts are identified, provided with a set of questions to answer, and scales on which to evaluate each country. The product is a comparative evaluation of countries along a scale, for example, from low to high investment risk. We might learn from a study that there is a higher risk in investing in Peru than there is in Brazil. It would also tell us how a country ranks on a number of different dimensions: it may be favorably evaluated on political factors but unfavorably evaluated on economic ones.

The use of subjective evaluations has been the subject of considerable debate during the last decade. Unfortunately, the debate over the use of this approach has played a less than central role in its application to political risk analysis. Subjective evaluation approaches fill a number of key gaps that inevitably appear in the attempt of researchers to analyze systematically a particular problem. They draw on a group of acknowledged experts in a field and provide an approach for aggregating their collective knowledge on a problem. They seem to provide a midpoint between totally qualitative, traditional case study orientation and a more quantitative approach. But, as will be pointed out in the following discussion, subjective evaluations, as they are currently applied, are hampered by severe problems that are likely to limit their usefulness to the overseas investor. To understand these problems, let us first briefly review a number of subjective evaluation approaches and the basic problems with each approach.

Several efforts that use subjective evaluations have received a significant amount of attention from the investment community: Assessment of Probabilities (ASPRO), developed by the Shell Oil Company; the BERI Index, developed by F. T. Haner; and the World Political Risk Forecasts developed for Frost and Sullivan by Coplin and O'Leary. (These approaches have been singled out only because they have received much attention in the political risk field.)

The Shell effort combined expert opinions collected through questionnaires. ASPRO does not force panel consensus, nor does it require respondents to provide direct quantitative probability judgments. It is used exclusively for assessing company-specific political risk. In this case, political risk is defined in terms of the specific industry risks at stake: the likelihood that a contract will or will not be maintained with a foreign country for the prescribed period of time, due to economic and/or political circumstances. Risk is assessed for only one industry, and the evaluation includes both best and worst-case scenarios. As an in-house product, ASPRO naturally has the benefit of working within the specific industrial milieu. The panel of experts still, however, must be drawn primarily from the outside, and the factors they are asked to assess are, for the most part, predetermined. Although the probabilities of various risk scenarios for a given investment are calculated, interaction between the assessment process and the investment decision-making process appears to be minimal. That is, there does not seem to be any mechanism, once the original investment strategy is weighed, for the risk assessors and the decision-makers to refine and reassess probabilities of alternative strategies. Yet it has served in the past as one of the most sophisticated in-house attempts.

Haner's BERI Index utilizes the Delphic method for assessing the overall political climate in a large number of countries. Variables that generally reflect societal conflict and political instability are aggregated into an index of political risk and are rated and then re-rated by members of a committee of analysts. Indices are constructed to represent both short- and long-term risk. Unfortunately, political climate and political risk are not necessarily synonymous. Although the index does provide a framework for cross-national comparisons of political climates, its general nature does not permit a closer scrutiny of a particular investment by a specific firm. Even with the addition of weighted criteria designed to "customize" analysis of an individual country's climate, the Index does not appear to have performed extremely well. As one of the pioneering efforts in this area, BERI has suffered the criticisms frequently leveled against new approaches and has benefited from several revisions.

Haner's index is based on a theoretical framework that may or may not be valid. In a 1979 description of his index, he draws an elaborate chart presenting causes and symptoms of political risk. Each factor can be weighted on a zero-to-seven scale to provide the capability for adjustment on a country-by-country basis. Thus, eight "causes" feed into two "symptoms." These symptoms—societal conflict and political instability—would seem to provide the ultimate indicators of risk. The link between risk and these symptoms is not described, however, except in the most general terms of "societal stress." Haner himself (1975) has pointed out that BERI cannot gauge special situations nor important factors. Because indexes are so general in nature, they have little capacity for adjustments to the specific investment. Whether they describe political climate or political risk, they cannot provide any sort of determination of the flexibility of an investment. Only knowledge of the specifics of the investor can aid in this kind of formulation.

The Frost and Sullivan service appears to incorporate yet another drawback: calculations and techniques used for the derivation of probabilities are nowhere clearly described. It is difficult to evaluate how finely tuned and timely the analysis can be without a clear presentation of such techniques. In addition, although the narrative is an attempt to relate short- and long-term trends, its infrequent revision belies its usefulness. Once again, then, the same question must be asked of their work as of all the other efforts: Can a firm have enough confidence in the output of such risk assessment services not only to subscribe to them, but to base decisions on their recommendations?

Up to this point we have discussed the major types of methods of risk analysis and very briefly referred to some of the leading examples. In many ways the pitfalls of subjective evaluations are even more important than the possible shortcomings of the specific risk assessment services. The use of subjective evaluation techniques (such as Delphi) has a number of critical shortcomings that are usually overlooked by an individual not familiar with the technique. Past research tends to indicate that respondents inadvertently make significant errors in their judgments. This conclusion is true of both the statistically sophisticated and the lay respondent and indicates that both professionals and lay persons fall victim to the same unconscious bias. In addition, errors made tend to be systematic rather than random: increasing the number of experts therefore does not lower the number of errors. The following additional errors have also been outlined in a number of works on subjective evaluation techniques:

1. Subjective data respondents tend to focus on individual cases rather than on relevant cases. This might include an overemphasizing a recent event, or series of events, that occurred in a country, instead of basing the evaluation on events over the past few years. Certainly, more recent events should be more heavily weighted than others, but in a conscious, systematic manner. An extreme case (one particular incident of violence) might make more of an impression on the expert than other, more ordinary cases. Also, an individual might focus more on specific cases where he has more intimate knowledge.

2. Respondents tend to suppress conflict. A small body of internally consistent data is often valued more highly than a larger body of less consistent data. Individuals tend to ignore the more controversial evaluation, even though they might think it is more valid, to avoid conflict.

3. Responses are often influenced by a process known as anchoring, where the first response tends to influence future responses. Evaluating a country on the low end of a scale of factors at the beginning of a questionnaire is likely to influence the rankings of later factors. The result is that later responses are influenced by the earlier, lower rankings.

4. Responses can be influenced by "hearsay" information. Opinions and experiences that have been relayed by colleagues are not necessarily accurate or inaccurate, but they are often given far greater weight than they deserve.

5. The projection of future events, if included in the analysis, often leads to a tendency toward optimism in the short range and pessimism in the long range.

6. Subjective evaluators are often not required to indicate their degree of confidence in a response. Research suggests that the less one knows, the more likely he is to be overconfident. Thus, the evaluation of a country along

a particular dimension should be interpreted according to the degree of confidence that the respondent(s) has in his evaluation.

7. Concepts being evaluated are often ambiguous to the respondent; i.e., each respondent on a panel might interpret the question or concept in a different way. The best example of such ambiguity might be the concept of stability. Depending on the way each respondent defines stability, the evaluation of a country along a dimension of unstable to stable will vary. In addition, where respondents' nationalities vary (which is likely to be the case in country risk assessments), this problem takes on even further significance.

These problems can be quite significant in their effect on the reliability of results obtained from subjective evaluations. Some of the pitfalls can be corrected by careful construction of questionnaires and scales and by informing the respondents of the problems. Nevertheless, a number of the problems, such as unconscious bias, are difficult to counterbalance and limit the reliability of the subjective evaluation approach.

Unfortunately, many of the consumers of such approaches are not well versed in the limitations of subjective evaluations. They are therefore prone to use the results in totally inappropriate ways and are likely to draw inferences the technique cannot support. Or they are likely to dismiss the value of the technique because they are not familiar enough with its strengths and weaknesses. Responsibility for the misuse of the technique must be shared by the producer and consumer alike; the producer has generally failed to explain the limitations of the approach, possibly for fear that if the limitations are explained, nobody will subscribe to the service. The consumer has, in some cases, failed to take the necessary steps to understand how the approach could be integrated into the risk assessment and decision-making process. It is not enough for a company to buy a "packaged" risk program. An accompanying educative process must inform the consumer of the full range of advantages presented by a system *and* of its limitations.

ALTERNATIVE APPROACHES TO RISK ANALYSIS

It should be evident that most of the work in risk analysis uses the judgments of experts usually chosen from a number of different fields of specialization. The use of experts as the dominant approach for the assessment of risk seems warranted: few other approaches have demonstrated enough validity and reliability to be seized upon as alternatives. This is not to suggest, however, that alternative approaches do not offer any additional information to the risk analyst, but that the use of experts should probably remain the mainstay of risk assessments.

The major issue confronting the political risk analyst is no different from the one faced by any analyst who wishes to utilize the judgments of experts: how best to tap their knowledge to produce reliable results. As has already been pointed out, a number of severe methodological handicaps can impinge on the reliability of expert judgments. There are ways to improve this reliability, but except for isolated cases, they have not been examined.

Models of Expert Judgments

We have discussed and criticized the way judgments of experts are used and analyzed to produce a "composite" of risk factors in various foreign countries. For the most part the approaches to using expert judgments have relied on methodologically unsophisticated, yet straightforward, techniques. Only in the case of a few select approaches are the judgments treated in a fashion that enhances their reliability and validity. What can be done to improve the validity of results obtained through expert judgments in a way that remains manageable and "believable?" Before a possible alternative is discussed it is necessary to elaborate on one major problem appearing throughout all research that makes use of the judgments of experts.

Research in psychology over the last 30 years has demonstrated conclusively that the human mind is capable of responding only to selective cues in the environment, usually placing overemphasis on more recent occurrences. Thus, the judgments of experts at a given point in time are never really comparable to an earlier set of the same judgments. Clinical psychologists questioned the degree to which human judgment could be used in the prediction of such variables as patient response to treatment, recidivism, or academic success. What could such judgment add to predictions that could be made on a purely statistical basis by, for example, developing linear regression models (Dawes, 1976:5–6). Dawes goes on to say:

> More recently, it has turned out that optimal statistical models are not the only ones that outperformed clinical intuition. In a business context Bowman (1967) and in psychological contexts Goldberg (1970), Dawes (1971) and Wiggins and Kohen (1971) have suggested that models based on the clinicians' judgment could outperform the clinician. That is, if a 'paramorphic' model of an expert judge can be built, there is the intriguing possibility' . . . that this model may in fact outperform the judge on which it is based. Empirical research overwhelmingly supported this bootstrapping idea . . . . The conclusion does not say a great deal for the human capability of intuitively integrating information from various sources to reach an accurate conclusion . . . the expertise of good judges lies not in integrating information but in knowing how to code the important variables.

What are "bootstrapping" models, and how can they be applied to the analysis of political risk? Models labeled "bootstrapping" extend from the basic premise that a mathematical model is only an abstraction of the process it models. The expert, regardless of his field of expertise, possesses valuable assets in terms of interpretation and judgment about the weights of variables. At the same time, he is subject to the influence of a number of factors that conspire to limit the reliability of his judgments. Goldberg (1970:423) summarizes this problem, and although he is referring to the clinician, the same problem holds true for any expert used as a "judge":

> For the clinician is not a machine. While he possesses his full share of human learning and hypothesis generating skills, he lacks a machine's

reliability. He "has his days": Boredom, fatigue, illness, situational and interpersonal distractions all plague him, with the result that his repeated judgments of the exact same stimulus configuration are not identical . . . If we could remove some of this human unreliability by eliminating the random error in his judgments, we should thereby increase the validity of the resulting predictions. The problem, then, may be reformulated: Can the clinician's judgmental unreliability be separated from his—hopefully, somewhat valid—judgmental strategy?

The objective of modeling exercises such as bootstrapping is to build the model by using the knowledge of experts to select the right variables. By selecting the variables without the input of experts, other approaches eliminate the most useful contribution of these experts; at the same time, the use of experts solely as evaluators of information enhances the unreliability of the results.

The basic approach of bootstrapping is to model the hidden cognitive process of the individual decision-maker(s). Paul Slovic (1976) describes the basic technique as one that requires the decision-maker to make "quantitative evaluations of a fairly large number of cases, each of which is defined by a number of quantified cue dimensions or characteristics." One example of this approach is the financial analyst who is asked to predict long-term price appreciations for each of 50 securities. The components of the securities that would influence appreciation, such as P/E ratios, corporate earnings growth trend, dividend yield, etc., are factored into a linear equation, and the analyst weights the various factors to reflect their relative importance. It is surprising that when the results from such linear equations are compared to the decisions made by judges without the use of any models, the models turn out as better predictors than the expert "intuitions" of the judges. The reason for this result is rather straightforward, as pointed out by Slovic (1976):

> A model captures the judge's weighting policy and applies it consistently. If there is some validity to this policy to begin with, filtering out the error via the model should increase accuracy. Of course, bootstrapping preserves and reinforces any misconceptions or biases that the judge may have. Implicit in the use of bootstrapping is the assumption that these biases will be less detrimental to performance than the inconsistencies of unaided human judgment.

How does bootstrapping relate to the problem of political risk analysis? It must first be pointed out that results from bootstrapping efforts are impressive, and the model has been applied in areas such as psychiatric and medical diagnosis, graduate school applications, financial soundness of business, judicial decisions, and roll-call votes. Still, there is no application that directly addresses the type of problem we have discussed here. This should not suggest, however, that the model is inappropriate. In fact, a strong case can be made that it combines the advantages of expert judgment approaches with a more consistent methodology for producing reliable results. The following specific factors make bootstrapping particularly applicable to the political risk analysis problem.

1. We have already pointed out that a number of problems are inherent in the use of experts. They are not usually consistent in the way they judge information, and the results obtained are usually not extremely reliable. Bootstrapping tends to remove these inconsistencies by building the model around the substantive expertise of the individual "judges." Once the model is operational, the conditions that cause variation in the reliability of expert judgment techniques are generally alleviated.

2. Turnover in experts, particularly among those within a company, cause fluctuations in the reliability of risk evaluations. Once again, because the analytic process is "institutionalized" through a bootstrapping-type model, changes in the individuals do not directly affect the reliability of results.

3. Bootstrapping makes maximum use of the experts, and psychological research convincingly demonstrates the importance of experts in the selection of variables. Dawes (1977:5) points out:

> people, especially the experts in a field—are much better at selecting and coding information than they are at integrating it . . . people are important. The statistical model may integrate the information in an optimal manner, but it is always the individual . . . who chooses variables . . . it is the human judge who knows the directional relationship between the predictor variables and the criterion of interest, or who can code the variables in such a way that they have clear directional relationship.

4. A final, but crucial, consideration is the role of outside consultants in evaluating risk. Models such as bootstrapping provide an approach to combining the knowledge of outside experts with the knowledge of individuals inside the company. Once the model is established the use of outside experts is no longer necessary, except to update the model periodically to include new variables. Thus, the outside consultant plays the "true" consultant role and does not force his own biases on the investment decision.

It is unfortunate that no examples of bootstrapping applications are highly relevant to the political risk problem. Nevertheless, one study by Hammond and Adelman (1976), cited by Dawes (1977), is worth summarizing to illustrate the dimensions that bootstrapping might encompass in the risk analysis field. The Hammond and Adelman study concerned the decision faced by the Denver City Police concerning the type of bullet to be used. Generally referred to as the round-nosed vs. hollow-nosed bullet controversy, it has been repeated in a number of police departments around the United States. The controversy basically revolved around the physical effects of the bullets and the social policy implications. Dawes points out:

> the disputants focused on evaluating the merits of specific bullets—confounding the physical effect of the bullets with social policy implications. That is, rather than separating questions of what it is that the bullet should accomplish from questions concerning ballistic characteristics of specific bullets, advocates merely argued for one bullet or another.

In other words, experts on social policy were evaluating ballistic characteristics, and ballistic experts were evaluating social policy considerations. Hammond and Adelman were able to elicit, from the respective experts, both the policy dimensions and the ratings of ballistic characteristics. Three dimensions appeared to be most significant: stopping effectivenesses, probability of serious injury, and probability of harm to bystanders. Dawes (1977:16–17) summarizes the remaining stages of the effort:

> When the ballistic experts rated the bullets with respect to these dimensions, it turned out that the last two were almost perfectly confounded, but they were not perfectly confounded with the first. Bullets do not vary along a single dimension that confounds effectiveness with lethalness. (Apparently, the probability of serious injury or harm to bystanders is highly related to the penetration of the bullet, while the probability of its effectively stopping someone from returning fire is highly related to the width of the entry wound). Since policy makers could not agree about the weights given to the three dimensions, Hammond and Adelman suggested that they be weighted equally. Combining the equal weights with the (independent) judgments of the ballistics experts, Hammond and Adelman discovered a bullet that "has greater stopping effectiveness and is less apt to cause injury (and is less apt to threaten bystanders) than the standard bullet then in use by the DPD."

The Hammond and Adelman study helps demonstrate the advantages of bootstrapping models by presenting evidence (consistent with all other bootstrapping models) that experts are best used in the identification of key variables and not necessarily in the combination of those variables. The approach is also useful because it provides a way to identify variables that might be overlooked in less systematic analyses or whose value might be overemphasized. In the Hammond and Adelman effort, some of the obvious relationships between policy and ballistics variables were never delineated due to the absence of a systematic effort to identify the variables themselves.

BOOTSTRAPPING FOR POLITICAL RISK ANALYSIS

A bootstrap model constructed in a practical, political risk analysis environment will undoubtedly improve on current methods of risk assessment. Studies that compare intuitive (i.e., unaided or clinical) expert judgments on multidimensional problems, such as risk assessment, to judgments based on bootstrap models have found, with no exceptions, that the bootstrap models improve upon the intuitive methods. Because these models depend on operationalized inputs and explicit rules for combining variables, they will lead in the risk assessment case to a more disciplined set of political risk models, which should increase precision and prediction power.

While we are not yet able to provide an actual example of bootstrapping, since this would require the active participation of investment experts, we can present the basic steps to be implemented to build such a model for the assessment of political risk.

1. Selection of Experts. First identify those individuals in any organization who normally participate in the foreign investment decision-making process. Regardless of how they are assessed, individuals from within an organization have developed some expertise in assessing foreign investment climates. The bootstrapping approach will systematically tap this expertise. No minimum number of experts is required to develop this approach, but it should include those individuals who are considered to have developed expertise and/or who have previously participated in foreign investment decisions. In addition to these in-house experts, add outside "substantive" specialists (e.g., area experts, product experts, etc.) to ensure comprehensive analyses of an investment problem.

2. Define Investment Risk. One criticism of existing risk assessment approaches is that they generally do not consider the different investment objectives of each investor. The evaluation of investment risk ("what is at stake") is closely tied to the determination of the parameters of a good (acceptable) investment. Some investors might define this as a specific rate of return on an investment; others might use a measure of productivity. Investors, if they are moving into new foreign investment ventures, might be willing to accept lower returns if they will lead to successful investments in the future. Thus, there are likely to be different definitions of the objectives involved in a particular investment decision, depending upon the nature of the investment, the country involved and the particular objectives of the investor. No set of political risk factors can be reliably generated independently of a definition of these objectives.

This definition of an investor's objectives provides the model with its dependent variable—one we call investment risk. By defining the objectives of a particular investment, the investor has also defined what is acceptable and, in turn, what is unacceptable. A bank's decision to lend money to a foreign government, for example, is most likely to be based on the expectation of repayment. The investment risk, to that bank, is some definition of the parameters of repayment—how many years, likelihood of extension of repayment time, etc. The task of this step is to define carefully what the bank considers an acceptable final outcome of the loan and what would be the minimum acceptable outcome from an investment standpoint.

The individuals identified in step one will independently define the investment objectives. It is entirely possible that these individuals will define objectives somewhat differently. Therefore, an integral part of this step is to confront the individuals with variations in their definitions so that a consensus can be attained on a single or coherent set of definitions. Once this consensus is achieved, approaches to measuring the investment risk (e.g. specific rate of return, level of productivity, etc.) will be identified.

3. Determine Relationship between Risk Factors and Investment Risk. After defining the relevant dimensions of investment risk, the experts provide their verbal impressions of the relationships between political risk factors and those dimensions. For example, what factors could occur that would affect

productivity? (i.e. labor unrest). This step attempts to specify in a systematic fashion the expert's baseline model of the causes and stages of investment risk.

An oversimplified example may clarify these first steps. Suppose an expert from a company involved in making a decision to build a factory in a foreign country identifies a relationship between labor unrest and the loss of productivity (productivity having been identified as a major investment risk). This labor unrest is generated by a loss of popular support for the current regime. Loss of support is, in turn, a result of a number of economic factors such as high inflation, increasing rates of population growth, etc. Figure 9.1 is a model for this hypothetical expert.

Step 2 separated the concept of investment risk into elements; for this expert, loss of productivity was the primary investment risk. Step 3 generates a model that specifies the causes and stages of changes in productivity. This step can also expand an expert's model. When confronted with this basic model, the expert is likely, in subsequent iterations, to modify the relationships. In addition, the outside substantive expert is likely to suggest modifications in the model.

4. Measurement. The development of a set of baseline models leads to the testing of the relationships specified by the experts. The first three steps have yielded lists of variables that relate political factors (which include social and economic) to various types of investment risk. These models must be tested against historical data (i.e. for the past five to ten years) for the country under investigation to determine how "valid" the relationships are for postdicting (predicting past events). At the end of this step, whose initial results are obtained based on the country's past performance, the initial bootstrap model is produced. By returning to the experts and exposing them to each other's models and variables and the tests against historical data, the models are clarified, refined, and possibly expanded.

5. Prediction. Taking these models from Step 4, three types of prediction scenarios are created. First, taking ranges of future values for variables in the models (such as projecting economic growth over the next several years), experts are asked to estimate the effects on investment risks. For example, the experts would estimate the levels of productivity that would result from changes in the variables in their models. Statistical analyses then examine the relationship between the variables and the experts' predictions of investment

Figure 9.1   A Hypothetical Model

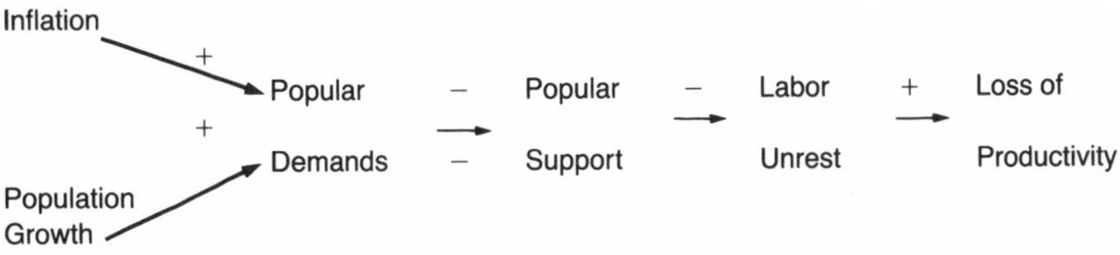

risk. These resulting "prediction bootstrap models" summarize the relations between the political factors and investment risk. A second procedure is to provide experts with a variety of future scenarios described along the various dimensions of investment risk and to ask them to estimate what variables produced each scenario. In the first exercise, the experts predict investment risk from different hypothetical levels of variables; in the second exercise, they estimate the values of variables from different hypothetical levels of investment risk.

A third possible scenario is to review actual past investment decisions made by the investor and to test their success or failure against the bootstrap models; in other words, to ask whether these models would have helped in the assessment of past investment decisions.

6. Refinements. The last step is to expose any differences between in-house and outside experts' models and to attempt to resolve them. By the end of this step, several products have been developed that contribute significantly to the systematic assessment of political risk:

- The procedure has produced a set of models that relate key variables to those kinds of investment risk which are meaningful to the particular investor.
- We have explicit information on future scenarios of investment risk in countries of interest to the investor.
- The consensus and dissension among experts have been explored.
- Specific indications of where information is lacking and where uncertainty is greatest have been exposed.

Most of all, the bootstrapping approach develops a model that is meaningful to each particular investor where the variables are carefully and systematically specified for each investment climate. It is a proven approach, which, in a field dominated by subjective and impressionistic evaluations, demands further attention.

REFERENCES

Bowman, E. H. 1967. "Consistency and Optimality in Managerial Decision Making." *Management Science* 9: 310–21.

Dawes, R. M. 1971. "A Case Study of Graduate Admissions: Application of Three Principles of Human Decision Making." *American Psychologist* 26: 180–88.

———. 1976. "Shallow Psychology." In J. Carrol and J. Payne, eds., *Cognition and Social Behavior*. Hillsdale, N.J.: Lawrence Erlbaum Assoc.

———. 1977. "The Robust Beauty of Improper Linear Models in Decision Making." Address to American Psychological Association. August, San Francisco, California.

Goldberg, L. R. 1970. "Man Versus Model of Man: A Rationale, Plus Some Evidence for Improving on Clinical Inferences." *Psychological Bulletin* 73, no. 6: 411–32.

Hammond, K. R., and L. Adelman. 1976. "Science Values and Human Judgment." *Science* 194: 389–96.

Haner, F. 1975. "On Measuring Political Risk." Unpublished paper.

Slovic, P. 1976. "Cognitive Processes and Societal Risk Taking." In J. S. Carroll and J. W. Payne, eds., *Cognition and Social Behavior*. Potomac, Md.: Lawrence Erlbaum Assoc.

Wiggins, N., and E. S. Kohen. 1971. "Man vs. Model of Man Revisited: The Forecasting of Graduate School Success." *Journal of Personality and Social Psychology* 19: 100–106.

chapter ten

The Frost and Sullivan Method: Applying the "Prince"

William Coplin
Michael O'Leary

This chapter will introduce the Coplin and O'Leary approach for the country studies published by Frost and Sullivan's Political Risk Service, which provides risk forecasts on 85 countries to its clients. One product of the system is a country study that provides information on the background factors and political actors determining risks to international business. It also contains three regime scenarios for the 18-month and five-year forecasts and what those scenarios will mean for political turmoil, restrictions on international business, trade policy, and economic policy. The majority of the report is narrative, but indicators are used for a risk rating score, for presenting the political structure operating within the system, and for economic background.

The approach involves using a 60-page questionnaire in which three or more country specialists write and review a country study. The degree of agreement and disagreement among the specialists is noted in the report, and a synthesis of the viewpoints is presented. The material contained in this chapter describes the basic questions asked our specialists for the 18-month section of the report, the Prince political forecasting model that is employed for the 18-month forecasts, and the procedure for calculating the 18-month risk indicators.

GUIDELINES FOR PREPARING THE NARRATIVE FOR THE 18-MONTH FORECAST

In preparing the 60-page narrative for our country reports, each item in the outline is placed at the top of a page, and the specialists are asked to discuss the major points raised by the question for the country which they are analyzing. The guidelines are listed below in outline form.

I. Background
    A. Discuss background factors that have *the most significant impact* on the way the political system works:
        1. Geographic factors, including (as appropriate) location, natural resources, topography.

    2. International political factors (such as relationships with neighbors and others in its region), involvement in major power conflicts, territorial disputes, alliances.

    3. Social problems, including (as appropriate) ethnic or racial conflict, inequality, regional differences, urban-rural conflict.

    4. Economic problems, including (as appropriate) growth, inflation, unemployment, international finance and trade.

B. Indicate the degree to which background factors such as economic performance, social conditions, or international events might affect the support for, and opposition to, this regime, and the likelihood of this regime being in power eighteen months from now.

C. Discuss the second most likely regime at the end of the next eighteen months. Describe under what conditions it might come into power. Indicate whether this regime will lead to major shifts in policies or will have a minor impact.

D. Discuss the third most likely regime. Make sure it is substantially different from the other two. Describe under what conditions it might come into power. Indicate whether this regime will lead to major shifts in policies or will have a minor impact.

II. Political Turmoil

This section forecasts the types and magnitude of politically motivated violence in the next eighteen months. Political turmoil includes general strikes, demonstrations, riots, terrorism, guerrilla activities, and civil and international war.

A. Describe the recent pattern of political turmoil and how it has affected society. Include both domestic and international sources of violence.

B. Forecast the magnitude and type of turmoil likely to occur over the next eighteen months under the most likely regime. Describe the actors and their capability to cause or deter turmoil. Discuss the impact of turmoil, including 1) the direct impact in which international interests serve as a target of turmoil, and 2) the indirect impact from disruptions in communications, transportation, labor supply, economic stability, and capital flight.

C. Forecast of turmoil under the second most likely regime.

D. Forecast of turmoil under the third most likely regime.

III. Restrictions on International Business

This section forecasts the likelihood that in the next eighteen months the government will change restrictions on the operations of international business through restrictions on ownership, management, labor policies, local operations, and the repatriation of profit or capital.

A. Describe the configuration of key political actors respecting general support for, or opposition to, restrictions on international business under the most likely regime. Also indicate what changes in the political configuration might occur under the second and third alternatives described in the regime stability section. Discuss other factors, such as economic changes or international conflict, which might alter the present configuration.

B. Forecasts of changes in restrictions:

    I. Restrictions on foreign equity ownership

        a. Current levels?

        b. Future policy under most likely regime?

        c. Future policy under second most likely?

        d. Future policy under third most likely?

    2. Requirements for personnel and procurement
       a. Current informal and formal restrictions on procurement, on using expatriates for management, labor, other?
       b. Future policy under most likely regime?
       c. Future policy under second most likely?
       d. Future policy under third most likely?
    3. Taxation discrimination
       a. Taxation discrimination for and against foreign business
       b. Future policy under most likely regime?
       c. Future policy under second most likely?
       d. Future policy under third most likely?
    4. Restriction on repatriation of capital and profits
       a. Current restrictions?
       b. Future policy under most likely regime?
       c. Future policy under second most likely?
       d. Future policy under third most likely?
    5. Exchange controls
       a. Current policy?
       b. Future policy under most likely regime?
       c. Future policy under second most likely?
       d. Future policy under third most likely?

IV. Trade Policies

This section forecasts the likelihood that in the next eighteen months the government will significantly change policies restricting imports.
    A. Describe the configuration of key political actors on the policies restricting imports under the most likely regime. Indicate what changes in support or opposition to existing policies might occur under the other two alternatives discussed in the regime stability section. Discuss what other conditions, such as current accounts difficulties, might alter the present configuration.
    B. Forecasts of changes in tariffs and non-tariff barriers:
       1. Tariffs
         a. Current levels?
         b. Future policy under most likely regime?
         c. Future policy under second most likely?
         d. Future policy under third most likely?
       2. Non-tariff barriers
         a. Current levels?
         b. Future policy under most likely regime?
         c. Future policy under second most likely?
         d. Future policy under third most likely?

V. Economic Policies
    A. Fiscal and monetary policy—Describe current government fiscal and monetary policies with respect to deficit spending, control over credit, and other stimulants to economic growth and limitations on inflation:
       1. Future policy under most likely regime?
       2. Future policy under second most likely regime?
       3. Future policy under third most likely regime?
    B. Labor Policy—Describe policies that directly and indirectly affect labor costs. Such policies include, but are not limited to, minimum wage legisla-

tion, benefit requirements, and constraints on the power of labor organizations:
1. Future policy under most likely regime?
2. Future policy under second most likely regime?
3. Future policy under third most likely regime?
C. Policies toward international finance—Describe the current policies of the government with respect to obtaining short-term and long-term capital from external sources. Include policies toward international financial institutions (such as the IMF and the World Bank), private sources, and other special sources (such as foreign aid):
1. Future policy under most likely regime?
2. Future policy under second most likely regime?
3. Future policy under third most likely regime?

POLITICAL FORECASTS THROUGH THE PRINCE SYSTEM

In addition to providing the narrative to conform to the outline presented above, the country specialists are also asked to complete what we dub Prince charts on regime change, political turmoil, restrictions on international business and restrictions on trade. A general, political forecasting model that can be applied to any collective action, the Prince Model has evolved over many years of refinement and application. It is useful in a wide variety of political situations, and is one of the few approaches to political forecasting that is both systematic and relevant to decision-makers. The model provides a means for the rigorous analysis of information, producing calculations that result in forecasts of the probability of specific political outcomes. At the same time, it uses the invaluable and unique expertise of specialists—both to supply information for the model and to adjust the calculations produced by the model according to qualitative, subjective knowledge about a given country.

The Prince Model has also been applied to areas other than political risk analysis by Coplin and O'Leary. In 1972, it assisted the Intelligence and Research Bureau of the Department of State in forecasting the probability of a successful agreement between North and South Korea concerning an agenda of outstanding issues. The model assisted the U. S. Army Corps of Engineers in estimating the likelihood of decisions affecting wetlands regulatory policy in the mid-1970s. More recently, it aided the Central Intelligence Agency in estimating the probable position of 52 countries on various issues at the 1979 World Administrative Radio Conference. The model has also been used by several local government agencies in forecasting political events.

Prince Charts

To obtain information for a country forecast, the first step in using the Prince Model is to conduct a survey of the team of expert analysts (at least three for each country). Each team member answers a questionnaire that includes several "Prince Charts," which are used to record the positions of major individuals, groups, and institutions on a particular action that could affect international business in the country. In completing the charts, experts are first asked to list at least seven actors that are able to influence each action during the next eighteen months. The actors selected may be individuals, groups or ministries within the government, opponents of the government, or groups in the society, such as business, unions, or ethnic organizations. Actors may also include foreign individuals or institutions, such as the International Monetary Fund or other governments.

The experts then indicate on the Prince Chart their estimates of the position of each actor listed, according to the following four categories:

1. <u>Orientation</u>—the current general attitude of the actor toward the action. The actor's orientation is classified into one of three categories: Support (S), Neutrality (N), or Opposition (O).

2. <u>Certainty</u>—the firmness of the actor's orientation. For group actors, certainty is a function of the extent to which there is consensus among the actor's membership in supporting or opposing the action. Certainty is measured on a scale ranging from 1 (little or no certainty) to 5 (extremely high certainty).

3. <u>Power</u>—the degree to which the actor can exert influence, directly or indirectly, in support of or in opposition to the action relative to all other actors. The bases of an actor's power, as well as the ways in which this power may be exercised, are varied. Power may be based on such factors as group size, wealth, physical resources, institutional authority, prestige, and political skill. Power is measured on a scale ranging from 1 (little or no power) to 5 (extremely high power).

4. <u>Salience</u>—the importance the actor attached to supporting or opposing the action relative to all other actions with which that actor is concerned. Salience is measured on a scale ranging from 1 (little or no importance) to 5 (extremely high importance).

The Prince Charts obtained from each of the team members are analyzed to measure the degree of consensus among the experts. If the team members differ significantly on estimates of an actor's position, additional information is sought. After obtaining a clear consensus among the experts, the individual charts are combined into a single set of estimates.

Decision Structure Charts

The information in the Prince Chart, which represents a consensus of experts' estimates, is used to create a Decision Structure Chart for each risk factor. Decision Structure Charts visually portray the forces supporting and opposing each factor, presenting an overall picture of the probable action concerning the factor. (See Figure 10.1.)

On the chart, each actor is placed along the vertical axis according to whether it supports, is neutral toward, or opposes the action, and by the certainty of the actor's support or opposition. The actors are located along the horizontal axis according to their importance in determining the outcome of a decision as measured by their power (ability to influence the decision)

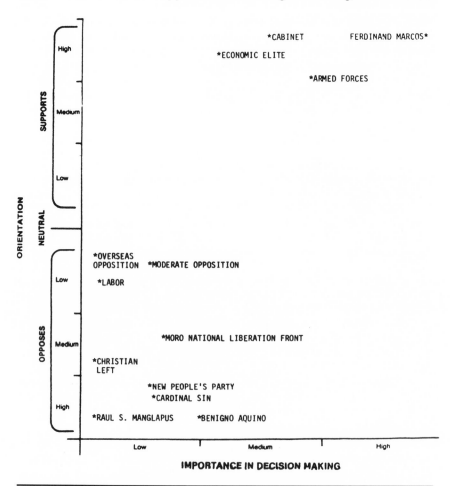

Figure 10.1   Decision Structure

and salience (the likelihood that an actor will use its power to influence the decision). Thus, the position of the actors in relation to the two axes indicates their roles in determining the action.

Actors located in the upper-right corner of the chart are those that exert the maximum weight in support of the action. Actors in the lower-right corner of the chart are those that exert the maximum weight against the action. Actors located in the middle of the vertical axis are either undecided or likely to shift positions. Actors located in the upper left are strong supporters of the action, but carry little weight in determining its outcome. Actors in the lower left are opponents with little influence. The chart was compiled before the assassination of Benigno Aquino.

In our Decision Structure Chart based on the Prince Chart for the Philippines there are significant differences among the actors in the Philippines concerning a regime change. One extreme position is that of Ferdinand Marcos, located in the upper-right corner of the Decision Structure Chart, not only adamantly in support of his regime but also having the capability to exert maximum weight to support his orientation. A different extreme position is that of Raul S. Manglapus, located in the lower-left corner of the Decision Structure Chart, who is opposed to the regime yet with little ability to bring about change.

The political analysis underlying the forecasts can best be understood by examining the Decision Structure Chart in conjunction with the narrative analysis provided for each estimate. The narrative appearing with the chart describes the factors underlying the positions and the importance of the actors, possible coalition changes, other actors that may become important, and the impact of the changes on international business.

While each Decision Structure Chart is unique in many respects, certain general patterns frequently appear. Each chart presents patterns of actor distributions that indicate quite different interpretations of the forecasts about the outcome. A summary analysis is always provided with each chart.

Probability Calculations

The estimates of the probability of the occurrence of an action in the next eighteen months come from the country specialists' analyses of the actors' positions. Each actor is assigned a total score in each Prince Chart. This "Prince Score" is the product of the firmness of the actor's orientation to the action (certainty), the actor's ability to influence the outcome of the action (power), and the importance of the action to the actor (salience). The score has a positive sign if the actor supports the action and a negative sign if the actor opposes the action.

In our actor-by-actor scoring for the Marcos regime (see Figure 10.2), we find that the major opponent of the regime, Benigno Aquino, is assigned a total of -50, while Ferdinand Marcos is assigned a total score of $+125$. These scores reflect the actors' opposition or support for the regime and also their respective importance in either opposing or supporting the regime. This Prince Chart indicates that Ferdinand Marcos's ability to support his regime is stronger than Benigno Aquino's ability to help bring about a regime change.

The chart also shows the large number of opponents of the Marcos regime. The ability of these opponents, each relatively weak, to coalesce and increase their strength is what constitutes a danger to the regime. The text accompanying the probability forecast discusses the factors that might result in such coalitions.

The Prince Chart numbers provide the basis of a formal estimate of the probability of an action's occurrence. This probability is defined as ΣW_s divided by ΣW_t. W_s is each of the positive Prince Scores. W_t is the absolute value (ignoring the minus signs) of each actor's Prince Score. To arrive at a probability score for an action, the absolute values of all the actor scores are added to produce a number representing the total weight in the political

CURRENT ESTIMATES

ORIENTATION   CERTAINTY, POWER, SALIENCE

✦ Supports	1 Little/None	4 High
O Neutral	2 Slight	5 Extremely High
— Opposes	3 Moderate	

ACTOR	ORIENTATION	CERTAINTY	POWER	SALIENCE	PRINCE SCORE
Benigno Aquino	—	x 5	x 2	x 5 :	—50
Armed Forces	+	x 4	x 3	x 4 :	+48
Cardinal Sin	—	x 5	x 1	x 5 :	—25
Christian Left	—	x 5	x 1	x 3 :	—15
Economic Elite	+	x 4	x 3	x 2 :	+24
Moderate Opposition	—	x 2	x 2	x 3 :	—12
Labor	—	x 3	x 1	x 3 :	—9
Raul S. Manglapus	—	x 5	x 1	x 3 :	—15
Ferdinand Marcos	+	x 5	x 5	x 5 :	+125
Moro National Liberation Front	—	x 3	x 2	x 2 :	—12
New People's Army	—	x 5	x 2	x 2 :	—20
Cabinet	+	x 5	x 2	x 4 :	+40
Overseas Opposition	—	x 2	x 1	x 3 =	—6

Figure 10.2   Prince Chart. The Continuation of the Marcos Regime (June 1, 1980)

system that could influence the action's occurrence (ΣW_i). This number is divided into the sum of the positive scores, which represents the total weight in support of the action (ΣW_s). The resulting fraction is the probability score. The greater the weight of actors supporting an action relative to all weight in the system (as defined by the Prince Chart), the higher the probability of the action's occurrence.

If an actor is neutral toward the action, his potential score (the product of power, salience, and certainty) is added to the sum of the absolute values of all the other scores (the denominator in the probability equation, ΣW_t). Half of the neutral actor's score is added to the sum of the scores in support of the action (the numerator in the probability equation, ΣW_s). Adding only half the neutral actor's score to the numerator is based on the assumption that there is an even chance that the actor will eventually either support or oppose the action.

In the Philippine example, the total weight in the political system affecting the support for the regime was 401. This is the denominator in the probability equation. The numerator, the sum of the positive actor scores, was 237. The quotient, the probability of the Marcos regime's remaining in power for the next eighteen months (following June 1980) was 59 percent. As will be described in the next section, the model can be applied to forecasting the likelihood of regime stability, political turmoil, restrictions on international business, and trade restrictions.

Using the Prince Model

The Prince Model is applied in several ways throughout the Country Reports. A Decision Structure Chart is also included in that section. Furthermore, Decision Structure Charts on political turmoil, restrictions on international business, and trade restrictions appear in the report's respective sections. Finally, the probabilities calculated according to the Prince Model appear on the page introducing the political actors. That page summarizes the influence of each actor on the three conditions by reporting both the actors' Prince Scores and the resulting probability calculation.

Because the Prince Model is generic, it can be applied as a framework for analyzing other political decisions that may affect a business project. Some users of Frost and Sullivan Country Reports have their field staff complete Prince Charts, either for routine monitoring or for analyzing specific decisions. In addition to being used by individual analysts to complete a Prince analysis on their own, the Prince framework can be used in planning or decision meetings in which members of the group share their knowledge about political conditions.

CALCULATING RISK RATINGS

In addition to using the narrative and the forecasts to inform their assessment of political risks for their company, our clients also require a standardized measure of risk that can be used for general cross-national comparison. These measures or risk ratings greatly simplify the results of the political risk analysis, but they are important because they force the analysts to standardize their conclusions so that others can judge the relative riskiness of various countries. Many of the schemes ask analysts to rate countries on a series of numerical scales (e.g., 1 to 10), and a single score is determined by taking the average of the ratings. This approach ignores essential complexities and should be used only as a last resort in most cases.

The scheme presented below was developed by the authors of this package for Frost and Sullivan's Country Reports. In the discussion, we will present the calculation procedure that takes the information from a country study and produces a letter grade for countries that ranges from A+ to D− for three categories of risk—financial, manufacturing and extractive and export.

Meaning of the Risk Indicators

Before looking at the calculation procedures, let's examine the meaning of the risk indicators. Table 10.1 briefly describes the ratings and business sectors or categories of risk.

Table 10.1   Description of Risk Ratings for Three Business Sectors

Future Conditions and Policies

Risk rating	Finance	Direct investment	Export
A+,A,A−	Favorable attitude to international business. No restrictions on exchange and payments. Prudent international financial policy.	Stable country. Favorable attitude, especially with respect to equity, loan participation, and taxes. Restraint in fiscal and labor policy.	Stable country. Tariff and other barriers to trade and payments are minimal. Prudent international borrowing policy.
B+,B,B−	Generally favorable attitude, but some selected restraints on currency flows.	Limited but possibly dangerous turmoil or moderate restrictions on business activity. Modest increase in labor cost and power.	Limited but selectively dangerous turmoil or policies restricting trade and payments.
C+,C,C−	Widespread (but restrained) pressures for restrictions on international business. Financial policies leading to questionable international debt.	Moderate to high turmoil, creating security problems. Policies focus on special controls on equity, repatriation, or other controls on foreign business. Labor policies leading to escalating labor costs.	Sufficiently high turmoil to create risks to delivery or payment. Policies restrict or increase the cost and difficulty of trade and payments. International financial policy causing declines in currency value.
D+,D,D−	Widespread hostility to foreign business. Tight controls on international payments and other transactions. Financial policies leading to excessive international debt.	Turmoil presents serious security concerns. Foreign business a handy scapegoat in politics. Severe (though sometimes inconsistent) restrictions on all phases of business operations.	Turmoil creates serious problems for the fulfillment of contracts. Inconsistent and restricted payment. Currency fluctuates widely as a result of international finance policies.

The *Finance* category weighs government actions affecting the flow of money in and out of the country. It encompasses risks that result from poor economic conditions, in which foreign debt and currency weakness may affect the ability of the government or local businesses to pay debts in a timely fashion. This ranking summarizes the information of greatest interest to banking clients and to related companies, such as insurance and investment. Finance officers for all types of businesses also find this category highly relevant.

The *Direct Investment* category weighs government actions that affect the supply of materials and labor as well as the control of equity, capital, profit, and operations. It deals with a wider range of risks than the Finance category and is of most interest to clients who have current or planned overseas facilities.

The *Export* category weighs government actions affecting exports to the country. It deals with trade restrictions and factors affecting payment. Marketing and credit managers within exporting companies are the users who typically are most interested in this category.

It should be emphasized that the ratings apply to the sector in a general way; specific businesses even in the same sector may have different risks that would require the adjustment of the ratings. The rating of A, B, C, or D is provided to allow the reader to quickly see the overall conclusion of the country report as it pertains to the general categories of risks pertaining to each sector.

Calculating Risk Indicators

The letter grades are determined by taking the results of a country study and applying them to a worksheet. Table 10.2 and Figure 10.3 provide examples of part of the summary of a study on Nigeria completed in February 1982.

Table 10.2   Summary of 18-Month Forecast

Risk Ratings by Sector: Finance, C+   Manufacturing/Extractive, C   Export, C+
Risk Factors under Three Most Likely Regimes (with Each Regime's Likelihood)

	Current level	Shagari stays (80%)	UPN regime under Awolowo (10%)	Military takeover (10%)
Political turmoil	Moderate	Same	MORE	MUCH MORE
Restrictions on international business:				
I. Equity	Moderate	Same	MORE	MORE
II. Personnel/Procurement	High	Same	MORE	MUCH MORE
III. Taxation discrimination	Moderate	MORE	MORE	MORE
IV. Repatriation	Moderate	MORE	MORE	MORE
V. Exchange controls	High	MORE	MUCH MORE	MUCH MORE
Trade Policy:				
I. Tariffs	Moderate	Same	Same	MUCH MORE
II. Non-tariff barriers	High	Same	LESS	Same
Economic Policy:				
I. Fiscal/Monetary Expansion	Moderate	Same	Same	Same
II. Labor cost expansion	Moderate	Same	MORE	LESS
III. International Borrowing	Moderate	Same	LESS	Same

<u>NIGERIA</u>   <u>1/15/82</u>   <u>A.H.</u>
Country   Date   Person

Eighteen-Month Calculation

Variable	Calculation Process	Score	Finance	Man'f./ Extract	Export
1. Political Turmoil Probability	$\underline{1}$ + $\underline{0}$ (.80)+ $\underline{2}$ (.10)+ $\underline{3}$ (.10) =	1.5		1.5	1.5
2. Equity Restrictions	$\underline{1}$ + $\underline{0}$ (.80)+ $\underline{1}$ (.10)+ $\underline{1}$ (.10) =	1.2		1.2	
3. Personnel/Procure-ment	$\underline{2}$ + $\underline{0}$ (.80)+ $\underline{1}$ (.10)+ $\underline{2}$ (.10) =	2.3		2.3	
4. Taxation Discrimination	$\underline{1}$ + $\underline{1}$ (.80)+ $\underline{1}$ (.10)+ $\underline{1}$ (.10) =	2.0		2.0	
5. Repatriation Restrictions	$\underline{1}$ + $\underline{1}$ (.80)+ $\underline{1}$ (.10)+ $\underline{1}$ (.10) =	2.0		2.0	
6. Exchange Controls	$\underline{2}$ + $\underline{1}$ (.80)+ $\underline{2}$ (.10)+ $\underline{2}$ (.10) =	3.2	3.2	3.2	3.2
7. Tariffs	$\underline{1}$ + $\underline{0}$ (.80)+ $\underline{0}$ (.10)+ $\underline{2}$ (.10) =	1.2			1.2
8. Non-Tariff Barriers	$\underline{2}$ + $\underline{0}$ (.80)+ $\underline{-1}$ (.10)+ $\underline{0}$ (.10) =	1.9			1.9
9. Fiscal/Monetary Expansion	$\underline{1}$ + $\underline{0}$ (.80)+ $\underline{0}$ (.10)+ $\underline{0}$ (.10) =	1.0	1.0		
10. Labor Cost Expansion	$\underline{1}$ + $\underline{0}$ (.80)+ $\underline{1}$ (.10)+ $\underline{-1}$ (.10) =	1.0		1.0	
11. International Borrowing	$\underline{1}$ + $\underline{0}$ (.80)+ $\underline{-1}$ (.10)+ $\underline{0}$ (.10) =	.9	.9		.9
	TOTAL		5.1	13.2	8.7
	MEAN		1.7	1.89	1.74

Notes

1. Place current level in first blank and scale: Low=0; Moderate=1; High=2; Very High=3.

2. Scale forecast change in next three blanks so that Less=-1; Same=0; Slightly More=.5; More=1; Much More=2.

3. Parentheses contain probability of each of the three regimes.

4. Letter rank scaled as follows from numerical score:
0.00-25=A+	.76-1.00=B+	1.51-1.75=C+	2.26-2.50=D+
.26-.50=A	1.01-1.25=B	1.76-2.00=C	2.51-2.75=D
.51-.75=A-	1.26-1.50=B-	2.01-2.25=C-	2.76-3.00=D-

Figure 10.3. Worksheet for Calculations

part four

FINANCIAL STRUCTURING AGAINST RISK AND POLITICAL RISK INSURANCE

chapter eleven

Managing Financial Risk: Assessing Devaluation, Foreign Exchange Controls, and Debt Repayment

Fariborz Ghadar

It is becoming increasingly clear that in an era of political and economic instability, those who do business in developing countries must exercise unusual prudence and foresight. Successful risk management is a necessity in a world of rapid and complex change. The variety of difficulties met by international banking institutions, multinational corporations, and those corporations that insure overseas investments has been well documented; their struggles to extricate themselves from their problems have been complicated, costly, and only partially successful. Although the management of these firms has recognized for some time the need to put risk management on more than an ad hoc basis, there has been little agreement—and not enough discussion—about *how* to do it. Clearly, successful risk management depends upon good judgment and excellent information—keen practical insight, in short, into the variables that affect risk. But where, exactly, does such insight come from? What kind of information is relevant to risk assessment and what is to be done with it? This chapter poses some specific answers.

Financial risk involves such phenomena as devaluation, inconvertibility, rescheduling of external debt, cross-default, and deposit blockages. Roughly speaking, political risks can be said to be liabilities to changes brought about by political (ideological) motivation, whereas financial risks are liabilities to economically (nonideological) motivated changes. We need to manage financial risks to prevent them from deterring us from pursuing profitable and reasonably secure investment opportunities in developing nations. First we will consider the range, complexity, and the parameters of financial risk in order to learn how to define, quantify, interrelate, and manage those risks.

The financial risk management problems faced by multinational corporations can be thought of as a complex matrix of key, interrelated variables. For example, any corporation with assets and liabilities as well as cash flow surpluses and deficits in various currencies will face problems presented by foreign exchange rates. While any effective interest rate may be considered as the nominal yield plus foreign exchange gains or losses—the net effective yield related to the base currency interest rate, purchase power parity states that the forward premium of the currency should bring the net effective interest differential on many currencies to zero. Nevertheless, in imperfect markets like those found in developing countries, where the parent corporation or its subsidiaries do not have access to domestic and external markets in the same manner, the net effective yields on individual currencies will vary. Local interest rates combine a real rate and an anticipated inflation rate. Relative inflation, as compared to the rest of the world, may eventually result in the depreciation of the currency, but there may be no simple correlation between relative inflation and depreciation in each time period. Financial risk in such a context obviously involves a complex assessment.

We can, however, isolate three major types of exposure experienced by multinationals where foreign exchange risks are a factor: transaction exposure, translation exposure, and economic exposure. *Transaction exposure* exists when cash flows require conversion in the exchange market. *Translation exposure* occurs when net assets in the balance sheet are translated at current rates or at varying historic rates. *Economic exposure* is the impact of exchange fluctuations on a company's future operational cash flow. A firm may adjust to these exposures by means of the structure of its relationships with suppliers, customers, or other members of the corporate group. The company may also counteract exposure by hedging in the forward or money markets. For example, when there is an expected foreign exchange loss, the company may achieve a balanced position or even create a gain by operating in currencies that would offset the anticipated loss. The success of these operations depends, of course, on a company's ability to predict the relative movement of these currencies. Making these kinds of forecasts falls within the purview of the company's political and economic risk analysts, as well as that of the firm's treasury.

The ability to predict foreign exchange movements is also crucial when affiliates deal in different nonconvertible currencies. In this situation, the only efficient way to obtain an accurate picture of the aggregate foreign exchange position of the company is through a centralized reporting system. This mechanism eliminates the need for many hedging transactions, since given currency receivables from one unit may be used to compensate liabilities from another. The alternative of each unit covering its own exposure would be too expensive. This centralized reporting system also reduces dependence on simple, uniform guidelines, which have often proved unworkable. A policy of stretching local credit terms and reducing the receivables of local customers in the event of an expected depreciation is bound to provoke strong opposition from operating personnel as limiting their flexibility. A hard and fast rule that subsidiaries in devaluation-prone countries pay intercompany accounts as soon as possible and delay paying intercompany accounts receivable while subsidiaries in revaluation-prone countries do the opposite would also encounter resistance and for the same reason.

A compromise between decentralized decision-making and centralized exposure management must be achieved. One quite successful arrangement is for the parent corporation to act as a bank for its subsidiaries. Under this system, any manager who wishes to cover his exchange position can obtain forward rates from the treasury department of the parent. In this way, the manager guarantees the exchange rate for his reports. It then becomes the parent company's responsibility to decide whether it will obtain a forward exchange contract from a commercial bank. To make this decision, the treasury department must determine whether the exposure is compensated by the position of another operating unit. It is essential, however, that the centralized banking unit, in this instance the corporate treasury office, have recourse to an international risk management system for assessing country risk and for formulating a coherent strategy for cross-border exposure. This is particularly true in developing nations where forward markets and other financial arrangements are neither well developed nor readily available to the firm. Such a policy must be founded on reliable intelligence gathered and compiled by those possessing not only expertise and experience, but also the will to make impartial and exact judgments. This effort requires extensive interaction between the treasury department and corporate risk department. Although it is impossible to foresee with absolute certainty what risks investment in a particular country entails, it is possible for the treasury with the assistance of the political risk department to develop accurate, up-to-the-minute assessments of those factors—foreign exchange inconvertibility and controls, devaluation and fluctuations in the value of the currency, and payment delays—that bear most closely on investment and to maintain and update these analyses at short intervals. These assessments, if scrupulously researched and carefully organized, can be presented in a comprehensive, though concise, form.

In fact, most corporations carry out such assessments to forecast foreign exchange rates. Surveys of multinational corporations have shown that nearly 80 percent prepare formal exchange rate forecasts on a regular basis, and some 15 percent prepare irregular forecasts. Of the remaining, 3 to 4 percent rely exclusively on purchased forecasts, while only 1 percent make no forecasts at all. While four out of five companies surveyed carry out foreign exchange forecasts, on average half believe forecasts to be the weak link in the foreign exchange management process.

In a particular survey of corporate exchange rate forecasting practices in 1975, Michael Jilling and William Folks, Jr., found that 1.9 percent used probability distribution, 8.4 percent prepared internal estimates, 30.8 percent made point estimates, while 37.4 percent forecasted only the direction of foreign exchange rate movements. The remaining 13.1 percent used other forms. This survey reinforces the expectation that the forms of foreign exchange forecasts vary significantly from one organization to the next. In general, most foreign exchange projections were for no more than one year, while occasionally forecasts up to five years were carried out.

The percentage of multinational banks that carry out foreign exchange forecasts is expected to be much higher than 80 percent. In fact, many of the multinational companies rely on banks for assistance and information in preparing their forecasts. Chemical Bank, for example, has quite an extensive foreign exchange forecast service. Yet reports from subsidiaries, financial publications, academicians, and consultants also play a role in the process of foreign exchange forecasting in numerous organizations. In general, however, it is clear that most multinationals are not satisfied with their forecasting system. Jilling and Folk's 1975 survey indicated that less than half were satisfied with the frequency of the forecasts, less than a third with the content of these forecasts, and even fewer with the actual forecasts' accuracy.

Forecasting under fixed or managed exchange rate systems is even more difficult. Under these systems the movement toward equilibrium in spot, forward, and, often, interest and inflation rates that occur under the floating rate system is artificially prevented from occurring by the government.

The central banks in effect are willing to absorb and counter the market pressures. Even government intervention has its limits, however. Governments ultimately must resign themselves to some degree of market discipline. The difficulty in forecasting fixed or managed exchange rate systems is to guess when this devaluation will occur and to what extent. Often these decisions are more political than economic. It is true that the political leadership in countries with managed currencies must respond to economic pressures to devalue; however, the response might be delayed. The probable political response requires familiarity with the political system and a feel for the environment. Often if the government finds it necessary to assert that no devaluation will occur, it is an indication of the pressures on the exchange rate system. In many instances just before or after a change of government, devaluations could occur. The devaluation of the Mexican peso fits neatly in this category. In these instances either the previous government has bitten the bullet and devalued, removing foreign exchange pressures on the new regime, or the new incumbent can blame the ill-adjusted actions of predecessors and bring about a devaluation.

Despite the uncertainties that political considerations place on the managed foreign exchange system, certain economic indicators are quite useful in evaluating the pressures on the exchange rate. The economic and market pressure can be evaluated; only the timing and size of change may be political in nature and sometimes less predictable. The parameters will be briefly described below.

Balance of Payments and Current Account

If the country spends abroad more that it earns or acquires from abroad over a sustained period of time, the likelihood of devaluations increase. Various measures, including various line items in the balance of payments, indicate the extent to which the flows of foreign exchange might be in disequilibrium. The current account position of a country is the net balance (exports less imports) of all transactions of merchandise goods, services, and unilateral transfers with all other countries within a specified time period. Consequently, it is a good measure of the foreign exchange flow into and out of a country. This measure is often normalized (i.e., as a percentage of exports) and becomes a parameter followed in many financial evaluation and forecast systems. Often imports and exports are further scrutinized to evaluate the stability of the country's earnings and expenditures. In particular, the nature, diversity, and essentiality of the import and export baskets are reviewed in detail.

Differential Inflation Rates

A high domestic inflation rate eventually will render a country's exports noncompetitive in the world market and imports less costly than domestic products and cause large current account deficits. The normal remedy is to devalue the local currency and reverse the trend. As an economic indicator, the differential rate of inflation cannot predict the timing of a devaluation. In a world of political intervention, a country experiencing relative inflation may adopt tariffs, export subsidies, and import quotas to forestall deterioration of the balance of payments. These policies will be only stopgap measures, however, unless the inflation differential is reduced. Currency competitiveness measures the extent that local inflation has been compensated for by the exchange rate movement.

Often the growth of the money supply predates the likelihood of exchange rate changes. The money supply is thus a leading indicator and is often used by financial forecasters as a delayed inflation measure in the evaluation of future currency competitiveness.

Level of Reserves

The international reserves—a country's holdings of gold, special drawing rights (SDR), and its foreign exchange and reserve position in the IMF—are used to protect the country from fluctuations in foreign exchange earnings. Reserves normalized by months of imports produce a useful indicator called the "reserves-to-import" ratio. This ratio is often used to measure a country's ability to weather temporary balance-of-payments difficulties. In interpreting this measure, the volatility and diversity of the nation's export and import baskets must be considered.

Often a combination of these parameters is used to measure the availability of foreign exchange in the short run. For example, the vulnerability index measures the ability of a country to meet its short-term external commitments; namely, imports and short-term debt repayment reduced by the nation's reserves less gold holdings (since gold is considered not particularly liquid) as a percentage of exports.

These parameters measure the economic and market pressures present on the system. If the government decides to ignore them, it is more likely that foreign exchange controls must be imposed, and the nation sacrifices the convertibility of the local currency. Controls often cause the fall in confidence in the local currency, and market forces result in a parallel market rate—one in which a free rate is technically not allowed but nevertheless is tolerated. Often it is illegal to exchange the currency in the local market. Nevertheless, black markets do exist, and parallel market rates may be quoted abroad or in neighboring countries. The stricter the government is in imposing foreign exchange controls, the greater the spread between official and so-called "free market" rates.

A shortage of foreign exchange often is accompanied by payment delays. While the government may decide to prioritize payments, the private sector payments for dividend royalty and management fees often end up with the lowest priority for payment.

Many resources are available to those interested in assessing the risks of various forms of investment in developed nations with readily convertible currencies. There are also comprehensive analyses of risk in developing nations, such as the rankings prepared by the American Express Bank and other banks. American Express assigns countries ratings from A to E based on quantitative and qualitative analysis of the sovereign and transfer risks present. Appended to the letter rating is an asterisk rating that reveals possible deterioration in a country's economy. This system has many advantages. One is that it avoids labeling entire countries as either acceptable or unacceptable risks, while simply suggesting the type of reward necessary to make investment in a particular country worthwhile. For example, a B rating commands a certain return over LIBOR, and the loan officer prices in line with this rating. Another advantage of this rating system is that it enables those company officials responsible for foreign investment of loans to rely on commonly held, clearly defined assumptions in their discussions of a particular transaction as well as in their development of a well-balanced portfolio. The American Express Bank's rating system, although comprehensive, is, however, inherently reductive (a problem its creators tried to surmount by adding the asterisk warning system). The very presence of a rating, even when combined with an assessment of supplemental factors, tends to reduce the discussion of a country's risk to a static abstraction. Furthermore, systems like the American Express Bank's report often rely heavily on political data and ignore such relevant financial parameters as devaluation, foreign exchange controls, and payment delays, which the treasury of a non-bank multinational might find relevant. What is needed for optimum financial risk management are in-depth country reports that concentrate on the areas of concerns that vary depending on the financial exposure in the country. Clearly, ongoing investments present a different set of concerns than a bank involved in only letters of credit financing. Therefore, it is not surprising that 80 percent of multinationals carry out their own individualized foreign exchange risk analyses.

In conclusion, we must add that no risk assessment is foolproof or guaranteed, but to be useful a risk assessment must be as precise as possible and custom-tailored to the needs of the multinational manufacturing company, bank, service company, or even insurer. Their concerns and needs are clearly varied. While political and economic/financial risks are interrelated, the financial aspects of country risks are somewhat more readily measurable, quantifiable, and addressable than so-called political aspects of country risks. In countries with freely convertible currencies, active exports, and forward exchange rates, the multinational enterprise analysis is straightforward. In countries with fixed or managed currencies and in environments where government intervention in the capital markets is extensive, forecasting and responding to financial risks is more difficult. Often the pressures on the economic system can be quantified, but the response is political. These responses often do not uniformly impact trade investments or loans, thus the need for a specialized and customized approach to financial risks is not only desirable but essential.

chapter twelve

Political Risk Insurance

Felton McC. Johnston

If we disregard the activities of banks—and bankers will tell you, rightly, that they have "insured" political risks for centuries—modern political risk insurance is an infant phenomenon. It has, and is showing, great potential for growth, but in the meantime it has problems of capacity, availability, and cost. We are in the fairly early evolutionary stage of the market for political risk insurance and correspondingly for those who sell it and those who use it. This chapter will describe what political risk insurance is, its utility, what is available, and who offers it in various marketplaces. Also described are the motivations and constraints that influence those insurers and what they provide, and how the practices and performance of the marketplace seem likely to develop over the coming decade. In conclusion some suggestions will be offered about how to approach the marketplace, what for, and when.

WHAT THE MARKETS OFFER

In general, potential political risk losses are categorized by insurance buyers and sellers by the type of exposure to loss—sales and contracting overseas, and investment—and by the type of coverage available for such exposures. The accompanying table of insurable perils (Table 12.1) provides a general description of these exposures for which coverage is available, all of which are generally one form or another of loss due to (a) inconvertibility or transfer risk coverage, (b) expropriation, confiscation, or other "wrongful" or simply inconvenient behavior by a government, and (c) various forms of political violence along a spectrum from international war to strikes, riots, and civil commotions. If it occurs to the reader that the latter two categories of risk are not peculiar to other people's countries, this simply confirms the reality that "political" risks are not peculiarly foreign by nature. Nevertheless, that is the way the market, for the most part, treats them.

THE MARKET PLAYERS

The markets for political risk insurance can be divided into the private versus the public official markets, and the private markets in turn are separated by location (Europe [principally Lloyd's] versus America), and by the philoso-

Table 12.1   Insurable Perils

I. Selling and Contracting Abroad
   A. "Wrongful" calling of bid, performance, advance payment, and similar guaranties or other "on demand" instruments posted by a seller in favor of a buyer.
   B. Contract frustration: action taken by a government, not allowed by terms of the contract itself, including:
      i. contract repudiation
      ii. export embargo/license revocation
      iii. import embargo/license revocation
   C. Nonpayment or other default due to:
      i. currency inconvertibility (active or passive)
      ii. political violence
   D. Loss due to other causes:
      i. confiscation or deprivation of equipment or inventory
      ii. damage or non-payment due to political violence

II. Investment Abroad
   A. Currency inconvertibility due to active or passive measures (devaluation protection is generally unavailable). Coverage may extend to repatriation of capital, earnings, debt service, and various contractual payments.
   B. Expropriation
      i. nationalization or confiscation of an enterprise or of assets without adequate, effective, and timely compensation
      ii. "creeping" expropriation (e.g., confiscatory taxes or price controls)
      iii. other governmental action or condonation of actions, resulting in deprivation of the investor's assets, rights, or ability to operate.
   C. Political Violence
   (Coverage from private entities generally excludes land-based war, although strikes, riots, and civil commotion are generally covered, and coverage for losses due to civil war and insurrection may be selectively available.)
      i. damage loss
      ii. nonpayment or default
      iii. other losses consequential to political violence
      iv. kidnap and ransom (available from private carriers only)

phies and motivations of the players. All are evolving in relation to each other: they are obliged to adapt their policies and practices to each other even though their separate existence is likely to continue.

The official markets are made up principally of the export credit agencies whose purpose is to facilitate the sale of goods from their countries to others. While these agencies principally serve to offset export risks rather than investment risks, they may also offer protection against the latter in some instances, and of course "investment" and "export" risks are not mutually exclusive categories. These agencies tend to pursue the same aims in much the same ways, although important differences do affect what may be obtainable from them and the terms on which it is offered. They are to be found in every industrialized country and in many less developed countries.

Most of these agencies will insure—on a whole turnover or a more selective basis—a domestic manufacturer's export receivables against political risks and, in some cases, commercial risks as well. (See Table 12.2 for a list of the principal agencies.) They may—and often do—provide political or comprehensive risk protection for term loans as well; indeed, they may make the loans themselves. The scope of their political risk coverages is generally described in Table 12.1, under "Selling and Contracting Abroad." They may in fact be private entities doing business both for their own account and for the account of their governments.

These agencies, or in some cases other national agencies in the same countries, may offer insurance, guaranties, and loans for overseas projects in pursuit of other, additional objectives, either to secure access to goods and resources or to promote economic development in third countries. These objectives are of course not mutually exclusive. Thus the export credit agencies of many capital-exporting countries or associated agencies now cover "investment" risks as well.

The private political risk (non-bank) insurance market had its origins at Lloyd's of London in the "marine" market centuries ago. A little over a decade ago, syndicates at Lloyd's began reinsuring the inconvertibility and expropriation portfolios of the U.S. Overseas Private Investment Corporation (OPIC) and commenced offering policies directly to companies doing business abroad. More recently, U.S. firms, led by AIG, CIGNA, AFIA, Chubb, and a few others, have developed broad programs for insuring firms' export and investment risks against political perils. Additional non–U.S., as well as new U.S., participants in this market may be anticipated.

It is now possible for an American firm, for example, to cover its sales and investment risks not just with government agencies such as Eximbank and OPIC, but in the private domestic and Lloyd's markets also. Still, the ability of that firm to obtain the desired protection may be constrained in both public and private markets, in different ways and for different reasons.

MOTIVATIONS AND CONSTRAINTS OF POLITICAL RISK INSURERS

Although many of their goals and interests are common, public and private sector entities do have distinctive motivations and operate under separate constraints. The distinctions between these two markets will continue, although each is increasingly coming to share some of the other's approaches.

Public entities are not involved in political risk insurance *primarily* to make money (although they are increasingly interested in enhanced revenue generation, loss avoidance, and loss control). Their involvement principally serves national or international objectives—export promotion, international economic development, and other foreign policy goals. They commonly also have subsidiary objectives or interests that may favor the investor or not. For instance, most public entities will do business with smaller domestic firms on terms at least equal to those offered to larger firms, even though the smaller firms' business is not profitable. The public entity generally will be willing to consider individual items, i.e. to be the victim of adverse selection, if those items otherwise fit its criteria. And the public entity may be willing to assume some (but not all) risks the private market would shun for underwriting or other reasons, and to write business at rates below "market." Also, other terms and conditions may be more favorable in the public sector market. For instance, investment insurance is commonly available in public markets for up to 20 years but is generally limited to up to 3 years in the private market. Some of these differences for "investment" risks are summarized in Table 12.2.

The private insurers' motivations, while exclusively commercial, are not simply to make the most possible money from any particular transaction. Their willingness and ability to respond to the needs of businesses operating abroad reflects, in any instance, a variety of considerations, including particularly:

1. the absolute limits on the insurer's capacity to insure political risks. Any insurer is constrained by regulations imposed by governmental authorities, rules of voluntary associations (such as Lloyd's Council), and by its own board and management. Since the overwhelming practice in insurance (and especially in catastrophic lines like political risk) is for a primary insurer to reinsure his own risks and retain only a portion of them, an insurer must be sure that individual items underwritten and cumulative exposures fall within the terms of his reinsurance; otherwise, he must be sure that he is willing and able to retain them for his own account. If a particular transaction or group of transactions does not fit within the insurer's reinsurance "treaty" (the agreement covering a broad range of transactions for which the insurer does not need to have the reinsurer's individual approval), then he may seek to arrange "facultative" reinsurance for the transaction(s). Finally, the insurer will have a set of rules by which he governs his own behavior generally. For instance, while he may be able to lay off 90 percent or more of a given risk with reinsurers, he may nevertheless be unwilling to retain 10 percent of a risk that individually or in combination with other assumed risks will cause his exposures (with respect to countries, perils insured against, industries, or other categories) to exceed some level with which he is comfortable.

2. the insurer's attitude toward political risk insurance and his reasons for being in the business. What the insurer is willing and able to do has much to do with his reason for underwriting *any* political risks. It is a simplification, but a valid one, to say that there are two basic reasons why insurers will assume political risks, given the "catastrophic" nature of those risks and their unpredictability, which causes most insurers to shun them. The first is simply that there is money to be made, and in an industry characterized for the most part by low margins (and, at the bottom of a cycle, by no margins or worse), earnings and earnings growth may be found in new, exotic, and perceived higher-risk products such as political risk insurance. In these lines, where there are fewer players, demand generally exceeds capacity, and insurers may be willing to pay handsomely to hedge their exposures, the attraction for some insurers is obvious.

The other motivation (which does not necessarily exclude the first, of course) is competitive. To retain valuable business in their other (especially)

Table 12.2   Principal Official Agencies Insuring Export and Investment Exposures

Country	Agency	Export coverage?	Investment coverage?
Australia	Export Finance and Insurance Corporation	Yes	Yes
Austria	Oesterreichische Kontrollbank Aktiengesellschaft	Yes	
Belgium	Office National du Ducroire	Yes	Yes
Canada	Export Development Corporation	Yes	Yes
Denmark	Eksportkreditradet	Yes	Yes
Finland	Vientitakuulaitos	Yes	
France	Compagnie Française d'Assurance pour le Commerce Extérieur	Yes	Yes
France	Banque Française du Commerce Extérieur	Yes	Yes
Germany	Hermes Kreditversicherungs-Aktiengesellschaft	Yes	
Germany	Treuarbeit Aktiengesellschaft		Yes
Hong Kong	Hong Kong Export Credit Insurance Corporation	Yes	
India	Export Credit and Guarantee Corporation Ltd.	Yes	Yes
Israel	The Israel Foreign Trade Risks Insurance Corporation Ltd.	Yes	Yes
Italy	Sezione Speciale per l'Assicurazione del Credito all'Esportazione	Yes	Yes
Italy	Societa Italiana Assicurazione Crediti SPA	Yes	
Japan	Export Insurance Division, Ministry of International Trade and Industry	Yes	Yes
Korea	The Export-Import Bank of Korea	Yes	Yes
Mexico	Fondo para el Fomento de las Exportaciones de Productos Manufacturados, Banco de Mexico SA	Yes	
Netherlands	Nederlandsche Credietverzekering Maatschappij NV	Yes	Yes
New Zealand	Export Guarantee Office	Yes	Yes
Norway	Garanti-Instituttet for Eksportkreditt	Yes	
Portugal	Companhia de Seguro de Créditos	Yes	
Singapore	Export Credit Insurance Corporation of Singapore Ltd.	Yes	

Country	Agency	Export coverage?	Investment coverage?
South Africa	Credit Guarantee Insurance Corporation of Africa Ltd.	Yes	Yes
Spain	Compañia Española de Seguros de Crédito a la Exportación SA	Yes	
Spain	Compañia Española de Seguros de Crédito y Caución SA	Yes	
Sweden	Exportkreditnämnden	Yes	Yes
Switzerland	Geschäftsstelle für die Exportrisikogarantie	Yes	
UK	Export Credits Guarantee Department	Yes	Yes
UK	Trade Indemnity Company Ltd.	Yes	
USA	Export-Import Bank of the United States	Yes	
USA	Overseas Private Investment Corporation		Yes

property and casualty lines, some insurers feel obliged to be in the political risk business, like it or not. This is particularly true for insurance companies catering to firms that are heavily engaged in international trade and investment.

3. the insurer's relationship with the business seeking insurance and with the broker, if any, representing the insured. An insurer's view of a particular transaction or group of transactions is obviously colored by his view of the prospective insured. Is the company one with which his firm does a large volume of business, or is the insurer seeking to win new business from this company? Is that business particularly desirable? Conversely, is the prospective insured not a regular customer, merely shopping for the lowest rate, seeking to cover only his worst risks, and perhaps known to be a troublesome or accident-prone insured? A new or irregular customer not particularly sought after may nevertheless obtain reasonably priced cover for an acceptable risk, especially if he is represented by a skillful, vigorous, and influential broker; but other positive elements can have an important bearing, especially in marginal situations.

4. the insurer's view of the particular transaction and related business, and how it fits his overall book of business. Naturally, if an insurer has an opportunity to insure a broad class of business—such as the expropriation risk associated with a company's investments in eight countries—the insurer will normally find that opportunity more attractive than the risk on any one of those investments, not just because this brings him more business but because it helps him to develop a broader book of business and avoid adverse selection. Accordingly the insurer may offer a blanket or "global" policy: the insured pays premiums on some investments he considers "safe" and might not otherwise insure, but his average cost per dollar of insurance coverage

obtained is brought down. In this case, the company's confidence in its own judgment about what is or isn't safe (and, of course, whether coverage is reasonably available otherwise for what is considered unsafe) may determine whether a global policy is chosen. Otherwise the insurer looks at the potential opportunity and the inherent risks it poses, much as the prospective insured should, except that the insurer focuses on the likelihood of loss, the value insured, and the prospects of salvage, with less regard for the overall effects of loss on the insured.

THE FUTURE DEVELOPMENT OF POLITICAL RISK INSURANCE MARKETS

While it is not easy to predict the future evolution of political risk insurance markets, evidence and logic point to certain likely political risk market trends.

First, while there have been retrenchments by some active participants and continued unwillingness by most companies to become involved directly in political risk underwriting, over the long haul the private market seems likely to grow in overall capacity, to attract more participants, and to offer broader and more effective protection. For sheer competitive reasons, this should be true at least for large companies seeking to obtain coverage; and as the market develops to serve and retain these important customers, its ability and willingness to serve less favored buyers is likely to increase generally, although not correspondingly.

How smoothly and rapidly this market development progresses will depend in large part on the experience insurers enjoy. Major losses will always drive some participating insurers and reinsurers from the field. Very profitable experience will attract new participants—and increased involvement by existing ones—as will the threat of losing an important customer to more aggressive competitors.

The growth of the private market is already having an impact on public sector underwriters—both in political and commercial (credit) risk fields. The private market has focused on export (versus investment) risks, as have the public agencies. Although lacking the advantage of the fiscal backing of the state, private insurers are correspondingly free of many of the constraints imposed by the state and some of its bureaucratic burdens. This has enabled private insurers to capture markets previously served exclusively by public agencies, even though those agencies in general offer coverage at lower rates. At the same time, as they have suffered extraordinary losses, the public agencies have come to recognize that their official role and support of the national interest does not assure unlimited tolerance for their losses, and most official agencies have been obliged recently to review critically their terms and conditions and their strategies for reconciling public policy goals and their own commercial interests.

It is likely that public entities will strive increasingly to conduct their affairs on a sounder commercial basis. This may mean less generous terms for insureds in some instances, but more flexible and otherwise beneficial terms for others as those agencies seek to preserve markets and market shares. Over the long term it seems likely that public and private entities will develop not just in competitive reaction to each other, but that new and interesting arrangements for cooperation between them will be found. This is true already where major projects are involved and neither public nor private market capacity alone is sufficient to accommodate insurance demand.

APPROACHING THE MARKETPLACE

A broad and important set of issues, many discussed in the opening section of this book, relates to the process by which a company assesses political risks and decides what to do about them. Although there is no single, correct methodological approach to assessing political risks nor a single correct approach to dealing with those risks, there can be no doubt that every firm doing a substantial part of its business overseas should have an articulated, coherent, and effective process for recognizing and coping with overseas political risks. The absence of such an approach is likely not only to expose the company to risks it should not assume and might cost it dearly, but also to result in bad decisions about risk-taking generally (including foregoing opportunities that could safely be seized) and less than optimal solutions to risk mitigation and control. And although larger companies are more likely to have the resources and sophistication to assess and address political risks, their bureaucratic complexity may be an obstacle to an effective process. Whether or not the firm has such an approach may determine not just what and how effective a role political risk insurance plays in the firm's efforts to cope with risk, but how beneficial that insurance is, and at what cost. We know that, given the practices and motivations of insurers, companies that take a careless, casual or simply episodic approach to purchasing political risk insurance are not likely to obtain the best terms and conditions the marketplace offers.

It is fundamental that a company having major exposures in overseas markets not only consider the role of political risk insurance at an early stage of decision-making, rather than as an afterthought or a last-ditch solution to political risk problems, but that the company consider it as part of the risk environment itself. This is not to say that every firm needs to have political risk insurance—larger firms with a broad spread of risk may well be able to self-insure most if not all risks—or that other solutions to risk problems, including various financial techniques, may not be superior. But a strategy for analyzing and coping with political risks that does not take carefully into account the availability of political risk coverage and other techniques for coping with risk will at best be a flawed strategy. It will either involve the company in risks that could and should be avoided, or dispose the company to avoid risks that could, with the proper measures for protection, be undertaken profitably.

What is suggested is a continuous process by which the company considers and reconciles its general business strategy, the associated political risks, and its approach to those risks. The company may, for instance, decide that a blanket political risk insurance policy is well suited to its overall strategy, and that negotiation of such a policy, if it is available on reasonable terms, could permit the firm to undertake substantial risks that otherwise it would have to avoid. It may discover that the incremental cost of insuring some risks is so great that they should either be self-insured or avoided altogether.

Such a process is no less important for a firm whose overseas exposures are more concentrated or otherwise less suited to a blanket or global insurance policy. Even a firm with a single overseas exposure—an investment in one factory abroad—needs to contemplate the present and future implica-

---

Table 12.3　Public and Private Markets for Insurance of Investment Risks

General and Principal Distinctions

	Private commercial markets	Public agency markets
Perils insured	While limited revolution, insurrection, or civil strife coverage may be obtained from selected sources, it is generally unavailable for events on land and immobile assets.	Generally no exclusions for loss due to any warlike event.
Terms of commitment	Although rarely beyond 3 or 4 years, established operations will normally roll coverage forward annually, and will renew, at some price, even when adverse conditions have developed.	Up to 15 or 20 years from many entities.
Cost	Highly variable, based upon underwriting judgments, relationships with insured, capacity considerations, reinsurance arrangements, etc.	Varies widely among national agencies, but generally below those of commercial insurers.
Capacity	For individual projects, perhaps up to $100 million, but limits are highly variable among insurers and with respect to individual insureds.	Varies widely by agency or program involved.
Geographical availability	In theory, anywhere, but subject to reinsurance restrictions, country capacity limits, and underwriting judgments, and likely to be more elastic for buyers of global or blanket coverage.	Generally limited to "friendly" countries with which special arrangements have been reached governing rights and salvage, or to those having "acceptable" legal regimes or practices. Attention is often concentrated on former colonies or other countries with which there are special economic relationships. "Global" coverage is generally unavailable.

	Private commercial markets	Public agency markets
Investor eligibility	No particular requirements; regular customers are favored.	Nationals of the agency's country and companies domiciled therein, in some cases with national ownership requirements.
Investment or project eligibility	Normally no distinction as to new or existing investment.	Coverage is generally available only for new investment (including earnings reinvestment) or for creation or expansion/modernization/improvement of an existing one. Projects may be ineligible for various public policy reasons; e.g. adverse domestic economic effects, military implications, etc. Correspondingly, undertakings having particular benefits (especially economic) for the agency country are often favored, and such benefits may actually be required for coverage to be available.

tions of that investment and its associated risk. What does the investment mean to the company? What is the true sum of the company's risk exposures associated with that investment—both current and contemplated? What would its loss or the prolonged interruption of its operations imply for the parent firm? What means are available to mitigate those exposures, and what does that imply for that investment in the future? How should the investment be structured and financed? Should its profits be reinvested, or should they be remitted home promptly?

Early consultations with insurers and brokers may cause the firm either to lower its sights or raise them. An insurer may be willing to combine, on an attractive basis, political risk coverage with the insured's overseas property and casualty coverage. "Manuscripted" policies with terms and conditions designed for the insured's particular needs and concerns might be negotiated. No coverage may be available for some exposures. It may be possible to obtain expropriation or contract frustration coverage, but inadequate coverage for transfer risks associated with the same project(s).

Insurers may offer more than the mere plug to fill the risk gap. The insurer (or the broker) may help the company to identify and cope with risks it has not previously recognized. Over time, the more sophisticated insurers will be providing, on a regular basis, assistance to companies in risk identification and in loss control, as they now regularly do in property and casualty insurance lines. Public sector insurers in particular may, by their very association with the project, discourage harmful foreign governmental actions or enhance the potential for recovery when they occur—an especially important element when the investment's operations are intimately and significantly linked to those of the insured.

But insurers may also offer less than what is appropriate, or simply the wrong thing. A buyer of insurance (and his broker) needs to look closely and critically at the policy he is offered. What are important exceptions and limitations? Is the deductible appropriate? What are the insured's duties and rights in the event of loss? An insured can pay for coverage and be in a position to collect, and yet have to forgo compensation because actions required to collect are inconsistent with other corporate interests in a given situation. It is also necessary to consider the motives and behavior of the particular insurer. What is the claims experience others have had? How prompt, flexible, and efficient is their claims management? How strong a company is the insurer? Why are they in this market? Can they be counted on to renew the policy regularly on reasonable terms, even if the risk environment worsens? What is the insurance company's overall relationship with the insured?

SUMMING UP

Political risk insurance is a risk transfer tool whose availability from both public and private entities is increasing. Nevertheless, the market for this insurance is fragmented, in the early stages of its development, and characterized by capacity constraints and relatively high costs. The availability of insurance varies not just with the perceived risk of a particular investment, but with the specific character of the insured and the insurer, and their relationship. A wise company will not merely utilize political risk insurance to cope with particular problems as they arise, but will continuously incorporate political risk insurance and other risk transfer and control devices into its business strategy and planning.

part five

CONCLUSION

chapter thirteen
Conclusion

Take calculated risks;
that is quite different from being rash.
—Gen. George S. Patton

Since the reader by now has perused either the whole book or the sections of interest to him, a tapestry woven from the various chapters is unnecessary here. A theoretical, interdisciplinary foundation for "country risk analysis" has been laid, and some of the more salient variables have been amplified in the concrete country case studies. Some of the studies can stand on their own and serve as examples for economists and political scientists to demonstrate how their own formal disciplines can be bent and interwoven to have a direct impact on bolstering profits in the business world. Armed with an understanding of the more generalizable variables (and important new questions will emerge in different countries and localities) derived from adapting an interdisciplinary, social science approach to international business needs, the reader should conclude from the section on methodologies either that the attempt to develop uniform quantitative models is spurious, reductionist, and even counterproductive, or that there is hope for developing the discipline of "country risk analysis" still further and for creating models that help rather than limit or hinder. Other methods for qualitative forecasting, such as the use of a "decision tree" or scenarios, have been omitted here since, I believe, predicting political outcomes is less important than alerting executives to those political, social, commercial, and economic problems which, alone or in dynamic combination, might have a deleterious impact on a type of business investment. Nevertheless, as the substance of the discipline develops, further refinements of forecasting techniques will be useful. Finally, this book has introduced the reader to established financial management techniques for protecting currency exposure and to the insurance options available when less expensive strategies for investment protection cannot be utilized.

How do we proceed to explicate and legitimize political, or country, risk analysis as a profession? How do we prevent it from atrophying in the face of hard-nosed businesspersons who want to be convinced that it is an indispensable tool for bolstering the bottom line? Used properly, political risk analysis can contribute to the definition of marketing strategies and, most important, alert the planner to protect assets and secure payments as circumstances warrant.

First, it is important to choose the right personnel: individuals with a solid background of comparative politics, international relations, and economics or finance, who have had experience in, or are flexible enough to adapt to, the culture of big business. The Iranian revolution led to a population explosion in the political risk field, comprised of both in-house analysts and outside consultants. In business on their own were former Central Intelligence Agency agents and analysts, diplomats, academics, and even a group of Oxford dons. In more recent times, the field has begun to consolidate.

Second, it is crucial that the country risk manager establish a communications flow within the whole corporate entity that will ensure that the political risk analysis function serves the real needs of the corporation and serves them well. It is important that the manager leave his desk and do a personal selling job on behalf of his program to operational officers in the subsidiaries and at the field level (even if he must fly to Singapore to meet with key Far East regional marketing executives); a give-and-take exchange must ensue over the utility of risk analysis to them and what factors are most meaningful to them. The manager must integrate his program with strategic planning and the identification of priority markets, with the treasurer's office, and with the political risk insurance selection process. A formalized channel of communication might be established on a simple level with regional operations officers: for the purpose of eliciting input on a given country, getting feedback on analysis, and "involving" the operations officer in the process. The central purpose is to *educate*, not to predict the future; the best sort of education always involves a two-way flow. Many larger corporations also map out future target markets, strategies for penetrating them, and ways to reduce the need for, or avoid, political risk insurance on the basis of political risk assessments *early* in the process of decision-making.[1] If proper channels of communication cannot be established among different departments at the corporate center or between the political risk program at the corporate center and the field areas, a lot of interesting reports might be written, but needs will be inadequately fulfilled.

Third, each business must develop a method for garnering and managing data. I recall a conversation, three years ago, with a senior executive of a major insurance company about to set up a political risk coverage department. He remarked to me that his problem really was not so much collecting the information as figuring out what to do with it. Clearly, once the parameters of risk or investment disincentives for one's company have been crystallized, the management of data becomes easier. The mere concretization or structuring of relevant questions may help the analyst organize information.

Access to the best sources of information is also vital. The key to analyzing situations seemingly as arcane as the business climate in Zimbabwe or post-independence prospects for the sultanate of Brunei lies in knowing how to obtain the best periodicals and journals worldwide and how to draw on knowledgeable human resources within the reach of your corporation or bank. Regional officers of your own business entity, local agents, or business contacts in a country of interest often can offer special insights concerning conditions there. At home, government officers and—for smaller corporations—international banks often can be helpful. The Washington, D.C. office of one multinational corporation maintains files on every country in the Third World and on subjects ranging from anti-boycott information to international terrorism, to evacuation plans, to the pan-Islamic movement. These files contain clippings culled from newspapers and magazines around the world (including unclassified C.I.A. publications, such as daily translations of the Chinese press and radio transmissions). The most important research performed by this office revolves about questions that the easily accessible literature does not answer—the "loose ends" and contradictions in the more conventional source materials. For this purpose, the corporation's political risk analysis unit has made it a particular point to cultivate good relationships with people at the Department of State, the Department of Commerce, the Department of Treasury, OPIC and the National Security Council, as well as key officers in embassies, international banks, and regionally specialized academicians. In a recent instance, this office was able to do a project-oriented political risk and financial analysis related to a dam in Sierra Leone in just two days with appropriate phone calls to sources at both the State Department and the World Bank. On another occasion, the office located a professor at the University of California who was the acting editor of a journal on Asian Studies. He had just rejected an article on Brunei because he did not believe the subject large enough then to warrant coverage. After a few phone calls to a Ph.D. student in Southeast Asia, the California-based academician was able to assist this corporate risk analysis center in piecing together, in less than a week, an analysis that was fundamental to a major investment.

From a positive standpoint, we have noted that political, or country, risk analysis has been used by larger companies for strategic planning—targeting international markets and developing strategies for penetrating those markets. For these companies, whether a decision process regarding one particular country is even begun may require that the country's political and investment climate be acceptable. In some of the larger firms, such screening may involve formal analysis in which all the factors discussed in Part I play a role. While it is desirable that the political risk analysis function develop more in this direction, such a result can be achieved only on a company-by-company basis as each political risk analysis unit establishes its own reliability.

From a more defensive perspective, political risk analysis identifies areas in which risk must be managed or covered in some way. Chapter 11 explored methods for managing currency exposure. In addition, when war, insurrection, civil strife, and expropriation or default become real, potential problems, the corporation may opt for political risk insurance cover or *avoid* the business opportunity altogether. Political risk insurance frequently is just too costly. A survey commissioned by OPIC three years ago noted that firms "whose strategy and structure is global" and have a greater and more diversified spread of international operations may well decide to absorb the cost of the risk because of the diversity of its portfolio of subsidiaries.[2] The key to deciding early in the game whether to avoid a particular international opportunity, whether to choose one opportunity over another, or just what strategies to pursue to protect oneself is good intelligence and more good intelligence. Political risk insurance should not be poured like water on a fire; it should be used selectively. Intelligence through political risk analysis may not reduce actual risk, but it can reduce uncertainty.

NOTES

1. "A Study of Additionality of OPIC Assistance to U.S. Private Direct Investment in Developing Countries," an unpublished paper for OPIC by Arthur Young & Co., May 28, 1982, II-17.
2. Ibid., II-22.

Index

About the Author/Editor

David M. Raddock, a specialist in Chinese and Soviet politics and in political psychology, is currently based in Washington, D.C. as a private consultant to several major corporations. He did his undergraduate work at Cornell University and received his doctorate in comparative politics from Columbia University. He has conducted research in East Asia, Africa and Latin America. Dr. Raddock began his career on the faculty of the University of Texas. In his years thereafter as the in-house political risk analyst for a multinational corporation, he developed its corporate program in country environment analysis.

Dr. Raddock has been a frequent contributor to academic journals, magazines and newspapers. He has written for *China Quarterly, Journal of Asian Studies, Contemporary China, China Report, Worldwide Projects, Arts Magazine, Art News, Far Eastern Economic Review, Newsday* and the *New York Times*. His first book, *Political Behavior of Adolescents in China: The Cultural Revolution in Kwangchow*, was written in part under a grant from the National Endowment for the Humanities after two years of field research in Hong Kong doing interviews with former Red Guards. The author currently is working on political cultural aspects of the PRC's modernization process.

About the Contributors

Henry Albinski is Professor of Political Science at Pennsylvania State University. Author of eight books and numerous journal articles, he is also Director of the Australian Studies Center at Pennsylvania State University.

William D. Coplin and **Michael K. O'Leary** are the original developers of the Frost and Sullivan Political Risk Services. Both Professors of Political Science at the Maxwell School of Syracuse University, they have authored, individually and jointly, more than twenty books and articles on political analysis.

Gustavo Coronel is affiliated with the energy division of the Inter-American Development Bank in Washington, D.C. A former Member of the Board of Petroleos de Venezuela and Maraven, Mr. Coronel is the author of *The Nationalization of the Venezuelan Oil Industry.*

Hermann Frederick Eilts, a career foreign service officer, was U.S. Ambassador to Saudi Arabia from 1965 to 1970 and Ambassador to Egypt from 1973 to 1979. He is chairman of the Department of Political Science at Boston University.

Zvi Gitelman is Professor of Soviet Politics at the University of Michigan, Ann Arbor. He is the author of *Jewish Nationality and Soviet Politics* and other works on the Soviet Union and Eastern Europe.

Fariborz Ghadar teaches international business at George Washington University and is a consultant in international finance. He was Deputy Minister of Finance before he left Iran on the eve of the revolution.

Felton McC. Johnston is Vice President for Insurance of the Overseas Private Investment Corporation. Formerly a banker with Morgan Guaranty, he has also served as chairman of the investment insurance committee of the Bern Union.

Robert O. Slater has been affiliated with Mathematica and other private research organizations and has published in the *American Political Science Review* on coups in Sub-Saharan Africa. He directs the Foreign Language and Area Studies Program at the Defense Intelligence College.

Kim Woodard was a research associate at the East-West Center of the University of Hawaii and authored a major book on China's petroleum and energy resources. Dr. Woodard is now President of China Energy Ventures, a consulting firm in Washington and Houston.